12.95

D0405400

Law and Social Change in Postwar Japan

Thomas J. Wilson Prize
The Board of Syndics of Harvard University Press has awarded this
book the seventeenth annual Thomas J. Wilson Prize, honoring the
late director of the Press. The Prize is awarded by the Press each
year to the best first book accepted that year.

Law and Social Change in Postwar Japan

FRANK K. UPHAM

Harvard University Press
Cambridge, Massachusetts, and London, England

Copyright © 1987 by the President and Fellows
    of Harvard College
All rights reserved
Printed in the United States of America
10 9 8 7 6 5 4 3

Library of Congress Cataloging-in-Publication Data

Upham, Frank K.
  Law and social change in postwar Japan.

  Includes index.
  1. Justice, Administration of—Japan—History.
  2. Civil rights—Japan—History.   3. Japan—Social
conditions—1945–   . I. Title.
LAW   347.52'009   86-19472
ISBN 0-674-51786-5 (alk. paper) (cloth) 345.207009
ISBN 0-674-51787-3 (paper)

To my parents

Acknowledgments

I AM very grateful to the many people who have helped me in completing this book. The following institutions generously provided financial support: the East Asian Legal Studies program at Harvard Law School, the Japan Foundation, Ohio State University, the Japan–U.S. Joint Friendship Commission, Boston College and Boston College Law School, and the Program on U.S.–Japan Relations of the Center for International Affairs of Harvard University. My debt to Ezra Vogel, Philip Jones, Dick Finn, and the staff of the Program on U.S.–Japan Relations is particularly great; they have not only supported me for two semesters over the last four years but also provided an environment that enabled me to draw on the knowledge and experience of many of the Japanese bureaucrats, scholars, and businessmen who have served as Program Fellows since 1981. Indeed, this book is in many ways a product of the Program.

I am equally indebted to those whose support was purely intellectual. Rick Abel, Mary Ann Glendon, Duncan Kennedy, Sally Falk Moore, Mark Ramseyer, Michael Reich, Jim Rogers, Richard Stewart, Uga Katsuya, Urata Masutarō, and Michael Young all critiqued early drafts of the book and provided invaluable encouragement. Lawrence Beer, David Engel, Whitmore Gray, John Haley, Hanami Tadashi, Miyazawa Setsuo, Omichi Masao, Joel Rosch, and Sugeno Kazuo reviewed later versions and enabled me to eliminate at least some of the errors in the manuscript. Although they were not directly involved in this book, I also want to express my gratitude to my early teachers of Asian law, Jerome A. Cohen, Fujikura Kōichirō, Morishima Akio, and finally Tanaka Hideo, who was my first teacher of Japanese law and whose intellect and spirit have greatly influenced my career. I would also like to acknowledge the ongoing support of my colleagues and students at Ohio State and Boston College law schools.

A very concrete debt is owed to those in Japan without whose help I would never have been able to begin my research. Doshisha University has twice extended hospitality to me and my family, and its law faculty, especially Professor Igeta Ryōji, has provided much-needed advice and guidance over many years. The law faculties of Tokyo and Kyoto universities have also been extremely helpful, and I am particularly grateful to Professor Shiono Hiroshi, Dean of the Faculty of Law of Tokyo University, whose guidance was indispensable in researching Chapter 5.

Perhaps most of all I want to thank the dozens of people involved in the specific events that I studied for sharing their time with me. I regret that I cannot thank all of them individually, but two lawyers, Orita Yasuhiro and Gotō Takanori, deserve special commendation for their patience and willingness to teach. The staffs at the Buraku Problem Research Institute and the Buraku Liberation Research Institute, although often presenting opposing viewpoints, were equally hospitable to me, as were the officials of the cities of Kyoto and Osaka and at the Ministries of International Trade and Industry and Labor.

The preparation of this book was made as pleasurable as possible by the help of Michael Aronson, Maria Ascher, and Mary Ellen Geer at Harvard University Press; the able research assistance of Madoka Etoh, Pete Michaels, Nakamura Reiko, Okada Hideichi, David Sneider, and Thomas Wexler; and the consistently reliable support of Betty Capstick, Sandra Cooper, Fran Piscatelli, and the staff of the Boston College Word Processing Center.

Finally, I want to extend special thanks to my friend Rob Evans for his good-natured editorial help, and to my wife and family for their patience and support.

Contents

x   Contents

Law and Social Change in Postwar Japan

ONE

Models of Law and Social Change

THIS BOOK is about law and social change in contemporary Japan. It examines the way in which elites use legal rules and institutions to manage and direct conflict and control change at a social level. Given the common view of Japan as having little conflict and less law, this topic will strike some as unusual. In most accounts of postwar Japan, social life is portrayed as virtually conflict-free, the result of a society where the Confucian ideals of social harmony and antipathy toward law have been internalized by a loyal and cooperative population. In this view fundamental schisms in Japanese society are rare, the occasional individual disputes are handled quickly and effectively by traditional means such as mediation or conciliation, and lawyers and litigation are eschewed as socially disruptive.[1]

With this view of society prevailing, it is not surprising that observers of Japanese law have traditionally been concerned primarily with demonstrating and explaining its insignificance. When Japanese law has been dealt with at all, the focus has been on the minimal role that it plays in ordinary dispute resolution—on the low rate of litigation, the small number of lawyers, and the prevalence of mediation and conciliation. To explain these phenomena, most accounts have relied on cultural characteristics: a low legal consciousness and strong traditional values that predispose the Japanese to compromise. At their most extreme such accounts resort to mystical abstractions, such as "the gentle aesthetic of the Japanese mind," which their authors claim make the cold rationalism of litigation inappropriate in Japanese society.[2]

Recent scholarship, however, has attacked this description of the Japanese legal landscape. Legal scholars have argued that the definition used in determining the number of Japanese lawyers excludes large numbers of professionals who do what would be considered legal work elsewhere, and that the supposedly low litigation rate is actually within the normal range for industrialized democracies. Others have directly challenged the cultural approach and have instead attributed any relative Japanese disinclination to litigate to deliberately created barriers that render litigation less cost-effective than mediation or conciliation. They maintain that much that is considered traditional in Japanese legal phenomena is in fact a postwar creation, pointing out, *inter alia*, that litigation rates were higher in prewar than in postwar Japan. These scholars dismiss the cultural explanation as a politically convenient myth used by Japanese elites to legitimate the suppression of conflict.[3]

This critique has been enormously important in giving us institutional and political alternatives to the cultural explanation of Japanese legal phenomena. By freeing us from the relative immutability of culture, it has enabled us not only to explain more fully why certain phenomena exist but also to question whether law in Japan is in fact as irrelevant as conventional assumptions would have us believe. Emerging alongside this legal scholarship is a growing body of literature on Japanese social conflict that has revealed Japanese society to be much more complicated and contentious than the popular perception of harmony and consensus would imply. Many of these works give a good deal of attention to the role of law in particular instances of social and political conflict, but few have focused on the general role of law in social conflict or made an explicit argument for greater attention to law in the ordinary study of Japanese society or politics across a range of substantive areas.[4] It is the primary purpose of this book to build on both these bodies of scholarship to demonstrate not only that the assumption of law's insignificance is fundamentally incorrect but also that any description of Japanese society, particularly one that attempts to explain the process of social change within Japan, is incomplete without an account of how legal rules and institutions influence the course of conflict and the direction of social change.

To make this argument it is unnecessary to choose between the cultural and institutional theories of Japanese dispute resolution or to analyze the motivation of ordinary Japanese involved in individual instances of conflict. Unlike most other works on Japanese law, this book is not primarily concerned with individual dispute resolution. Instead, it focuses on how legal rules and institutions are manipulated to create and maintain a framework within which social conflict and change occur in Japan. The social conflict examined does not involve the everyday disputes of landlord and tenant, creditor and debtor, or husband and wife; rather, it is conflict among organized groups of people with inconsistent interests: pollution victims as a group against polluting firms, minorities demanding social equality against the majority, women workers protesting discriminatory employment practices, and one industrial sector against another in the formation of national economic policy.

These are examples of conflict that results from conscious efforts to achieve group goals and that often demands significant change in the social order. The line between individual, diffused conflict and organized social movements is not impermeable: the former may develop into the latter; the latter may disintegrate into the former. Indeed, a clear conceptual demarcation between the two may not be possible. But there is a qualitative difference between a dispute between two neighbors over one's late-night piano playing and a dispute involving several hundred area residents organized to oppose the construction of a waste incinerator in their neighborhood. The difference is not only one of relative resources but of social importance and consequence as well. The pollution dispute has a greater chance of becoming a broad movement with implications beyond the particular dispute. It is more immediately threatening to political and social harmony, partly because it already involves more people and partly because it has the potential of challenging the prevailing social norms and order on a general rather than a particular level and in an organized rather than an ad hoc manner. It is the description and analysis of such conflict that form the bulk of this book, and it is the role of law in directing and managing the accompanying pressures for change that is its analytical focus.

Whether a series of discrete grievances coalesces into a broad social movement (or an established movement fragments into myriad individual disputes) will depend ultimately on the existence of political allies, the depth of commitment and political resources of the disputants, and the normative appeal of the underlying issues.[5] Such outcomes are, in other words, largely determined by politics, not legal doctrines or institutions. But the latter can play a substantial role in influencing the manner in which individual grievances develop into social conflict and emerge in the political arena. Within a given society, it is the legal system that determines what forums are available to disputants and what forms of conflict are appropriate. Form and forum in turn will affect the identity and number of potential political allies, the mode of internal organization within groups, the chance of alliances among groups, and the way in which the parties' divergent normative positions are presented to each other and to the public. By influencing these variables of social conflict, law can influence the shape and direction of social change. Although politics may ultimately be the controlling factor, formal legal rules and institutions are not irrelevant, even in Japan.

To investigate how law affects the course of social conflict and change in Japan, this book examines four case studies: the evolution of the antipollution movement and the development of government pollution control policy; the struggle by an outcaste group to overcome and eliminate social discrimination; the elimination of sex discrimination in working conditions, wages, and personnel practices; and the formation and implementation of economic policy by the Ministry of International Trade and Industry. These areas were chosen because, to varying degrees, they are areas of conflict and change in all industrialized democracies and thus provide a basis for comparative analysis.

The presentation and analysis of the case studies focus on the legal framework within which social conflict develops and evolves. I shall examine, therefore, not only whether the aggrieved parties chose litigation, mediation, or violent self-help but also what their options were and how those options were broadened or narrowed by legal doctrine or government policy. In analyzing the government's responses to the appearance of social conflict, I shall focus not only on its response to the substantive grievances and the persons who articulated them but also on its response to the tactics used. Throughout I shall be looking at the social role of the courts and legal doctrine not only when the former become the vehicle for protest, but also when the latter ostensibly precludes any recourse to the courts. In the first three case studies, innovative and independent avenues of social protest were developed, and I shall look closely at how the government has attempted to close these avenues by manipulating their legal environment so that subsequent groups and individuals will find them unavailable or unnecessary for the effective redress of their grievances.

The first case is the Japanese experience with industrial pollution from the 1950s to the 1980s. It is well known, there is a wealth of material available, both factual and interpretative. The tactics chosen by the pollution victims include not only the expected mediation but also both violent confrontation and litigation, two forms of protest that are much more significant in Japan than most Westerners believe and that figure prominently in the other case studies as well. But its status as a completed event makes the pollution experience particularly valuable because it can serve both as a model against which we can measure the other three cases and as a prologue because, although the litigation's direct long-term influence on environmental policy appears minimal, a political event of the magnitude of Japan's antipollution struggle inevitably changes the political and social context within which it occurs. It was a warning to the government that change was occurring, and it is probably not coincidental that the late sixties and seventies also saw the appearance of social conflict in many other areas, including minority and women's rights, the independence of local government, and even industrial policy. Although none of these areas has threatened the social fabric or the Liberal Democratic Party's political control to the extent that the antipollution movement did, they do provide additional opportunities to analyze the role of law in social change in Japan.

Three subsequent areas of inquiry have been chosen. Two concern the management of ongoing social conflict: the Burakumin liberation movement and the struggle of women against employment discrimination. The last area, the creation and implementation of industrial policy, concerns the prevention of conflict by the manipulation of administrative procedures and legal doctrines and the management of interest-group formation. The first two were chosen not only for their intrinsic interest, comparative importance, and availability of materials but also for the contrasting tactics of the groups involved, particularly their attitudes toward and use of litigation. The Burakumin, ethnic Japanese who are the descendants of Tokugawa Period (1603–1868) outcastes, adamantly reject the formality of the judicial process. Instead they use a tactic called "denunciation" (*kyūdan*), which draws on the tradition of symbolic violent protest that also underlay the confrontational tactics of the pollution victims. Japanese women, on the other hand, have pursued a litigation campaign reminiscent of the civil rights and environment struggles in the United States, using the courts to press for basic social reforms not easily attained solely through political means. The two different movements provide complementary views of the role of the legal system in ongoing social change in Japan in terms of both the effectiveness of the different tactics and the government's and the judiciary's reaction to them. Their study can help us learn more about the use of traditional versus liberal legalistic modes of protest and specifically about the former's continued viability in the 1980s for achieving nontraditional goals such as equality of opportunity and treatment.

The fourth case study, administrative practice in the context of industrial policy, approaches the interaction of law and social change from a different perspective. Rather than analyzing how the legal system is involved in ongoing conflict, a study of industrial policy can show us how the effective preclusion of litigation by restrictive legal doctrines can hinder the emergence of conflict by helping maintain an informal relationship between the government and business interests, by limiting and controlling access to the process of policymaking, and by discouraging the formation of interest groups that might disrupt the process. My focus will be on the legal nature of the making and implementing of government policy, specifically the constant consultation with affected industry representatives, and the legal doctrines governing judicial review of administrative action.

The selection of industrial policy as the fourth case study may at first appear anomalous. Not only is overt conflict almost totally absent, but industrial policy covers a different set of issues. The first three phenomena have to do with disadvantaged groups struggling for either material existence or legal rights against entrenched, powerful groups with totally different backgrounds and interests. Industrial policy, on the other hand, directly involves only a small number of businessmen and bureaucrats, whose interests are often complementary and whose backgrounds are substantially similar. But if we look beyond the immediate parties to the industrial policy process and ask who might become involved if the legal rules governing participation were changed, we can surmise that the entry of new groups, including environmentalists and consumer advocates, would quickly transform the current seemingly smooth process into one with abundant overt conflict. The legal exclusion of such groups is part of the government's strategy for maintaining control over the issues in the industrial policy debate and parallels the analogous development of legal rules and institutions to hinder the further emergence of independent players in the antipollution and antidiscrimination movements as well.

Two Western Models

The constant theme throughout these four case studies is the role of law in the government's struggle to control the process of social conflict and the nature and direction of social change. To find and keep this thread through the mass of detail in the case studies that follow, it will be helpful to have in mind two models of the role that law might play in the process of social change. Although both combine elements of the normative and the descriptive, neither represents a legal system that exists, has ever existed, or ever will exist in any society. They are introduced here neither as alternative visions of the proper role of law in social conflict and change nor as descriptions of other legal systems with which Japan can be compared; their role is solely to act as intellectual reference points against which the Japanese phenomena can be evaluated.[6]

The first model emphasizes the role of rules. It hypothesizes a legal system where legal professionals use specialized techniques to find and apply unambiguous rules to clear fact situations independent of external influence. Judicial decisions are reached through specialized modes of legal reasoning proceeding from established rules or principles uniformly applied to all cases. Under the rule-centered model there is a clear differentiation of law from other sources of normative learning, and law eventually supersedes all other state-sponsored forms of conflict resolution. Laws are obeyed largely because they are enacted in a procedurally correct manner, are rationally applied, and are so perceived by the public.[7]

Individuals in this imaginary world are willing to submit to the legal process because they believe in the desirability of formal procedures guaranteeing that universal rules will be followed in the official resolution of all disputes. Neither the government nor the society, in the form of social customs or mores, has the power to intervene in the uniform application of universal norms by the legal system. Since obedience is to the impersonal order of law rather than to the particular loyalties of social life, informal or nonlegal control of social behavior is difficult in those spheres of life that the law purports to control. Even in those spheres that law leaves untouched, informal social controls are limited by the legal rules controlling the process of conflict resolution, so that even outside its formal purview a rule-centered legal system weakens if not displaces other means of social control.

This model has profound implications for the independent existence of social values that have not been enacted as formal legal norms. The conditions of rule-centered law—the universal rules uniformly applied, the specialized and independent corps of professionals, and the appearance of rigor and inevitability of its law-finding technique—make it the only legitimate mode of authoritative dispute resolution. Indeed, dispute resolution is not only the courts' monopoly but also their paramount role in society, and litigation under a rule-centered regime can be termed dispute-resolution litigation. Because the courts apply norms created independently of the judges and parties in the immediate dispute and because the formality and procedure of litigation prevent the judge from distorting the norms or their application, the dispute is resolved in accord with universal norms. And because the norms are knowable in advance and the process of judicial decision making is consistent, the parties to a dispute or potential dispute can accurately predict its results. Legal predictability in turn makes economic planning possible and has frequently been associated with the rise of capitalism. But the ability to predict with confidence when and how state authority can be called upon to intervene coercively in private affairs, an ability that the model assumes for all citizens, is also an extraordinarily destabilizing weapon in ordinary social disputes except in those rare situations where the norms of acceptable social behavior correspond exactly with the formal legal rules.

The social role of the legal system under such conditions is both revolutionary and limited. It is revolutionary in the sense that it removes the state and society from the dispute process by creating a private world where individuals can act contrary to all social and political values not formalized in legal rules. Under other forms of political domination, the state can intervene in individual disputes to fashion ad hoc resolutions appropriate to its own social and political agenda at that time and place. Even if the state should choose not to intervene, the disputing parties and the third-party decision maker are subject to the informal pressures of the society of which they are a part. Whether one calls such pressure traditional values or elite domination, without the formal rationality of rule-centered law the parties are not free to act in their own interests or the judge to decide in accord with universal norms.

In a society where citizens' actual behavior is at odds with the legal norms or where the government wishes to play an active role in directing and controlling social behavior at all levels, therefore, the rule-centered model liberates the individual and threatens collective control. The legislature provides the legal rules and the government enforces the courts' judgments, but the litigation process itself is insulated from the state. The parties, their rights, and the reasoning process by which those rights are derived exist within a private sphere of individual behavior that is radically distinguished from the public sphere of political action and social policy. The government, should it enter this private world through contract formation or tortious conduct, is bound by its rules and can claim no special brief to speak for the greater good. Nor can it or a social elite stand outside the private sphere and influence litigation, either by direct intervention as a party or indirectly through a private party using visions of the public good to bolster his or her own case.

In contrast to the power of legal rules, the roles of legal process and legal professionals are profoundly limited under the rule-centered model. When a norm is broken and conflict occurs, the aggrieved individual goes to court and the judge determines whether the apposite norm has been broken and, if so, orders the indicated remedy. The judge makes the decision, but only in the sense that an electronic calculator "decides" when it adds a column of numbers. If the society changes and conflict increases because generally accepted social behavior no longer conforms to the norms (or the norms were inconsistent with social behavior from their creation), the judge has no power to make the formal law fit social practice and values either by evading the old rules or by creating new ones.

The second model, though equally hypothetical, presents a radically different perspective on law. Instead of formal rules and specialized personnel independent of political and social influences, it emphasizes the role of judges as political actors and litigation as the forum for broad-based social controversies. It denies the possibility of mechanistic fact-finding and the "black-box" scientism of classic legal reasoning and replaces them with judicial policy judgments based not on the uniform application of unambiguous rules but on the judge's vision of wise public policy. In contrast to rule-centered litigation, where the parties supposedly operate independently and separately of the government and public policy, the state is frequently directly involved as a party, and even when the parties are all private entities, government policy is the focus of the substantive inquiry.[8]

The political nature of the decisions and the legislative style of judicial reasoning make the courts' role in judge-centered litigation illegitimate from the perspective of the rule-centered model.[9] Under the latter, litigation has no independent normative impact on society; it is merely machinery for the social application of legal norms, and judges and lawyers are only cogs in this machinery. Under judicial domination, however, the explicit utilization of litigation to pursue social change rather than private interests is both legitimate and inevitable. The judicial value judgments are such that they cannot be hidden behind the mask of legal reasoning, and the issues and remedies are such that judges are involved not only in the declaration of social values but also in their formation.[10]

Although the assumptions of the judge-centered model lead to greater power for the process of litigation and for the judiciary as an institution, they weaken the independence and insulation enjoyed by the parties in the traditional model and render impossible the uniform penetration in society of formal legal norms. Because legal rules no longer mechanically control the result, the parties are no longer in complete control of the process. Loss of party control occurs procedurally as the public nature of the controversy leads to the intervention of additional parties and as the judge assumes a more active role; it occurs substantively as the balancing tests and legislative judgments of policy science replace the "black box" of formalist legal reasoning. Interests replace rights, and flexible ad hoc policymaking replaces the general application of universal norms. In this sense the theoretical power of plaintiffs under rule-centered law to force the general application of legal rules throughout the jurisdiction, independent of government policy or social values, is lost and replaced by an overtly political but normatively less consistent power on the part of the judicial system and those groups that can persuade it to do their bidding.

Despite the fundamental differences between these heuristic models, they have one common characteristic that is central to their function in this book: the limited role of the state in litigation. Under rule-centered law, the legislature provides the legal rules but then loses all control over the degree and speed of their penetration into social life. Even more relevant to the Japanese comparison, the administrative apparatus of the state has no role in either the creation of the norms or their penetration throughout society. Given the foreign origin of many fundamental legal norms in Japan and the central social role of the bureaucracy, the creation of a private domain of dispute resolution that is completely beyond its influence can be socially and politically threatening. Under judicial domination, on the other hand, the state, usually through its administrative agents, is an active party to the decision-making process, but it is only one party. Given the indeterminate nature of legal rules in this model, the legislature has lost much of its power to set consistent norms and the bureaucracy is only one of the myriad interests that appear before the courts. Because of the ad hoc nature of judicial decision making, the threat of the uncontrollable and complete penetration of legal norms throughout society is eliminated but is replaced by a powerful judiciary that effectively hampers the government's ability to control social conflict and direct social change.

At this juncture it should be reiterated that the models presented here are at best rough sketches of more complex ideal types developed in detail by others. Although they both have roots in Western concepts of law, they are neither descriptions of actual legal systems nor formulas for potential ones.[11] But despite their artificial nature, they represent contrasting ideals and accounts of the role of legal rules and institutions in social conflict and change, and most observers would agree that elements of both models are present in all Western legal systems. Virtually all observers of Japan, however, would agree that the Japanese legal system plays neither role to any substantial degree and that even the partial realization of either model would threaten the present structure of Japanese society.[12] To understand the nature of this threat and how both models are perceived in Japan, it is necessary to examine the origin of legal rules in Japan and the relative roles of the legislature, judiciary, and bureaucracy in setting the social and political agenda.

With many notable exceptions,[13] the fundamental norms of Japan's legal system were either written by foreigners, like the Constitution of 1947, or derived from Western legal models, like the Civil Code of 1896. Those who would explain Japanese legal phenomena by reference to Japan's cultural traditions make much, perhaps too much, of this foreign origin. They contrast the Civil Code's emphasis on individual autonomy and economic choice, products of its nineteenth-century German heritage, with the neo-Confucian emphasis on loyalty and duty of Tokugawa Japan (1603–1868), and they contrast the panoply of civil rights and liberties and the New Deal public-welfare liberalism of the current Constitution with the political repression of prewar Japan. With this history, the traditionalists argue, it is inevitable and natural that the Japanese have little interest in enforcing legal rights: not only the process but the norms themselves are too foreign for the Japanese psyche.

Japanese political and legal history is much more complex than this account indicates: the law was never quite so foreign nor Japan's history so monolithic.[14] The necessary qualifications, however, should not obscure the undeniable fact that Japan's legal norms are basically the result of foreign imposition or conscious, at times uncritical, imitation and not the result of internal social evolution. And even though the origin and magnitude of the gap between Japanese social behavior and the legal norms may be debatable, there is no question that it exists and that the norms assume legal and social behavior and attitudes considerably more individualistic, egalitarian, and assertive than many Japanese feel comfortable with or consider appropriate.

If we assume that current social behavior and attitudes are congenial to Japan's elite, the implications of the rule-centered model become clear. Let us assume, for example, that a common way to resolve minor neighborhood disputes is intervention by a higher-status third party, usually either a local political leader or a police or government official.[15] Mediation has two implications for the social and legal order. First, unless the parties have a thorough knowledge of their legal options and the resources to pursue them, applicable legal norms may be replaced by social norms, most likely those of the higher-status intervenor. Second, in addition to strengthening the social penetration of elite norms, such mediation engenders dependence on local notables or government officials and reinforces the power structure of local society. The effect is similar whether the dispute is minor (for example, late-night piano playing) or life-threatening (industrial pollution), and, with some qualifications, whether the mediation is informal and ad hoc or part of a government mediation bureaucracy.

Litigation as idealized in the rule-centered model, on the other hand, would not only bypass the current power structure but would destroy it whenever, as is frequently the case in Japan, the formal norms of the legal system were substantially at variance with those of the elite. Contested divorce is a good example. Japanese law includes an irretrievable breakdown of the marriage, regardless of fault, as one ground for divorce.[16] According to the legislative norm, in other words, divorce is preferable to forced continuation of marriage when one of the spouses wants divorce and there is no hope for reconciliation. This norm is not, however, shared by all Japanese, and judicial hostility and compulsory mediation have effectively nullified the statutory norms and replaced them with an ad hoc system of institutionalized mediation that generally favors the legal continuation of marriage and that usually allows contested divorce only on the basis of fault on the part of the party opposing divorce. Both the family court judges, who not only frown on no-fault contested divorce but sometimes also deny divorce even with clear evidence of fault on the respondent's side, and the family court mediators, who at times consciously and explicitly attempt to represent "social values," are from a very narrow range of the elite in Japan. Whether or not this antipathy toward divorce is shared by most Japanese, it is certainly not reflected in the legal norms; indeed, divorce by mutual consent has long been readily available in Japan. Nor is it shared by the many disappointed petitioners whose desire to vindicate the legal norm is consistently frustrated by the imposition of social rather than legal values. A further important implication of the mediation method is the haphazard nature of the normative system. Because of the judges' attitudes and the inconsistency of their decisions, an adjudicated divorce is extremely difficult and unpredictable, and mediation is the only real alternative for most spouses. Although most mediators are generally against divorce, they do at times successfully recommend it in contested cases; however, their lack of legal training and the ad hoc and confidential nature of mediation mean that consistent standards for divorce simply do not exist and would not be available to the public if they did.

The result of the current system is the replacement of statutory norms by a haphazard patchwork of individual decisions that sometimes merely reflect the relative strengths of the spouses and at other times are a result of the imposition of upper-class values in a way that would be impossible under rule-centered law. Uniform application of norms would destroy the discretion of both judges and mediators to fashion each case to its own facts. It would also, of course, mean that the judges and mediators would be bound by the legal norms regardless of their congruence or lack of congruence with their own values or visions of social welfare. The result would be the social penetration of legal norms regarding divorce and the family that are perceived by many Japanese, certainly by the majority of the upper class, to be inimical to social stability. Even when we remember that the two models are only ideal types and that phrases such as "irretrievable breakdown" are hardly self-defining, it remains likely that a substantial increase in the adjudication of contested divorce cases and the concomitant increase in judicial articulation of the reasons and justifications for departures from the statutory norms would decrease the current gap between marriage behavior and the legal norms and weaken the discretion of judges and mediators.

Just as the foreign origin of much of Japanese law helps to explain the social threat posed by the rule-centered model, attention to the historical role of the bureaucracy illuminates the implications of the judge-centered model. Japan has a long history of institutionally separating the functions of reigning and ruling and of clearly distinguishing between sovereign authority and political power. Following the Tokugawa pattern of imperial reign and feudal rule, the Meiji Constitution of 1889 located sovereignty in the Emperor but ratified a political structure that allowed substantial power to reside in the national bureaucracy and very little in the person of the Emperor. Similarly, the Constitution of 1947 locates sovereignty in the National Diet as representative of the people and establishes a separation of powers that relegates bureaucrats to the simple implementation of legislative policy. In actuality, however, the national bureaucracy remains one of the preeminent political groups in Japan, often rivaling or even dominating the Diet in the formulation and implementation of policy.[17]

The conventional description of Japan's political structure, though recently criticized as oversimplifying a complex series of relationships, remains that of a triumvirate consisting of the leaders of the Liberal Democratic Party (LDP), top business management, and elite bureaucrats.[18] These three groups are tightly interlocked and economically interdependent. The LDP politicians possess supreme formal authority: they vote on legislation; they constitute the Cabinet; and as ministers and parliamentary vice-ministers, they are in legal control of the bureaucracy. In matters of great political sensitivity or periods of severe interministerial conflict this formal authority becomes important politically, but in ordinary times the government of Japan is firmly in the hands of the bureaucracy. The Diet's legislative role normally consists of enacting bills drafted by the bureaucracy with little or no revision. Furthermore, since the minister and parliamentary vice-minister are the only political appointees in a ministry, they are, despite an increasing level of sophistication and experience among LDP politicians, substantially dependent on the career bureaucrats for the formulation as well as the implementation of policy. Top bureaucrats, on the other hand, cannot safely ignore the politicians' views, not only because of their formal authority and influence over top bureaucratic appointments but also because many bureaucrats enter politics directly upon retirement in their fifties. Retired bureaucrats constitute 30 percent of the membership of the Liberal Democratic Party in the Diet, a fact that underscores the two groups' interdependence.[19] The economic power of business completes the triangle of the business–LDP–bureaucracy relationship: the politicians are directly dependent on business for campaign funds, and those bureaucrats who do not enter politics generally retire to high positions in private firms with which they have developed a close relationship during their government service.

The legal doctrines and institutions that enable these relationships to function as they do constitute a major theme of this book and are treated in particular detail in Chapters 2 and 5. Here I need only point out that the powerful and independent judiciary hypothesized in the judge-centered model would present a threat to both the continuation of the triumvirate in its present form and to the bureaucrats' wide discretion in policy formation and implementation. Although the Japanese judiciary has a long and well-deserved reputation for political independence and a willingness to make decisions unpopular with the government, this political independence has not developed into an effective judicial review of discretionary administrative decisions, even or perhaps especially those with important distributive or political consequences.[20] In those exceptional cases where a plaintiff is determined enough to overcome the doctrinal and practical obstacles and succeeds in getting judicial scrutiny of discretionary acts, the courts almost invariably do two things: first, they reject the government's claim that the decision is totally discretionary and assert the court's right and obligation to review for abuse of discretion, no matter how broad; second, they determine that, in this case, the government's decision was within its scope of discretion.[21]

If we recall that the prime characteristics of litigation under the judge-centered model are a multiplicity of parties and interests represented, an active judge using legislative-style reasoning to fashion prospective social policy, and a focus on the government and its policies as the central issue in the litigation, the model's implications for administrative discretion in Japan are clear. While the bureaucracy's interdependence with business and political elites limits its discretion informally, judicial power of this type would limit it legally and publicly. Instead of behind-the-scenes compromises worked out among long-time associates with fundamentally complementary interests, administrative policy would be exposed to the glare of the media and open conflict of the courtroom, with hostile outsiders representing various interests that the bureaucrats had heretofore been able to ignore or deal with only on their own terms. Even in those instances where litigation did not occur, and they would be the vast majority, administrative decision makers would have to consider the possibility of litigation, with the result that the administrative process itself would become more multipolar and formal in an attempt to avoid judicial scrutiny and intervention.

As administrative processes became more open and formal, the informal give-and-take that is the social glue holding the business–bureaucracy–LDP coalition together would be threatened. Even if the substance of its decisions remained unchanged, the bureaucracy would be forced to explain and justify positions now left ambiguous; previously unspoken political compromises would become issues of popular debate; and the interdependence of the ruling triumvirate would be severely undermined. If we accept one political and legal scholar's characterization of Japan as "an administrative state, wherein the alliance of the LDP, the bureaucracy, and business, by their best light, plan and administer the resources of the nation for national progress and public welfare . . . with only minimal concessions" to their opponents,[22] the implications of the judge-centered model begin to reach beyond the bureaucracy to the structure of Japanese politics in general.

A Japanese Model

The identification of litigation as a threat to the political and social status quo is implicit in all writing on Japanese law and society, and recent scholarship argues persuasively that self-interest has led the Japanese elite to take deliberate steps to discourage litigation.[23] Whether these legal and institutional measures were taken out of self-interest or out of a sincere desire to preserve unique cultural values and avoid the economic and social cost of litigation is less important for our purposes than the fact that, though effective in a quantitative sense, these measures have failed to prevent litigation from playing an important social and political role in contemporary Japan.

What elite hostility has done, however, is to influence the development of litigation's role in such a way that it has evolved in directions largely different from either of our Western models. The process of that influence and the resulting form and role of litigation in Japan will be presented in detail throughout the case studies that constitute the bulk of this volume. For now it will suffice to sketch from selected perspectives a necessarily tentative and partial view of what one might call the Japanese model of litigation. Though heavily influenced by the data of the case studies and therefore more descriptive of an actual legal system than rule-centered or judge-centered law, this model, which I shall call bureaucratic informalism, is also meant to serve as an intellectual reference point to guide the reader through the detail of the following chapters. It is not meant, however, to explain or account for all that occurs within Japanese law and society.

Central to the Japanese model of law generally and of litigation in particular is the elite's attempt to retain some measure of control over the processes of social conflict and change. The vehicle for that control is a skilled and dedicated bureaucracy, itself one branch of Japan's tripartite elite coalition, which has a long history of active intervention in Japanese society. But social control, even the indirect control favored by Japanese governments since the Tokugawa Period, is extraordinarily difficult in democratic societies. Japan enjoys not only representative government but also a high degree of social and economic mobility, a vigorous and irreverent press, and an independent and respected judiciary and private bar. Even if the bureaucracy wished to exercise direct social control—and there is no reason to believe that the bureaucrats are any less committed to democratic values than any other segment of Japanese society—it would impossible to do so.[24]

Given these limitations, the bureaucracy does retain a surprising degree of control over the pace and course, if not the substance, of social change in Japan, and one of its major instruments for such control is the manipulation of the legal framework within which social change and its harbinger, social conflict, occur. The institutional barriers to litigation already well documented by recent scholarship are part of this framework, but they are only the beginning of the story; they cannot help us understand the nature and the role of the litigation that nonetheless occurs nor explain why there is so little demand, except perhaps among American social scientists and legal professionals, for more effective access to formal processes. For answers to these inquiries, one must analyze the way in which litigation is used today in Japan and the legal aspects of the governmental reaction to it in particular and to social conflict in general.

Unless one assumes that Japanese cultural traditions preclude the possibility, one will not be surprised to learn that litigation with elements of the rule-centered and judge-centered models occurs with some frequency in Japan, especially in politically charged areas such as freedom of speech, defense policy, or electoral malapportionment in the Diet, where opposition parties, particularly the Japanese Communist Party, are constantly searching for political leverage against the Liberal Democratic Party.[25] It also occurs in less ideologically polarized social conflict among groups and under circumstances with only ambiguous political implications. In varying degrees, litigation or potential litigation with strong elements of these models has arisen in each of the four areas of social life that will be examined in the case studies, but in each instance, using various doctrinal and institutional devices and with varying degrees of success, the Japanese government has attempted to prevent the development of litigation into an effective and ongoing vehicle for social change.

One consistent Japanese response to social conflict in any form is the creation of institutional mediation. Although recent empirical work has cast doubt on its accuracy, the conventional wisdom has been that disputes are usually resolved by the informal intervention of a trusted third party, most typically an older person of higher status. Whether or not such spontaneous intervention occurs successfully on a regular basis in contemporary Japan, the continuing belief that it does makes it politically easier for the government to establish bureaucratically controlled mediation schemes whenever informal means fail to prevent serious social conflict.[26]

Such was the case in two of the case studies presented here, where litigation played a large role in the articulation of conflict. In the antipollution case, victims of air pollution and toxic substance poisoning eventually became dissatisfied with what informal dispute-resolution methods could achieve and filed suit against the polluting companies. This litigation, which was known as the "Big Four Pollution Suits," became the focus for a social and political movement that ended the conservatives' rule in many local governments and threatened their majority in the National Diet. The lawsuits, which were all won by the plaintiffs, also spawned a second generation of environmental litigation that focused on government and business development policy and threatened to narrow the bureaucracy's discretion by formalizing the development process in a way that was inimical to the interests of both business and the bureaucracy.

The Japanese government responded in three ways. First, the bureaucracy drafted and the Diet passed a series of statutes that constitute a pollution control regime as strict as any in the world. Second, it established a polluter-financed but government-administered scheme to compensate officially certified pollution victims. Third and perhaps most significant for the present discussion, the government created a bureaucratically administered and staffed system of identifying and mediating pollution disputes. Since it began operating in 1971, the system has handled thousands of disputes of various kinds and degrees of complexity.

Whether each dispute mediated by the government is a lawsuit forgone—even whether the creation of alternative avenues for grievance articulation decreases litigation at all—is unclear, but the creation of the system and its staffing with competent and conscientious bureaucrats have combined with the compensation system and a dramatic decrease in urban pollution levels to defuse the antipollution movement and to return the locus of Japan's environmental and development policymaking from the courts to the bureaucracy. In doing so, the government succeeded in avoiding the continued development of litigation into a regular tactic of the environmental movement. Litigation is of course still available to potential plaintiffs—indeed, the antipollution regulatory scheme and the doctrines judicially developed in the Big Four and other early cases have arguably made pollution litigation easier doctrinally—and it does occur occasionally. But what appeared as a real threat in the early 1970s—that courts applying new pro-plaintiff norms would become the general arbiters of pollution disputes and that judges would increasingly intervene in environmental policymaking in pivotal cases of national importance—never materialized.

The official response to successful sex-discrimination litigation was not dissimilar, despite substantial differences in the nature of the litigation and its social and political context. In the mid-1960s Japanese working women began to sue their employers for what were initially blatantly discriminatory practices. In spite of daunting doctrinal problems, the plaintiffs attacked progressively more subtle and indirect methods of discrimination. This process gradually accelerated through the seventies, and at the end of the decade the Ministry of Labor began enforcing bureaucratically the most firmly established of the judicially developed norms. The process culminated in 1985 when the Diet passed without serious amendment the bureaucratically drafted Equal Employment Opportunity Act, which statutorily prohibits a wide range of practices already clearly prohibited judicially. The Act, on the other hand, left the Ministry wide discretion in devising and enforcing policy in areas that the courts had not yet fully developed, areas that, perhaps not coincidentally, are the most threatening to the fundamental employment practices of Japanese firms. Simultaneously, the Act created a system administered and staffed by the Ministry for mediating employment discrimination disputes.

It is too early to tell whether these measures will be as successful in recapturing the initiative in the antidiscrimination area as similar steps were in pollution. In the former area, substantially alleviating the underlying cause of discontent—the conflict between the rising aspirations of Japanese women and the fundamental structure of current employment patterns—may be much more difficult than it was in the case of pollution. Nor is there a clear national consensus for eliminating discrimination as there was for improving the environment. On the contrary, the nature and scope of equal-employment legislation was a matter of considerable partisan debate, and labor and management took opposite positions on various aspects of the bill. The Ministry of Labor is therefore likely to be criticized no matter what position it eventually takes on the issues deliberately left ambiguous in the statute. As a result, women may eschew government mediation and continue to sue at a greater rate than have environmental plaintiffs, particularly if the opposition parties decide to support such suits in a systematic manner.

It is important, however, not to underestimate the impact of the Equal Employment Opportunity Act. Although ambiguous on the definition and enforcement of equality for women in management, the law unequivocally prohibits long-standing discriminatory practices that have affected the vast majority of working women. The government will vigorously enforce these sections of the law, and the substantial and widespread beneficial effect for most working women will undermine popular support for litigation aimed at improving the status of the small minority of women who wish to compete equally with men, an aspiration that strikes many in Japan as selfish and harmful to family and society. Financial support from political parties, although enabling suits to be brought, will exacerbate the problem of broad popular support, particularly if the support comes exclusively from leftist parties. If one adds to these factors the Ministry's sincere willingness to mediate any discrimination complaints and a growing willingness on the part of many firms to hire women for the management track, albeit on their own terms and at their own pace, it is not hard to imagine the cutting edge of sex-discrimination reforms slipping smoothly out of the courts, where it has been up to now, into the Ministry of Labor. This need not mean the end of progress for equality in employment, but it will mean that its pace and course will be largely determined by the Ministry after informal consultation with unions and business, rather than by litigants pushing the courts to make social policy or apply norms that are inconsistent with the consensus of the bureaucracy, business, the LDP, and, in this instance, organized labor.

The aim of this and similar attempts to keep dispute resolution and social policymaking out of the courts is not direct bureaucratic control of Japanese society. Although influence over the direction of social change is central to these measures, the Japanese elite is neither mono-lithic enough to agree on detailed social objectives nor powerful enough to achieve them in the face of strong social or economic forces to the contrary. What Japan's tripartite elite has tried to accomplish, and what they have in large part succeeded in achieving, is the mainte-nance of a style of policy formation and implementation that empha-sizes bureaucratic leadership exercised through informal processes.

The terms *leadership* and *informality* require elaboration. Leadership is not meant to connote control in the sense that the bureaucracy can dictate private behavior, whether that of corporations or of individuals. As all four case studies demonstrate, the bureaucracy tries to gauge the fundamental direction of social change, compares it with the best interests of society from the perspective of the ruling coalition of which it is a part, and then attempts to stimulate and facilitate the creation of a national consensus that supports its own vision of correct national policy. Usually the initiative for a particular policy change comes from the ruling coalition itself; this was largely the case in both the creation of the affirmative action programs described in the Burakumin case study and the liberalization of the Japanese economy described in the industrial policy case study. At times, however, the impetus for change comes from social movements outside the bureaucracy–LDP–business coalition, and, as shown in the pollution and employment discrimina-tion instances, litigation can be the vehicle for making the elite aware of serious social discontent and spurring it to take remedial action.

In taking such action, however, the elite is conscious not only of the substantive aims of such litigation but also of the threat that it poses to the pervasive informality on which the triumvirate relies in setting and implementing its own policies. While litigation can thus be the vehicle for protest, it is not allowed to develop into an institutional channel for resolving disputes or setting national policy because either role would destroy the elite's control of the process as well as the substance of policymaking. In this context, therefore, informality means most of all legal informality and the avoidance of the formal processes implicit in litigation. Meetings may be scheduled and public testimony received, research commissions formed, reports published, elaborate plans of action drafted and approved by competent government officials, and concrete private action urged by powerful ministries; but nothing in the process will rise to the level of a legally cognizable act that could become the object of litigation challenging the process as a whole or any step therein.

Legal informality is maintained partially by the simple discouragement of litigation and the provision of the alternative avenues of dispute resolution accomplished by the creation of government mediation schemes and an effective response to the underlying problems. But these measures, while necessary, would not be sufficient. As we shall see in detail in the chapters that follow, legal informality also requires careful statutory drafting, not only to avoid the creation of private causes of action in statutes like the Equal Employment Opportunity Act but also to give bureaucrats both wide discretion to define their mission under a statute and the ability to carry it out through an administrative process that emphasizes informal consultation and compromise and avoids formal administrative acts that could trigger litigation. It further requires a body of legal doctrine that limits judicial review of bureaucratic action and a judiciary that is comfortable with administrative discretion and uncomfortable with the assertion of its own power. Finally and perhaps most important, bureaucratic informalism must be supported by an ideological vision of law and society that legitimates the various roles of courts, bureaucrats, legal rules, and social behavior and relates them to a vision of what society should be.

The importance of informality comes out clearly in the bureaucratic reaction to the litigation discussed earlier. The draftsmen were careful not to include in either the environmental or the employment opportunity statutes any cause of action that would strengthen the ability of private citizens to challenge legally government action taken under the statutes.[27] Nor is statutorily created governmental mediation controllable in any meaningful way through the legal system. Plaintiffs can still bring private actions against private defendants, but once the bureaucracy has intervened in a given field, whether it be environmental protection, employment discrimination, industrial policy, or affirmative action, the bureaucracy becomes the locus of the policymaking process and official policy the object of political debate, so that private suits against private defendants can no longer challenge the fundamental direction of policy.

The nature and implications of informality are perhaps best brought out by analyzing the evolution of conflict in the four case studies in terms of the contrasting roles of litigation and its informal alternatives in the articulation of social discontent. In both the environmental and employment-discrimination cases, litigation provided a forum for interests that had hitherto been ignored or discounted. In the pollution cases, plaintiffs and their supporters used the periodic court hearings to attract media attention and mobilize political allies, eventually succeeding in substantially weakening the national consensus for economic growth that had dominated postwar Japan. The employment-discrimination litigation, on the other hand, drew on a narrower band of the political spectrum and relied more on incremental doctrinal advances than on a dramatic reversal of national policy. But in both instances, the nature and rhetoric of the legal process gave the plaintiffs a chance to identify their own condition with universal principles agreed to by most Japanese. In both instances courtroom battles and moralistic judicial opinions upholding plaintiffs' positions contributed to the transformation of individual or local disputes into national issues that the ruling coalition could not dismiss.

The utility of litigation in broadening individual conflict into social conflict becomes clearer when we compare the Burakumin's struggle against discrimination with that of women. The Burakumin and their national organization, the Buraku Liberation League, have consistently eschewed litigation on the grounds that it fostered dependence on the state and its judiciary, both of which are believed to be infected with anti-Buraku prejudice. Instead of litigation, the League has mounted vigorous "denunciation" campaigns, using limited violence to force their opponents and selected bureaucrats to negotiate on issues ranging from liberation ideology to the types and amounts of transfer payments due Burakumin living in particular areas.

The substantial improvement in the economic condition of the Burakumin over the last two decades is evidence of denunciation's effectiveness in convincing bureaucrats to devote public resources to their cause, and the choice of denunciation over litigation gave League leaders greater control over the course and outcome of conflict than they would have enjoyed had they relied on the judiciary. The cost of rejecting litigation, however, has been an inability to identify the Buraku cause with universal principles held by all Japanese. Because each denunciation focuses on particular issues determined by immediate circumstances, they tend to resemble collective bargaining more than civil-rights struggles. Even when the rhetoric is highly moralistic, the nature of the denunciation process emphasizes the particularistic aspects of a dispute, often to the point where the universal nature of the issues is obscured and inaccessible to the greater public. As a result, the Buraku liberation movement has reached an impasse. Denunciation has achieved substantial material gains, but it has not enabled the Burakumin to universalize their complaints or gain the political support that would enable the movement to begin to bring Burakumin into the mainstream of employment and society. Instead, the League is locked into an informal relationship with local governments that in the long run may be more amenable to government control and manipulation than even the Ministry of Labor's policy toward sex discrimination under the Equal Employment Opportunity Act.

The industrial policy case study presents bureaucratic informality in a radically different context. Instead of open conflict between groups with contradictory interests, we largely find harmony and consensus among groups with similar interests and backgrounds. A close examination of the industrial policy process, however, reveals the same fundamental characteristics that dominate the government's legal response to the conflict of the first three case studies. Most important, the process is legally informal and unaccountable. Statutes establish extremely broad and vague parameters within which the Ministry of International Trade and Industry (MITI) shapes policy by private consultations with representatives of the relevant industry associations and individual firms. Only after a compromise has been reached that all major actors can live with does the process become formal and official, and even then administrative law doctrines restricting the standing to sue, the justiciability of government actions, and the close judicial scrutiny of bureaucratic discretion combine to put the results of the process effectively beyond the legal reach of dissatisfied outsiders. The bureaucracy exploits the informality of the process to allow it to exercise the same form of indirect leadership that we see in the other case studies. Just as the government uses institutionalized mediation, compensation systems, and affirmative-action grants to avoid or influence the course of conflict in the pollution and discrimination areas,

MITI mediates interfirm and interindustry conflict with the goal of facilitating eventual agreement on policy that is satisfactory to the participants and also within government guidelines. The relative power of the bureaucracy vis-à-vis the private sector may be significantly less in industrial policy than in the other cases, but the underlying role of the government as mediator and facilitator within an informal process of conflict management remains unchanged.

It should not be surprising that the same characteristics apply to industrial policy as to the other three phenomena; it is in many ways their mirror image. Whereas they represent the aberrational partial breakdown of social control, industrial policy represents the normal functioning of a system of social control that through the legal system and other devices strives to minimize open conflict. The response of the Japanese government to conflict that threatens its mode of governance is to reestablish informality as dominant in the structure of the conflict and thereby reassert influence over its direction. In industrial policy, MITI has retained the use of informality despite decreases in its formal legal power and profound changes in the structure of the Japanese economy. Thus, what we see in industrial policy is the routine reiteration of the same devices for conflict management that we see employed for crisis management and the reestablishment of control in the other case studies. For the real constant throughout this volume is the struggle for control of the process of social change, which entails control over the nature and course of social conflict, which in turn demands legal rules and institutions that allow informality in the process of conflict resolution and that encourage dependence on the government as a central player in that process.

Who has significant power over the process of social conflict and change is a central question in all societies. In democracies, furthermore, this issue is closely related to the forms and processes of the legal system. The two Western models presented earlier depict legal systems in which the management of social conflict is somewhat independent of government controls; whether it is left to the "black box" of rule-centered law or the balancing tests of judge-centered law, the bureaucracy under these models has limited control over the substance or process of conflict. Instead, initiative is in the hands of litigants and judges: the former force the application of universal norms in the first model and the latter determine broad social policy in the second. Under either set of circumstances, the role of the bureaucracy is limited.

Such laissez-faire pluralism is anathema to the Japanese elite, and it is not surprising that it strives mightily to preserve a legal system whose norms and processes support greater bureaucratic influence and involvement over the course of social conflict. In large part, this influence is exercised through the informal bureaucratic orchestration of private action rather than directly through compulsory state regulation. Sometimes this process takes place through institutions specifically created by statute to meet a particular need, such as family court conciliation or environmental mediation; at other times it occurs through an ad hoc consultation process with only the loosest legal framework, as is most common in industrial policy. The Japanese legal system is designed to accommodate either approach and is dependent on such informal administrative mechanisms to handle routine social conflict.

Occasionally, however, the informal systems of control are inadequate. Technological change may cause new problems that the informal system cannot understand or control: environmental pollution is one example. Or ideological, demographic, or economic forces may influence social norms in ways that the informal mechanisms cannot absorb. The aspirations of women and Burakumin for equal treatment are examples, and so, in a sense, is the demand for the liberalization and internationalization of the Japanese economy that has forced adjustments in the industrial policy process.

Sometimes, as in the Buraku and MITI examples, new forms of informality can be devised that accommodate the new social demands while retaining the fundamental social relationships of the previous system. In the Buraku instance, this new form was the informal negotiating process that has grown out of the Buraku Liberation League's development and the bureaucracy's and courts' toleration of denunciation as a routine vehicle for the articulation of grievances and demands. In industrial policy, the adjustment took the form of legislation that recognizes the new forces and players in economic policy but retains the informal consultative process that is the basis of policymaking. In both instances, substantive social change was accommodated without the sacrifice of bureaucratic influence over the process of change.

In other situations, however, change has been ignored or resisted. In both the pollution and sex discrimination instances, the informal systems of conflict management failed to adjust, partially because the bureaucracy underestimated the severity and breadth of the discontent and partially because it did not consider the possibility that victims of pollution and sex discrimination would successfully use litigation to advance their interests. As a result, these victims discovered for perhaps the first time in postwar Japan that the courts could provide a forum for the public articulation of the grievances of parties outside the ruling coalition and thereby enable outsiders to circumvent the elite control of the political and social agenda that is inherent in bureaucratic informality.[28] The plaintiffs used the judicial forum to gain media access to the public and the rhetoric of legal argument to connect their particular grievances to universal norms like benevolence and equality shared to some extent by all Japanese. Once it became clear that evocation by the elite of contrary norms like self-sacrifice and hierarchy had failed to negate the plaintiffs' appeal, the social and political battle had been won. The issues of female employees and pollution victims had become items on the national political and social agenda and would have to be dealt with.

Litigation in Japan can thus be the vehicle for the transformation of diffuse discontent or isolated instances of individual conflict into social issues. It can help disparate groups recognize common interests and form alliances, and it can help associate these interests with wider social values. To a certain extent, this process can occur regardless of the outcome of the litigation: the antipollution movement had achieved virtually total political victory before the Big Four suits had been decided. But in most situations, the judges' proclamations of support in the form not only of plaintiffs' victories but also of moralistic opinions endorsing the plaintiffs' cause are crucial to the political and social progress of the movement. The series of judicial opinions declaring employers' discriminatory practices illegal and, not incidentally, monetarily rewarding plaintiffs' perseverance may have taken longer and been less dramatic than the pollution cases, but their eventual influence was just as important.

In this sense of a judicial role in the development of social policy, the Japanese situation resembles the judge-centered model. The difference is in the state's reaction to the success of litigation. Instead of tolerating the continuation and expansion of the judicial role, the bureaucracy steps in to recapture control of the social agenda. It can do so only by recognizing the new direction of social change established partially by the litigation vehicle, but it need not and will not recognize an institutional role for the judiciary in shaping the ongoing course of that change. Although legally developed norms are recognized as socially valid and binding, the details of their implementation will continue to be worked out through the processes of bureaucratic informalism.

TWO

Environmental Tragedy and Response

SINCE its defeat in 1945, Japan has experienced close to forty years of virtually uninterrupted conservative rule. The Liberal Democratic Party (LDP), which despite its name is the most conservative of Japan's major parties, has been able to rely on electoral support from rural areas, which are disproportionately represented in the Diet, and small and large business interests. The party's continued electoral success has derived not only from directly serving these interests, but also from a strong national consensus that reindustrialization was vital to Japan's postwar recovery and from the LDP's success in achieving consistent real economic growth.

The policies that fostered this growth grew out of a political process dominated by three forces: the leaders of the LDP, and particularly the faction leaders with their strong ties to rural constituencies; the leaders of business, as represented on the macroeconomic level by organizations such as the Federation of Economic Organizations (Keidanren) and on the specific industry level by the various industry associations; and the elite bureaucrats, the graduates of Tokyo University Faculty of Law who hold most important positions in those ministries—Finance, Industrial Trade and Industry, Foreign Affairs, Agriculture and Forestry—that largely form and implement economic policy. The locus of political power was, and to a large extent remains today, in the constant formal and informal consultations among these forces and in the strong personal, political, and economic relationships binding the representatives of these groups to one another. With the exception of the 1960 U.S.–Japan Security Treaty crisis, this triumvirate enjoyed almost unchallenged control over national policy and the national social, political, and economic agenda throughout the 1950s and 1960s.

Much of its success was undoubtedly due to a lack of an alternative to economic growth as a focus for a national consensus—both the military and nationalism had been discredited by World War II, and the left-wing parties and unions were unable to present an effective alternative to the conservatives' program of industrialization and growth—but the lack of effective opposition was also due in part to Japan's failure to develop legal or political channels for challenging specific government policies or decisions. The legislative process is effectively dominated by the bureaucracy; the legal system, for various reasons to be considered in detail later, has not historically provided a forum for disputing official policies; and local politics have been dominated by particularistic loyalties to the *yūryokusha* ("the powerful people"), that is, heads of neighborhood associations, merchants' groups, or the support networks of national LDP politicians. Opposition by the minority parties was abstract and ideological, and issue-oriented interest groups such as those characterizing American politics were virtually nonexistent. The result was a "conservatives' paradise," where an occasional expressive and emotional protest like the Security Treaty riots maintained the appearance of vigorous opposition but where actual decisions on both broad policies and particular issues remained within conservative control.

Much of this situation changed in the late sixties and early seventies as unprecedented pollution shook, then destroyed temporarily, the consensus supporting high-growth policies. Postwar pollution began in the mid-1950's, but the strength of pro-growth sentiment, the polluting companies' consistent denials of responsibility, local and central governments' collusion in those denials, the victims' lack of political and financial resources, and their hesitancy to push their claims kept pollution from becoming a general social issue for more than a decade. Then in 1967 leftist lawyers filed the first lawsuit on behalf of pollution victims, which was quickly followed by three more. As these lawsuits progressed, they became the focus for an antipollution movement that soon grew to be national in scope and threatened the LDP's local and national legislative majorities and the triumvirate's informal and closed method of policymaking and implementation. The government's reaction was a dramatic turnabout in environmental policy. Legislative action, which had begun in 1967 as a palliative to the then weak movement, culminated in an extraordinary session of the national Diet in December 1970 known as the "pollution Diet," which enacted a series of amendments and new statutes that established

Japan as an innovator in environmental policy and a leader in pollution control. Perhaps most indicative of the political mood and the complete reversal of political and social momentum was the unanimous vote of the Diet to eliminate a clause in the Basic Law for Environmental Pollution Control of 1967 that limited environmental regulation to that consistent with economic growth.[1]

The aspects of Japan's pollution experience of interest here are the tactics of the pollution victims and their supporters and the government's response both to these specific tactics and to the movement as a whole. Through an examination of how the victims mobilized first themselves and later popular support, how they applied this political power to force substantial policy changes by government and business, and the role that the legal system played in these processes, we can see how law can be used by disadvantaged groups to articulate social grievances and to achieve social change in contemporary Japan. A subsequent examination of the elite's use of law to contain political damage and later to regain political control can show both the government's attitude toward the victims' tactics and the way it uses law initially to manage social conflict and later to prevent it from recurring.

Pollution in Minamata

Minamata is a small city in Kumamoto Prefecture on Kyushu, the southernmost of Japan's four main islands. The surrounding economy is largely dependent on fishing and agriculture, but since 1908 Minamata City itself has been the site of production facilities of the Chisso Corporation, which specialized initially in nitrogen-based chemical fertilizers and later in plastics. The presence of Chisso in the city was both an envied source of employment and financial support for the local citizens, and a frequent source of controversy as conflict between chemical production and commercial fishing developed. Beginning as early as 1926 local fishermen periodically demanded and received compensation for pollution damage to their fisheries, but it was not until the early 1950s that events proved pollution to be causing much more profound damage than a decline in the commercial fishing catch:

> By 1953, ominous evidence appeared in Minamata. Birds seemed to be losing their sense of coordination, often falling from their perches or flying into buildings and trees. Cats, too, were acting oddly. They walked with a strange rolling gait, frequently stumbling over their own legs.

Many suddenly went mad, running in circles and foaming at the mouth until they fell—or were thrown—into the sea and drowned. Local fishermen called the derangement "the disease of the dancing cats," and watched nervously as the animals' madness progressed.

Inexorably, the dancing disease spread to humans. By the early 1950's, a number of Minamata fishermen and their families were experiencing the disquieting symptoms of a previously unknown physical disorder. Robust men and women who had formerly enjoyed good health suddenly found their hands trembling so violently they could no longer strike a match. They soon had difficulty thinking clearly, and it became increasingly difficult for them to operate their boats. Numbness that began in the lips and limbs was followed by disturbances in vision, movement, and speech. As the disease progressed, control over all bodily functions diminished. The victims became bedridden, then fell into unconsciousness. Wild fits of thrashing and senseless shouting comprised a later stage, during which many victims' families, to keep the afflicted from injuring themselves or others, resorted to securing them with heavy rope. About forty percent of those stricken died.[2]

Because the symptoms were concentrated in the relatively poor fishing villages on the outskirts of Minamata City, residents of more affluent areas assumed that they were caused by hygienic deficiencies in the afflicted households. Their general reaction was to shun the victims and their families as carriers of a contagious disease. This reaction and the victims' own shame and guilt kept the symptoms from being medically discovered until 1956, and it was another year before probable causation was attributed to the consumption of local fish. But by 1957 the sale of Minamata fish had been banned, and suspicion had begun to focus on Chisso as the likely source of the disease.

In August of 1958 the victims of mercury poisoning, certain of both the cause of their suffering and the culprit, formed the Mutual Assistance Society to negotiate with Chisso, following the pattern of the previous fishery negotiations. Chisso rebuffed the Society's initial efforts, but the identification in 1959 by Kumamoto University researchers of organic mercury from Chisso's effluents as the causal agent had a drastic effect on fishing and brought the diseased patients powerful allies in the form of local fishermen. That August, members of the Minamata City Fishermen's Union demonstrated in front of Chisso's gates demanding compensation, purification of the bay, and pollution abatement. The company responded that, since causation of Minamata disease was "scientifically ambiguous," they could offer only a minor sum in the form of a solatium or sympathy payment (*mimaikin*) rather than compensation (*hoshōkin*). The fishermen reacted by storming the factory, and when a subsequent meeting brought only an increase in the total offer from ¥3 million (approximately $8,300) to ¥13 million ($36,000), they stormed it again, this time taking the plant manager hostage overnight. This act apparently impressed Chisso sufficiently for it to agree to mediation by a committee consisting of Minamata City's mayor and local delegates to the Kumamoto prefectural assembly.

The mediation committee took only ten days to propose an acceptable settlement whereby Chisso agreed to pay union members a total of ¥35 million ($97,000) immediately and ¥2 million ($5,500) annually thereafter. But adjacent fishermen's unions and the disease sufferers were specifically excluded. When in October and November 1959 Chisso refused to negotiate with the other unions, riots and plant occupations ensued, causing extensive property damage. The response was a second mediation committee, this time appointed by the prefectural governor. The committee's initial charge was only to address the unions' demands, but a widely publicized sit-in at the factory gates resulted in the consideration of the patients' demand for ¥230 million ($640,000, or ¥3 million [$8,300] for each disease victim) as well.

On December 16 the committee announced its recommendation: payment of ¥35 million ($97,000) to the fishermen and ¥74 million ($205,500) to the disease victims. The unions quickly agreed, but the Mutual Assistance Society initially rejected the recommendation as grossly insufficient. Persistent pressure from the mayor and city councilmen, the Japanese tradition of clearing the slate at the end of each year, and the threatened dissolution of the mediation committee were, however, too much for the victims, most of whom were unable to work and faced steadily rising debt, and on December 30 representatives of Chisso and the Society signed the proposed agreement and social peace was declared. As in the previous agreements with the fishermen, this agreement provided for sympathy payments or *mimaikin* rather than compensation. The amounts—¥300,000 ($830) for deaths, annual payments of ¥100,000 ($280) for adults and ¥30,000 ($83) for minors, and ¥20,000 ($55) for funeral expenses—were small even in the context of 1960 Minamata, but the true genius of the agreement from Chisso's point of view was its legal character.

Although the victims' reactions and the government mediation are consistent with the accepted perceptions of traditional Japanese methods of resolving disputes, the content of the agreement resembles the result of legal practice present in most societies. One searches in vain for the paternalism, communal sense of responsibility, and preference for legal ambiguity that stereotypes about Japanese law would lead one to expect. Clauses 4 and 5 clarify respective rights and duties under the agreement beyond peradventure:

> CLAUSE 4:   In the future, if Chisso's factory effluents are determined not to be the cause of Minamata disease, the solatium agreement will be dissolved immediately.
> CLAUSE 5:   In the future, even if factory effluents are shown to be the cause of the disease, no further demands for compensation will be made.[3]

The explicit characterization of the payments as *mimaikin* is further evidence of the company's close attention to the legal nature of the agreement and its determination to use legal doctrine to prevent continuing liability. Under the agreement Chisso does no more than express sympathy for the victims, who, in turn, forfeit all legal rights to compensation. Although this legal manipulation was eventually unsuccessful in shielding Chisso from tort liability, it determined the course of the conflict for many years thereafter.

The *mimaikin* agreement was intended to reestablish social harmony in Minamata, and it clearly bought several years of quiescence for Chisso and its government supporters. Had events elsewhere not dramatically altered the balance of power in Minamata, redirected the attention of the national media to Minamata disease, and brought the victims new political allies, the 1959 negotiations might have come to represent one more instance of successful Japanese informal dispute resolution. But even during this dormant period in the social history of Minamata, the main actors were busy maintaining the 1959 settlement, and the events of this uneventful period are one illustration of what "harmony" can mean and what is necessary to preserve it.

Direct governmental research on the mercury theory began in early 1959 with the formation of the Minamata Disease Food Poisoning Subcommittee of the Foodstuffs Hygiene Investigation Council of the Ministry of Health and Welfare (MHW). In its October report to the Minister, the Subcommittee agreed with the Kumamoto University team that the primary cause of Minamata disease was organic mercury. This conclusion was then reported to the Diet in November. Although the report studiously avoided any mention of Chisso as the source of the mercury, the government immediately thereafter disbanded the Subcommittee and removed the question of causation from the jurisdiction of the Ministry of Health and Welfare to that of the Ministries of International Trade and Industry and Agriculture and Forestry for "reexamination." The suppression of the Subcommittee report was followed in 1960 by the cancellation of government research grants to the Kumamoto University research team. For the next three years, the Kumamoto scientists' research was dependent on financial support from the United States National Institutes of Health.

Although it was not until 1968 that the government formally agreed that organic mercury was the causative agent, few outside of Chisso and the government disputed the role of mercury after 1959. There remained, however, the need both to demonstrate scientifically the precise process of poisoning and to trace the mercury to the Chisso plant. Industry-supported scientists put forward a series of hypotheses of both questions which, although tenuous at best, enabled the government to profess doubt as to causation and source. In fact, the government was no more in the dark than anyone else. Secret documents made public in court proceedings more than a decade later revealed that as early as July 1958, the Ministry of Health and Welfare had notified, *inter alia*, MITI and the Governor of Kumamoto Prefecture that research indicated that Minamata disease was caused by eating fish and shellfish contaminated by Chisso effluents.[4]

Despite this warning from the MHW, the Chief of the Public Procurator's Office for Kumamoto Prefecture repeatedly refused to investigate Chisso when, beginning in 1959, the Kumamoto University team asked for official help in their research. Even after a Kumamoto professor finally isolated organic mercury in samples of Chisso waste water and published his findings at a meeting of the Japanese Association of Hygienists in 1962, the Procurator's Office responded: "We cannot yet decide what to do. We have not been able to do anything so far because we did not know the precise medical cause, but when the medical researchers reach a conclusion, we will have to be very concerned with it, depending on the nature of the results."[5] The ironic denouement of the Ministry of Justice's role in this stage came in September 1968, after the MHW had finally officially recognized organic mercury from Chisso as the cause of Minamata disease. The Chief of the Kumamoto District Procuracy replied to questioning in the prefectural assembly by stating, "The statute of limitations on the crime of involuntary manslaughter and injury has already run out, but when new facts appear, we would like to examine them in detail."[6]

The "see no evil" attitude of the powerful government ministries and the continuing obstruction by Chisso reinforced the effect of the *mimaikin* agreement, and the victims and fishermen of Minamata had little choice but to suppress their frustrations and grievances. But the Minamata pollution was only one instance of a national problem, and the local settlement was doomed when another "strange disease of unknown cause" was discovered in 1964 in Niigata Prefecture on the island of Honshu. The symptoms were similar to Minamata disease; the victims' diet was largely fish from the Agano River; and investigation quickly revealed the presence upstream of an acetaldehyde factory owned by Shōwa Denkō using exactly the same process as Chisso. Japan's second case of mercury poisoning had been discovered.

The Ministry of Health and Welfare responded by commissioning the Niigata University Medical School to study the disease and determine its cause. The course of events that followed repeated the pattern set in Minamata. The medical school's interim report cited Shōwa Denkō's mercury wastes as the most likely cause of the disease, but the report was opposed by MITI and suppressed. In mid-1966, the government discontinued funding of the Niigata Medical School research team, and the scientists were forced to proceed at their own expense. For three years Niigata victims, like those in Minamata, encountered corporate denials, collusive obfuscation by government and industry, and the intervention of "objective" scientists who invariably supported the company's claims.

This time, however, events moved too quickly for the government to marshal effective countermeasures. The report of the Niigata University researchers was made public in April 1967, despite strong objections by senior Health and Welfare officials, and the victims' attitude quickly radicalized. With the support of leftist lawyers, who had moved to the area shortly after the initial discovery, and a strong local support group partially organized by these lawyers, the victims filed suit against Shōwa Denkō in June 1967. It was the first postwar pollution suit against a major company, but in many ways it was both the culmination of growing national dissatisfaction with pollution and the first of a flood of pollution litigation that was to occur over the next decade. Three months later suit was filed in the Yokkaichi air pollution case, then in July 1968 in the Toyama cadmium poisoning case, and finally, in June 1969, against Chisso by one faction of the Minamata disease patients. As these cases progressed over the next several years, they became known as the Big Four pollution cases.

By 1969 it had been sixteen years since the disease first appeared, thirteen years since its discovery as a discrete set of symptoms, eleven years since the MHW had first secretly identified Chisso as the probable cause, ten years since organic mercury's scientific identification as the causative agent, and seven years since the Kumamoto professors' conclusive demonstration of Chisso as its source. The reasons for this delay are complex; they include the socioeconomic status of the victims, their dispersal in several separate fishing villages along the Minamata coast, the economic and political domination of the area by Chisso, lack of access to legal resources, and a disinclination on the part of many victims to challenge authority, particularly through a lawsuit. I shall look at the last of these reasons more closely in the following section, but here I want to note two less obvious factors of particular importance to this inquiry.

The first is legal doctrine.[7] Clauses 4 and 5 of the *mimaikin* agreement were carefully drafted to discourage legal action by potential plaintiffs and undoubtedly played a role in the delay. Not only Chisso but also the government often referred to the Minamata problem as being settled privately by this agreement. Equally important were the doctrines of tort law—or at least the actors' perceptions of those doctrines—that would cover any litigation. As the Chief Procurator's doubts regarding the "precise medical cause" show, the victims' opponents were quick to discount the possibility of winning a tort suit on the merits because of a lack of what was referred to as "scientific" proof of causation. The belittling of the possibility of litigation in this manner not only discouraged litigation itself, but also had the important psychological effect of making any Chisso or government compensation a matter of grace rather than of right. This psychological leverage was at the heart of the use of the term *mimaikin* in the 1959 agreement and was reinforced constantly thereafter.

A second factor in the delay was the legal nature of the settlement process. Central to the creation of the 1959 agreement and its later maintenance was the manipulation of information made possible by the informality of mediation. Both Chisso and the central and prefectural authorities regularly suppressed information whenever it suited their interests. Not only did Chisso deny information requested by researchers, but it was revealed later in the course of the civil litigation that the plant had also ordered the halt of experiments conducted in 1959 by Chisso personnel who had recreated Minamata disease symptoms in cats fed Chisso waste water. The suppression of vital data was greatly facilitated by the informal methods of protest and dispute settlement used by the victims. Had the fishermen and patients relied on more formal channels, the total manipulation of information would have been much more difficult. Under the informal process of mediation, however, both the production of data and the setting of the mediation agenda remained under the control of Chisso and its allies.

The Choice of Tactics

The decision to sue is never easy, in Japan or elsewhere, but it seems to have been particularly painful for the Minamata victims. Their initial reaction was to conceal their own and their family members' afflictions. Japanese society, particularly the small-village society characteristic of the Minamata area, is strongly conformist. To be different is difficult, doubly so when the difference is a physical or mental handicap. Because marriage and employment decisions are based on family background as well as individual attributes, the victims' misfortunes implicated their families as well. Even whole communities feared ostracism should the presence of victims in their midst become known to outsiders. It is not surprising, therefore, that shame and fear were the victims' dominant emotions. By contracting the disease, the individual victim had damaged not only himself but also his community's reputation. To call attention to that fact by publicly demanding redress was only to put one's selfish interests over those of the community. Given the additional circumstance of Chisso's overwhelming economic and political dominance of the area—elected officials were likely to be either former Chisso executives or members of the Chisso company union; an estimated 45 percent of Minamata City tax receipts and 70 percent of its economy were directly or indirectly dependent on Chisso—it would have been remarkable had the victims' initial reaction consisted of vigorous demands for the vindication of their rights.

Even after the government's formal acknowledgment of Chisso's culpability and the successive suits in Niigata, Yokkaichi, and Toyama, which legitimated litigation in the eyes of many victims, most remained reluctant, and when the Ministry of Health and Welfare offered in late 1968 to mediate demands for additional compensation, the majority of patients' families accepted. For some victims, however, the Ministry's conditions—complete discretion in the choice of mediation committee members, little role in the mediation process itself, and a prior agreement to abide by committee recommendations—and bitter memories of the 1959 agreement ruled out further reliance on the government. Of these victims, 138 individuals from 30 families filed suit on June 14, 1969. A third group, many of whom were newly discovered victims or less severely afflicted, rejected both mediation and litigation in favor of direct negotiations with Chisso officials.

The split among the patients was extremely bitter and continues today. The litigation and direct-negotiation groups contemptuously refer to the mediation group, who accepted in 1970 a settlement with maximum awards of ¥2 million ($5,555) with a ¥50,000 ($140) annuity, as the "leave it to others" or "entrustment" group and are in turn condemned for their "selfish" willingness to pursue their own ends without deference to the greater good of other victims and residents of the Minamata area generally. Between the two nonmediation factions, the split concerned both tactics and political affiliations. Lawyers associated with the Japan Communist Party (JCP) dominated the team conducting the litigation, while the direct-negotiation faction was led by unaffiliated leftist lawyers and activists. The latter were highly critical of the JCP lawyers and the JCP itself for what they saw as the manipulation and exploitation of the victims for partisan political gain. They also were critical of litigation as a tactic, arguing that the court's only remedy—money—was both inadequate to compensate for the physical harm and inappropriate to achieve a psychological and moral resolution to the tragedy. Instead they turned to direct confrontation. The JCP lawyers countered that the perceived extremism and violence of the direct-negotiation group's tactics would discredit the antipollution movement and hurt the litigation. Despite these differences between their nonvictim supporters, the two groups were often able to coordinate activities successfully, culminating in the plaintiffs' eventual participation in direct negotiations after the end of litigation.

It seems likely that none of the plaintiffs in any of the Big Four cases sued solely for the money. Nor did they sue to vindicate legal rights; the prevailing notion at the time of suit was that the plaintiffs faced insurmountable doctrinal obstacles in all four suits. Instead, the suits are better interpreted as desperate, last-ditch efforts to preserve family and community. In the words of one plaintiff: "In general the first problem we had in relation to filing suit was the feeling that 'our lives are already past—we should just endure it.' But when it began to look like the precious land left by our ancestors might be encroached upon and our grandchildren's generation affected, we could no longer endure. 'Now, we must sacrifice ourselves!' became our cry. I think this trial was motivated by that attitude."[8]

Even in the face of extreme pollution and obfuscation by polluters and government, litigation was often unacceptable and individual action extremely painful. As explained by a resident of Isotsu, a small village near Yokkaichi City and the home of the nine plaintiffs in the *Yokkaichi* air pollution case, litigation was more an attempt to unify the group and incite unified action than a result of such action: "In Isotsu, as for the residents' way of thinking, everyone wants to do only what the others do. In whatever meeting, it's everyone together, following the group. So in the case of pollution damage, too, everyone must act together. If an antipollution suit is started, the whole group has to do it. This consciousness is very strong. Group unity forms very quickly, but it's a different story when it's a question of one of them stepping forward to take some positive action himself."[9] When someone did step forward, the community reaction was frequently to accuse him of selfishness—of damaging their community's economy and honor for personal gain. In Minamata that reaction took the form of demonstrations demanding the protection of Chisso against the patients' selfish demands and the description of the victims' leaders as "enemies of Minamata." In Yokkaichi the reaction was threatened ostracism, as related by a nonplaintiff discussing community attitudes toward a plaintiff named Fujida:

Because I knew [that air pollution would cause great hardship], I told Mr. Fujida that, for the sake of Isotsu, he had to let them say whatever they wanted. At the beginning, they called him a traitor and wanted to ostracise him [*murahachibu*—a traditional form of punishment was to isolate an individual from all social contact]. Even so, I encouraged Mr. Fujida and told him that I would stick with him to the end.

As for who was suffering . . . everyone in Isotsu was, but their way of thinking was "Why should I support some trial so they can make money off it?" The Patients' Association was different, however. They'd face up to that kind of talk—"What are you saying? Who do you think you have to thank for the higher smokestacks? . . . and the soot collectors? . . . for all the equipment the companies have installed? It wasn't until those nine [plaintiffs] came along that the companies woke up, that the stacks were raised. Now, was it?"

Back in 1963, you'd wash something, hang it out to dry and it'd be black immediately. You'd wash it again and a third time . . . and yet we still shut up and took it, didn't we? "For the sake of the country, for the sake of industrial expansion . . . there's nothing we can do." No one said anything. Even now you hear "those nine people know there's something in it for themselves"—that kind of thinking still exists.[10]

The plaintiffs' ignorance of the process of litigation and the pain involved in their decision to resort to litigation coexisted with extremely high expectations of its efficacy. Not only did they hope that it could help preserve the "precious land of their ancestors," but they also assumed it would give them a chance to confront their assailants personally and thereby gain moral justice in the form of a personal apology. As anyone familiar with litigation would guess, the formality of the proceedings completely frustrated this expectation and left victims, supporters, and observers disillusioned with the institution, as the following account of the *Yokkaichi* trial by a journalist-supporter illustrates:

> The trial had several surprises in store for those of us who hadn't seen one before. First was this thing called the advocacy system. It started with the physical arrangement of the courtroom. The two groups of lawyers sat opposite each other on either side of the bench. The plaintiffs themselves sat in the gallery in back. As for the defendants' side, no one even showed up—there were just the lawyers lined up looking professional.
>
> The significance the patients attached to this suit—it wasn't just money, just the compensation. It was to make the presidents of the companies that had inflicted this illness on them say just one word, "I'm sorry." The advocacy system pretty completely shattered this hope. At the very instant that the plaintiffs' lawyers were denouncing the defendants' crimes, at the very instant that the patients were making their embittered appeal, "Mr. President" was sitting in his nice, deep office sofa, not in court! Is money an excuse for even this?
>
> There was another problem for the plaintiffs' side. Of course no plaintiff can talk as well as a professional advocate. But it's also a fact that, no matter how talented the lawyer is, he can't relate 100 percent of the patients' feelings. There's the opportunity to testify directly, but even then the person himself is just asked questions—remains a "guest." Sometimes complicated expressions flickered across the patients' faces as they sat in the gallery listening to the give and take of the courtroom—"Why must this court thing be so far removed from the common people?"
>
> Of course, the suit had to be won nonetheless and the defendant companies defeated even if within the court rules, but as long as it was done in this phony way, there'd be no real victory. As long as the trial remained in this framework, "Mr. President" would be able to hire his lawyers to make excuses for him; even if he loses, it won't be anything

more than money. The guilty conscience, the pain he should feel as a human being, the recrimination, he will escape it all.[11]

The plaintiffs were further alienated by the terrible contrast between the tragedy outside the court and the cold formality within:

> As concerns the way the hearings went, we were made extremely anxious by the formalism. To take a living phenomenon like pollution, turn it into a series of documents, then discuss those while people are actually suffering and dying seems somehow arrogant or disrespectful. The plaintiffs' side would say, "It's terrible." The defendants' side would say, "It's not terrible." The judge would strike a balance and write his opinion. This is nothing more than haggling over the plaintiffs' appeal.[12]

Nor could they understand the reason behind the process of proof. As one victim explained later, for them the situation needed no further clarification: "The feeling that it was really slow was very strong. Such a lot of boring formality and verbosity—a trial for something that was so clear, so obvious from the beginning! If you went to the courtroom and watched, well, there'd be scholars lining up and spouting a bunch of meaningless jargon—really stupid stuff! You wanted to say, 'Stop! Stop! I can't stand it!' "[13]

In this sense the Minamata plaintiffs were more fortunate than the others. Their trial, of course, was just the same, but they had an alternative: the confrontational tactics of the direct-negotiation faction. One of these tactics was the "one-share movement," in which patients and supporters each purchased one share of Chisso Corporation so that they could attend the 1970 shareholders' meeting in Osaka. The victims' comments regarding this movement offer a vivid view of what their expectations of litigation had been. The following statement is from Onoue Tokiyoshi, who under the 1959 agreement had received a nominal solatium for the loss of his wife:

> I don't have much to say, but, if it's this small a sum, if a company executive is going to be this stingy, maybe the executives should talk about it and decide on one or two to be sacrificed, see? And drink the mercury. Then their eyes would be opened . . . So we should put water in a big keg, then put some mercury in it, take it up to the stage and say, "At this stockholders' meeting, if some of you important people at the top, some of you from Chisso Company sacrifice yourselves and become victims, then maybe we'll be ready to reconsider."[14]

Another victim, Hamamoto Fumiyo, who had lost both parents, looked forward to the meeting: "The Chisso Company is so hateful. When I go to Osaka, I'm going to say to [Chisso] President Egashira, 'I'm buying your life with ¥4 million.' I'm going to say something to him, I'm really going to go raving mad when I go to the meeting."[15] And she made the most of it at Osaka in front of national television coverage:

> You're a parent, too! Do you understand? Do you really understand my feelings? [Dead silence fills the auditorium.] What did you say, what did you say to me then [when he visited her home to express his sympathy—probably in 1969], have you forgotten how you bowed your head three times? [President: So I went to pray to your deceased . . .] Coming to the Buddhist altar is not enough! . . . [The people around them are silent and unmoving. She clings to the President's lapels.] . . . How much do you think I suffered? The suffering, it's so much, I can't put it into words! You can't buy lives with money! My brother's a cripple and people laugh! My parents . . .[16]

Moral indignation is not a uniquely Japanese trait, and the desire for moral justification and retribution is deeply rooted in Western tort law. What is remarkable in this situation is the plaintiffs' innocent faith in the legal system's ability to function as an instrument of moral justice, the apocalyptic and communal vision of litigation, and the total absence of the language of either legal rights or monetary compensation. The concept of a right to compensation or of the defendant's duty to pay does not appear in published discussions of the plaintiffs, and their disavowal of money itself as even a secondary motivation, at least at the time of filing, seems absolutely convincing. As the litigation proceeded and the plaintiffs realized that victory was possible, the amount of the award and how it should be allocated became a divisive issue among the victims, and their motivations grew more complex. Even so, the dominant theme of the post-judgment negotiations over the amount and form of compensation remained moral retribution, and it is hard to interpret the victims' initial motivation as either individual or pecuniary.

To a large extent the lawyers involved shared these views. Although their moral outrage was secondhand and their concern with broad social issues stronger than that of their clients, the lawyers certainly saw themselves as something more than detached legal advocates. To the extent possible, they became one with the victims, sharing their pain and experiencing their humiliation and shame. That personal involvement in the victims' life was necessary because the trial was to be the forum for the baring of the victims' suffering and for the moral condemnation of the defendants. Without experiencing that suffering the lawyers could not impart it to the court, and without the public drama of that presentation the litigation would degenerate into legal formalities and fail in one of its main missions, facilitating and strengthening the antipollution movement.

For Noro Hiroshi, the leader of the *Yokkaichi* lawyers' team, the trial was markedly deficient in this respect. Even more than the other three, *Yokkaichi* was a "science trial" and demanded considerable specialization and nonlegal expertise of the lawyers. As a result there was insufficient contact with local residents, and the lawyers did not adequately understand or express the plaintiffs' suffering:

> Because of that, when sometimes the plaintiffs themselves were attacked by the other residents in the area as being mercenary and selfish or they had similar simple problems, the lawyers couldn't get together with them and resolve them. Also, although of course they went to the site of the pollution and engaged in various negotiations, the lawyers did not establish an adequate level of mutual understanding with the inhabitants of areas other than Isotsu. My feeling is that this problem is due to the specialized division of tasks.
>
> Therefore, in the next suit like this, whatever happens, the first rule should be to have the lawyers fully experience and appreciate the life of the plaintiffs and other residents.[17]

Not all lawyers involved viewed the litigation in quite the same way as Noro. Some viewed the cases from the perspective of an ideal legal order—in the words of one, "as a strict question of human rights" rather than "an ideological struggle." Noro's view was strongly dominant, however, even within the *Yokkaichi* team, which was generally considered more narrowly legalistic than the other three. There were political variations as well—JCP lawyers were more likely to phrase their motivation in terms of exposing contradictions in capitalist society—but the general consensus was that a major function of the litigation was to aid the wider antipollution movement.

When the Big Four suits were filed, few of the lawyers were optimistic. Their pessimism was, of course, one factor in their relative disregard of the legal aspect of the cases, but as the cases progressed it became apparent that the plaintiffs had a chance of winning, and by the time of the *Minamata* decision, the opinions in the three previous cases had so relaxed tort doctrine that it was difficult to imagine a pollution victim who would not win. The *Yokkaichi* and *Niigata* opinions had dramatically liberalized the traditional standard for proof of negligence, and the *Yokkaichi* opinion's emphasis on care in industrial site selection and on the defendants' duty to use the best technology in the world without consideration of economic feasibility took negligence doctrine very close to strict liability. The *Minamata* court then completed this development by requiring polluters to suspend operations immediately whenever any doubt should arise as to the safety of their effluents. Perhaps even more remarkable was the Big Four courts' treatment of causation doctrine. All four opinions recognized that forcing plaintiffs to prove causation by the conventional standard—the demonstration by clinical and pathological data of the precise causal mechanism of the injury or disease, what the Chief Procurator had referred to as "the precise medical cause"—would pose insurmountable obstacles to judicial recovery by pollution victims. They responded by allowing the plaintiffs to use epidemiological studies to establish presumptive causation and then shifting the burden of proof onto the defendants to refute causation with traditional clinical and pathological evidence.[18]

The lawyers, true to their conception of the litigation, generally attributed this success to the complementary roles of legal and political action within the antipollution movement: to them legal victory would have been impossible without the strength and vigor of the extrajudicial activity accompanying the litigation. Although one can only surmise judicial motivation, the lawyers' view may be correct. From the opinions themselves it is clear that the judges were sensitive to the moral dimensions of the cases. The tremendous doctrinal leaps necessary to find for the plaintiffs, the unprecedented size of the compensation awards—the plaintiffs in the *Minamata* case got up to nine times the amount stipulated in the 1970 MHW-mediated agreement—and the judiciary's own official and unofficial comments about extrajudicial activity lead to the conclusion that the judges too were caught up in the moral momentum of these cases. Further evidence for this thesis of judicial motivation is found in the doctrinal evolution of environmental law begun with the Big Four. Although all four involved significant doctrinal innovations, only the *Yokkaichi* case has received much attention in this area, largely because of the similarity of the air pollution situation in Yokkaichi City with that in many other urban areas. The other three cases seem to have had little effect on tort doctrine generally, and even in the area of environmental litigation, plaintiffs' success has declined steadily since the mid-1970s, in close parallel with the decline of the political and social power of the antipollution movement.

The motivations of the victims in the direct-negotiation faction were quite similar to those of the plaintiffs, but perhaps their expectations of litigation were more realistic. Gotō Takanori, an activist lawyer who devised the one-share movement and was the leading outside adviser to the direct-negotiation faction, explains why many victims rejected both litigation and mediation:

> [On litigation:] The victims wanted a human apology from the President of Chisso and the legal system couldn't provide that. In this sense, the victims wanted to treat their assailant as a human being. They wanted to regain their human dignity through a human apology because they knew that compensation alone could not give them a reason for living. A lawsuit could give them only money—if they could get nothing, they might as well just sell their lives.
>
> [On mediation:] They never believed in the so-called "third committee" [the MHW Mediation Committee of 1969–70] chosen by the government to act as an independent arbitrator. They knew a third party would inevitably betray them, even if it were made up of government people, the governor, doctors, professors . . . They had experienced the history of Minamata disease and knew it was a history of perfidy by so-called third committees . . . For the victims there were only assailants and victims. They wanted everyone involved to clarify his position—whether he stood on the side of the victims or of the polluters. They could not allow anyone or any social system to claim to be a friend when it really was not. In this sense they didn't trust the court or the judges either.[19]

For Gotō the moral limitations of litigation—its inability to "restore a person's humanity"—were exacerbated by the activities of large corporations and the social conditions often caused by them. One possible response to this failure of law is direct action:

> The great struggle of the direct negotiation movement is the questioning of the basic foundation of our legal system, which is presently unable to punish corporations for their crimes. And to me, a man who practices "conventional law," the direct negotiation movement is questioning my obligations to the people in general and to my clients in particular. Should I be a lawyer who practices with so many limitations or should I step outside of the traditional role of lawyer and pursue another course?[20]

Gotō's point should not be misconstrued: he and his victim-clients saw direct negotiations as supporting the litigation, not opposing it. But as their activities progressed, Gotō and Kawamoto Teruo, the leader of the direct-negotiation faction, helped that group develop an innovative strategy and ideology of conflict independent of both government mediators and the courts.

The direct-negotiation faction grew out of a group of noncertified victims—those not yet formally recognized by the government as afflicted by Minamata disease. On June 14, 1969, the day of the filing of the lawsuit by certified victims, Kawamoto called the noncertified patients together. Their first objective was official certification, and it was not until October 1971 that they achieved this goal and could turn their exclusive attention to negotiating with Chisso. Between October 11 and November 1 they met with Chisso representatives three times in Minamata, but Chisso refused to open direct negotiations and referred them to the government as "an impartial third party." Their response was a sit-in outside the gates of the Chisso plant. When this proved ineffective, Kawamoto went to Tokyo and met with Chisso President Shimada Kenichi on December 7 and 8, but these discussions again broke down over the company's insistence on government mediation. At midnight on December 8, when the last session ended with Shimada carried out of his offices on a stretcher because of his hypertension, the patients refused to leave. This set the stage for more than 18 months of constant confrontation as the patients, although eventually removed from Chisso's premises themselves, pitched tents outside the building and daily stormed Chisso's fourth-floor offices demanding personal negotiations and atonement from Shimada.

The scene resembled an armed camp. Chisso erected a massive iron grillwork at the entrance to its offices and detailed forty male employees as security to fend off the victims' daily charges. Perhaps the atmosphere is best conveyed by the later description of one incident by the Tokyo High Court:

> Sakauchi Shin was one of several employees assigned to security duty at the Tokyo headquarters on the morning of July 19, 1972. At about 8:50 A.M., he went to the fourth floor landing to investigate a report that employees were being prevented from entering Chisso offices. When he arrived, he saw four or five employees surrounded by 17 or 18 patients and supporters. When he approached, he was first pushed back and then pulled forward, being seized by the collar by one of the supporters. While he was protecting himself, the defendant, who was in front of him on the left, came up to him and seized his right arm and then bit him on the lower inside of the shoulder joint. Sakauchi escaped from the bite of the defendant and again moved toward the supporters. He was again

pushed back and then grabbed by his right leg and pulled into the group of supporters.

While Sakauchi's associates were holding his shoulders in order to keep him from being pulled in, the defendant, with one of the supporters, seized Sakauchi's left ankle and pulled, lifting Sakauchi, off the ground. Then the defendant came up to Sakauchi who was hanging in mid-air and hit him twice in the stomach with his fist.[21]

Such incidents were frequent; although interspersed with short episodes of inconclusive negotiations urged on Chisso by various government officials, they continued through Kawamoto's indictment for assault and battery in December 1972 until March 20, 1973, when the Kumamoto District Court announced its judgment in the *Minamata* tort action.

The plaintiffs' total victory broke the impasse. On the same day, members of the litigation faction traveled to Tokyo to join Kawamoto's followers in pressing Chisso for compensation beyond that given by the District Court and a personal apology by Shimada. The judicial award was the largest in Japanese history, with individual awards of up to ¥18 million (approximately $60,000), but for the patients it was not enough. With the legal victory behind them, they pressed for annuities, medical expenses, and the guarantee that all patients, whenever certified and of whatever faction, would receive equal treatment. After five hours of negotiations on March 22, Shimada pledged that all damages would be compensated in good faith. But it was not until he had knelt before the victims and apologized that they accepted his promise.

Thereafter detailed and vigorous negotiations continued until July 9, when a final agreement was reached and signed by all factions of the victims. It went well beyond the tort award in providing for lifetime annuities to be adjusted biannually to the cost of living, a ¥300-million fund (approximately $1 million) to provide medical and economic assistance to victims, and promises by Chisso to search for and compensate unidentified victims and to cooperate with local officials in the cleanup of Minamata Bay. The agreement also went beyond the judicial settlement by including a full and public apology by Chisso:

CLAUSE 2:   Because Chisso did not take sufficient measures to prevent the spread of Minamata disease after its official discovery in 1956, did not undertake to investigate the cause of the disease, and did not provide patients with sufficient relief aid, the extent of the damages increased even further. Moreover, even when the causal substance had been confirmed and the disease became a social problem, Chisso continued to maintain a regrettable attitude toward its solution. Chisso will reflect upon these actions with heartfelt sincerity.

CLAUSE 3:   Chisso deeply apologizes to those patients and their families, already in great poverty, who experienced further suffering from contracting Minamata disease, who suffered as a result of Chisso's attitudes, and who experienced various types of humiliation and, as a result, suffered from discrimination by local society.

Furthermore, Chisso deeply apologizes to all of society ... for its regrettable attitude of evading its responsibility and for delaying a solution, as this caused much inconvenience to society.[22]

Three days later the tents pitched by victims outside both Chisso's Minamata plant and its Tokyo headquarters came down. After 18 months this chapter in the history of Minamata disease was over, and attention shifted to the criminal trial of direct-negotiation faction leader Kawamoto Teruo.

Kawamoto had been indicted on December 27, 1972, on five counts of assault and battery similar to the incident described earlier. It is important to reiterate that the acts for which Kawamoto was indicted were neither spontaneous nor isolated. Kawamoto was himself a victim of mercury poisoning and had lost his father to the disease, and rage was perhaps the dominant emotion motivating the direct-negotiation faction. But it was a controlled rage channeled and utilized by the demands of a social and political movement. Even if one assumes that the acts of individual patients like Hamamoto Fumiyo's clinging to former President Egashira's lapels can be best explained by uncontrollable emotions, those of Kawamoto, who orchestrated the entire approach to Chisso knowing full well that a certain level of violence would occur, cannot be similarly explained.

Recognizing the controlled nature of Kawamoto's acts is important in understanding both the concept of direct negotiations and the legal nature of his defense.[23] Because of the instrumental nature of the violence involved, a defense based on the doctrine of excuse was legally problematic. Excuse would have focused on the defendant's inability to control himself rather than on the magnitude of Chisso's crimes; it would have entailed admitting that Kawamoto's behavior was culpable and then arguing that somehow he was not responsible for it. Much more appealing to Kawamoto and his lawyer, Gotō Takanori, was the doctrine of justification. A justification defense would make the courtroom a forum for the recitation of Chisso's sins, and

Kawamoto's indictment could be turned on its head to become the moral indictment of Chisso.

Gotō and Kawamoto, however, went further, eschewing both excuse and justification in favor of an assault on the indictment itself. To them, Chisso's moral responsibility had been clarified by the tort decision and the later convictions of its executives for homicide. A justification defense, even if successful, would add little. Instead they chose to attack the central government, which they felt was equally culpable in the Minamata tragedy. Their approach was to demand the dismissal of the indictment on grounds of abuse of prosecutorial discretion and to premise that abuse on the government's systematic bias for Chisso throughout the fifteen years of the Minamata incident. By taking this approach, Gotō was able to transform the courtroom into a forum for the recitation not of Kawamoto's or even of Chisso's sins, but of those of the government. The Kumamoto District Court's opinion in the tort decision had not left the government unscathed, but only through a full-blown inquiry focused exclusively on the government's role would the public be able to grasp both the magnitude of official complicity and—vitally important to Gotō and Kawamoto—the need for a fundamental reorientation of Japanese society if such incidents were not to recur.

Needless to say the Japanese courts, reading their role somewhat more narrowly than did Gotō, were not eager to become part of the defendant's version of a contemporary morality play. The Tokyo District Court, although sympathetic to Kawamoto's situation and sensitive to charges of government misconduct, limited the inquiry to the immediate facts and circumstances of the incidents themselves. Given that Kawamoto acknowledged the facts in the indictment, the court had little choice but to find him guilty and give him a nominal suspended sentence. The Tokyo High Court, however, in its 1977 decision on appeal went well beyond the facts of the indictment to a detailed discussion of the etiology of Minamata disease, Chisso's negligence and bad faith, the twenty-year struggle of the victims for compensation and human dignity, and the role of local and central government in the creation and exacerbation of pollution. The court's treatment of the state's role, its appraisal of the defendant's actions, and the legal framework within which it analyzed these factors are central to understanding the judicial attitude toward confrontational tactics in Japan.

After noting the statutory and constitutional basis for its power to review the legality of the indictment, the court recounted the factual background of the indictment, stressing the government's role in early efforts to determine the nature and cause of Minamata disease. The recitation of the frequent and alarming reports of growing pollution and disease beginning as early as 1952, when juxtaposed with the government's consistent and calculated refusal to take any action, painted a damning portrait of official negligence and callousness. The court noted that from 1952 to 1962 there had been eleven official reports concerning the disease and its causation, some of which had explicitly cited Chisso waste water as the probable cause. Despite the fact that each subsequent report pointed more conclusively toward Chisso, it was not until 1968 that the government officially recognized Chisso's role.

The court then noted that despite the clear and early evidence of causation, both the prefectural and national authorities made no attempt to prosecute Chisso or any of its employees until 1975, when charges of negligent homicide were filed against two former Chisso executives. The court could find no justification for the delay, since the facts underlying the indictment were available to the authorities as early as 1960. Nor was the government able to offer any plausible explanation even after the court took the unusual step of formally inquiring of the Kumamoto District Procuracy and Prefectural Police if they had been aware of the various reports and investigations. Given the lack of a satisfactory reply, the court concluded that no investigation was ever carried out during that period.

In contrast to the authorities' lenience toward Chisso, the court cited what it deemed the vigorous prosecution of those harmed by pollution—fishermen, Minamata disease patients, and particularly the defendant and his supporters in the direct-negotiation faction—whenever they took direct action against Chisso. Such incidents ranged from the plant occupations of 1959 to the actions of Kawamoto himself. Despite injuries to both sides and at least one incident of "senseless" violence against victims and their supporters in which the American photographer Eugene Smith was blinded, only patients were ever prosecuted. Reinforcing the appearance of government bias was the timing of the defendant's indictment. According to the court, it came at a crucial stage in the negotiation process when the defendant's presence was particularly needed. Although the court made no attempt to show that the timing was consciously intended to disadvantage the patients, it concluded that, intentional or not, the indictment "took the part of"

Chisso and "dealt no small blow" to the patients involved in the independent negotiations.

The concluding section of the court's opinion begins with an inquiry into the nature of justice. Aristotle, Ulpianus, Radbruch, Bentham, Marx, and Fichte are all cited to the general effect that equality and fairness have been the foundation of justice in Western jurisprudence since the Greeks. The Anglo-American maxim that a good judge tries a case with fairness and virtue and bases his decision on equity rather than the strict dictates of the common law is set forth and illustrated by the U.S. Supreme Court's decision in *Cox v. Louisiana*. The court then finds these values embodied in the Japanese Constitution and characterizes a judge's role as implementing them in each concrete case, particularly by preventing the state from abusing its power. This judicial duty is to take precedence over the punishment of every guilty defendant.

This declaration of judicial philosophy left little question as to the court's ultimate conclusion. Citing the severity of the mercury poisoning and the government's inaction, the court characterized the local and national authorities as bearing half of the responsibility for Minamata disease. The government, therefore, stood in the same position as Chisso as an assailant of Kawamoto and the other victims.

Although the prosecution's bias became the ultimate legal basis of its decision, the court also evaluated the defendant's conduct and the tactics of the direct-negotiation faction that he led. For the court, the negotiations were not to be understood as simply part of a two-dimensional dispute over compensation for civil wrongdoing. The whole history of the Minamata incident had to be considered—the cruelty of the disease, the government's neglect, Chisso's insincerity during the negotiations, the ostracism of the patients, and the factional splits among the patients—as well as the value of the negotiations themselves. The court seemed to ascribe considerable weight to the fact that the defendant's efforts finally led to the agreement of July 9, 1973, which not only gave all patients compensation equal to the tort award but also provided additional economic security in the form of annuities and medical assistance. These terms were characterized as "good results" and evidence that Kawamoto's strategy had been more successful than mediation.

Nonetheless, the tactics used to force negotiations remained troubling. The court acknowledged that, however useful they may have been, direct negotiations did have inherent limits as a method of dispute resolution and that litigation remained as the appropriate final resort in case of an impasse. However, Chisso Corporation itself did not receive much sympathy from the court, which said that Chisso should have been extremely forbearing of patient violence. Kawamoto's individual victims presented a slightly more difficult question; the injuries suffered could not be lightly dismissed, and the victims' status as Chisso employees did not justify the defendant in injuring them. But the court then drew back from the implications of these findings: "However, since these assaults occurred between a person who was frantically demanding a meeting as the first step toward compensation and those who were trying to prevent the meeting, the assaults were not undertaken with personal animus toward the victims. If the accused's acts are considered as a protest by the many Minamata disease sufferers, especially by those who are unable to speak for themselves, anger against the defendant may lessen."[24]

In conclusion, the High Court found the defendant's behavior insignificant when compared to the government's misconduct. The indictment was in the court's eyes irretrievably unjust and the inference of intentional bias or gross negligence unavoidable; in fact, the court pointedly admonished prosecutors to refrain in the future from "bullying" the populace. The court's duty was thus clear; for although dismissing the indictment would cause no social harm, it would be terribly harmful to allow the state to continue to take the part of the assailant Chisso by maintaining the prosecution. The High Court thereby reversed the trial court and dismissed the indictment as a violation of Article 248 of the Code of Criminal Procedure.

The First Petty Bench of the Supreme Court dismissed the prosecution's appeal on December 17, 1980, in a 3-to-2 decision.[25] Although it explicitly rejected the High Court's use of the doctrine of prosecutorial abuse to dismiss Kawamoto's indictment, the majority refused to reverse the High Court and reinstate the District Court's sentence. The brief opinion sheds little light on its reasoning:

> In addition to the extremely unusual background of the case apparent from the record, much time has passed since the commission of the crime. During that time compensation for the Minamata patients has been settled, the dispute between the patients and Chisso Company has ended, and the victims of defendant's conduct no longer desire his punishment. The defendant has lost his father to the disease and is himself suffering ill health from its effects. Considering all these factors, it cannot

be said that the failure to reverse the High Court would be manifestly unjust.[26]

As one of the two dissents forcefully pointed out, the special circumstances of the case relied on by the majority were amply and properly considered by the District Court in its nominal sentence. To reject the High Court's reasoning but simultaneously affirm its dismissal of the indictment was, in the dissents' opinion, fundamentally nonsensical and would be construed as judicial toleration of the use of violence.

The Supreme Court's opinion may well be incoherent legally, but viewed from the wider perspective of Japanese society, the majority's disposition of the case begins to look like a political masterstroke. The options open to the Supreme Court were, after all, quite limited and all unsatisfactory. To reinstate the District Court sentence would have deeply offended society's sense of justice; to affirm the High Court's broad interpretation of the doctrine of prosecutorial abuse, on the other hand, would have been doctrinally difficult given the conservative approach of the Supreme Court to judicial intervention in the activities of the executive.

Through the ambiguity of the majority opinion, the Supreme Court was able to a limited extent to satisfy everyone politically while preserving what it saw as the doctrinal integrity of criminal law and procedure and at least the illusion of judicial reluctance to interfere with prosecutorial discretion. Kawamoto and his supporters were, of course, happy with the result, and even the prosecutor was at least able to praise the part of the opinion that rejected the application of the doctrine of prosecutorial abuse. Perhaps the most apt reaction, however, was that of Judge Terao, the author of the High Court opinion. He noted that the Supreme Court had after "considering and agonizing over this case from a broad point of view" eventually "understood my feelings on the case." If we in turn consider this opinion from the perspective of managing social conflict, that is, that of the reestablishment of social peace and the final putting to rest of a severely divisive chapter in Japanese postwar history, it is difficult to see how the Japanese Supreme Court's approach could have been improved.

The Government's Response

The magnitude of the apparent threat to the social and political status quo in Japan during the late sixties and early seventies should not be underestimated. The movements mobilized by the Big Four cases formed the core of a development that by 1973 was being heralded as a radically new form of political action, one that directly challenged not only the limited-access, consensus-based style of the governing elite but also, what is perhaps more important, the self-image of the Japanese as preferring harmony to conflict. In addition to exposing underlying social conflict, the pollution experience had also demonstrated that rights assertion and litigation could be valuable tools in achieving social justice. In this section we shall see how the government and its allies used legal rules and institutions to respond to this threat, not only to maintain their political control but more fundamentally to restore the faith in both the existence and efficacy of the tradition of mediation, conciliation, and trust in authority that has supposedly been the secret of Japan's postwar success.

The Big Four and the activities accompanying them were the forerunners of a grassroots political and social phenomenon known as citizens' movements (*shimin undō*).[27] Perhaps the best way for Americans to appreciate the excitement and fear generated by this phenomenon is to compare its impact with that of the civil rights movement in the United States. Although the latter resembled citizens' movements in that they both demanded political participation for excluded minorities—blacks and pollution victims—the civil rights movement was aiming to add one more player to the already recognized game of pluralistic politics. Citizens' movements can also be viewed as pluralistic in that they consisted of politically mobilized groups operating outside the traditional channels of political expression; what made them threatening in Japan is that there is no recognized tradition of pluralistic politics. In the United States, to allow access to blacks or environmentalists would dilute the power of the prior political actors, but it would not threaten the conception of American politics as interest-group politics channeled into democratic political institutions. In Japan, on the contrary, the citizens' movements were seen as fundamentally disruptive to the established ways of power.

First, these groups were local while the accustomed mode of governance was centralized control. Citizens' movements formed around local or regional environmental issues and focused on local governments for relief and political response. Only in rare cases like the Big Four did they become national in scope, and even then they consisted more of ad hoc cooperation based on recognized shared goals and interests than a single organization with which the central government could deal directly as a representative of the movement in general. One result of the local nature of citizens' movements was to strengthen the local governments vis-à-vis central authority. Local conservative governments either became willing to resist centrally pushed industrial initiatives in favor of environmental protection measures or were voted out of office and replaced by coalitions of the traditional opposition parties. Because the opposition parties had success in dealing with pollution issues, their local power began to be felt in national elections as well, and the Liberal Democratic majority in the national Diet weakened substantially even though the antipollution movement itself remained a basically local phenomenon.

Second, the citizens' movements developed outside the historical channels of political action in Japan. Not only were they outside the LDP–business–bureaucracy triumvirate, but they also remained free of strong affiliations with the opposition parties or labor unions. They were strongly supported by the Communist Party and the Komeito (Clean Government Party), but neither was successful in capturing the movement ideologically or organizationally. Instead, the various citizens' groups were genuine grassroots organizations with political attachments based on local issues rather than on the network of personal allegiances that characterizes Japanese political groups. As such, they threatened to destabilize the established political actors in Japan—the parties, the bureaucrats, the unions, and the business associations. The opposition parties to a certain extent welcomed this development, but for the LDP it held no possible political gain whatsoever.

Third, the tactics of the antipollution groups, especially the calculated combination of litigation, instrumental violence, and political mobilization, presaged a new vehicle for social protest that would bypass the traditional modes of dispute resolution epitomized by the 1959 solatium agreement in Minamata. The use of the courts and some judges' enthusiastic embrace of their new role meant that these new and uncontrollable interests would have access to a national forum for the presentation of their grievances. Even if they were ultimately unsuccessful, the very posing of fundamental social questions as legal issues meant that they would be thoroughly debated in the media; that public positions on particular issues would have to be taken, and these issues would thereby threaten to become national in scope and universalistic in nature; and that the informal, closed, particularistic decision-making process enjoyed for so long would be subject to public and judicial scrutiny, if not actual judicial usurpation.

To make matters worse, the synergistic combination of political movement and litigation meant that the latter could not be ignored and left to run itself into the sands of arcane doctrine and judicial passivity and incapacity. The political power of a successful movement would both force the judiciary to take action in the particular case and enable the activists involved to get the maximum political mileage out of any given legal decision. In this manner, the perceived institutional weaknesses of the Japanese judiciary—the lack of equitable remedies and class actions or the doctrinal obstacles to effective judicial review of administrative action—would be overcome politically by using the legally limited judicial declarations of rights and duties in a particular case as standards for political action and propaganda. Inherent in that process was the possibility that the use of litigation and politics would forge the fragmented local citizens' movements into a nationally based movement which, although initially limited to environmental issues, would eventually extend to other issues as well.

To combat this development the ruling coalition had to do three things: eliminate the pollution that was the underlying cause of political dissatisfaction, discredit or weaken this new model of social action, and settle the moral accounts unbalanced by the actions of business and government in the course of the pollution episode. To a great extent, government measures have succeeded in all three areas.

Of the three tasks, pollution control was the easiest. Official Japan may have been unconscionably slow in initially reacting to pollution, but once forced to move it acted quickly and effectively. In less than a decade Japan was transformed from clearly the most highly polluted advanced country to one that compares well with most other industrial societies. The remarkable drops in the levels of most major air and water pollutants were achieved by vigorous regulation of all significant sources of air and water pollution, using essentially the same legal tools employed elsewhere.[28] Although this discussion will focus on three other aspects of the government's response, it is important to remember that without the substantial alleviation of the very real grievances of urban Japanese, the complementary measures intended to divert environmental activism and conflict from the courts and citizens' movements would have been inconsequential.

The first of these complementary measures, the Law for the Resolution of Pollution Disputes (the Dispute Law),[29] established a comprehensive, three-tiered system for the identification, investigation, and resolution of pollution-related disputes. The first two tiers, Pollution Complaint Counselors and Prefectural Pollution Review Boards, are at the local level. The former is a complaint-processing system whereby prefectural governors and urban mayors appoint local officials to consult with residents, investigate reported pollution incidents, and provide guidance and advice. Counselors are usually local civil servants and cooperate closely with the pollution control offices of local governments.

The Prefectural Pollution Review Board is separate from the complaint system and is designed to settle complaints that have already escalated into disputes. It has jurisdiction over disputes between private parties and between citizens and the government and is empowered to conduct mediation, conciliation, and arbitration. Board members are appointed by the governor with the consent of the prefectural assembly and are generally law professors, retired judges, or practicing attorneys.

The third tier is the Central Pollution Dispute Coordination Committee. It too conducts mediation, conciliation, and arbitration but also has specific investigatory and fact-finding power beyond that of the Prefectural Boards. For example, it conducts on-site inspections and frequently requests documentation on contested issues from parties to a dispute. In serious cases it can and does initiate dispute resolution even when not expressly requested to do so by the parties and may permit the participation of affected individuals not originally parties to the dispute.

The basic approach of the Dispute Law—the provision of government officials charged with the identification, investigation, and resolution of small-scale conflict before it escalates—is consistent both with previous efforts in environmental statutes and with mediation schemes in other substantive areas. The stated purpose was to provide relief to pollution victims that would be cheaper, faster, and more effective than litigation, but the drafters' goals were clearly more ambitious than simple dispute processing. Third-party intervention, particularly governmental intervention, was also touted as consistent with Japanese tradition and responsive to the Japanese preference for informal, noncontentious modes of conflict resolution. Before one assumes, however, that the Dispute Law is another result of the strength of traditional values—that it was in a sense inevitable given Japan's history—it would be wise to inquire briefly into the process that led to the creation of the law.

That process began with the creation in 1966 of a Ministry of Health and Welfare advisory committee charged with investigating the problem of pollution and proposing alternatives for dealing with pollution disputes and victim compensation. The committee's initial interim report is surprising in light of the common wisdom on both the strength and content of traditional values: it recommended legislation establishing strict liability for pollution injury and emphasizing compensation through the established tort system. This approach met with immediate opposition from business groups led by the Federation of Economic Organizations (Keidanren), who urged that concern with environmental protection be tempered by recognition of the continued primacy of industrial development, and later from the Ministry of International Trade and Industry and other agencies, who argued for a comprehensive system of extrajudicial dispute resolution rather than reliance on the tort system. The final committee report was a compromise, recommending strict liability but emphasizing compensation through mediation and conciliation. Moreover, by the time the report was fashioned into a draft statute, which in 1967 became the Basic Law for Environmental Pollution Control (the Basic Law), the Keidanren, MITI, and their allies had succeeded in deleting the strict liability provisions and substituting provisions requiring the government to establish systems both for the mediation and arbitration of pollution disputes and for the administrative compensation of pollution victims. The development of the mediation system, therefore, was less the result of traditional values than of political will.

The Law for the Compensation of Pollution-Related Health Injury (the Compensation Law)[30] was the second of the measures aimed at diverting social conflict from the courts and from citizens' movements. It was enacted in 1973 when the political and legal momentum created by the plaintiffs' successive victories in the Big Four convinced the government that preexisting local and national schemes had failed to compensate the victims adequately or to slow the rush to litigation and protest. This law distinguishes between two categories of pollution diseases: nonspecific diseases caused or exacerbated by air pollution, such as bronchitis, asthma, or emphysema; and those caused by specific toxic substances, typically encountered as water pollution, such as mercury or cadmium poisoning. To qualify for compensation a person must satisfy certain administrative criteria and be certified by local boards comprised of medical and legal experts. Upon certification victims become eligible for substantial benefits, the entire cost of which is borne by polluters.

The payout of benefits has been substantial. By 1980 more than 80,000 certified victims had received over ¥85 billion (approximately $425 million) in compensation, and there is no question that the Compensation Law has resulted in industry's bearing a significant portion of the total social cost of pollution. Indeed, the compensation scheme has become the focus of considerable international interest for precisely this reason, but it has fared less well domestically. Japanese industry has criticized the formula for calculating compensation for air pollution diseases, arguing that their burden has risen while pollution levels have fallen. In the toxic-substances category, environmentalists point out that except for the designation of two areas of chronic arsenic poisoning in 1973 and 1974, no area or disease has been officially recognized except those areas involved in the Big Four cases—mercury poisoning in Minamata and Niigata and cadmium poisoning in Toyama—despite the subsequent discovery of widespread chromium poisoning in several areas and several incidents of more acute toxic substance contamination by substances such as PCB. It is quite clear that the prospects for future designation of such substances, whatever the strength of the objective case under the statutory criteria, are remote. To many in government and business, the recent decline in environmental protest has meant that the compensation and mediation schemes have not only served their purpose but also outlived their usefulness.

The third important response of the government was the introduction of citizen participation and environmental concerns into development planning.[31] There are two major aspects of this response, both adapted from American legal practice: the preparation of environmental impact assessments modeled on the National Environmental Policy Act (NEPA), and the holding of public hearings modeled on the legislative hearings of the Administrative Procedure Act. The fascinating role that these American devices now play in Japan illustrates how superficially similar legal forms can have radically different effects when placed in different social and legal contexts.

The Japanese version of environmental impact assessment found its impetus in two sources: political pressure in the form of citizens' movements and opposition-party proposals for the emulation of NEPA's provisions; and legal pressure in the form of the *Yokkaichi* opinion, which sharply criticized the lack of environmental planning that produced the air pollution in the Yokkaichi area, as well as several later judicial decisions that enjoined public projects for inadequate planning. The government's initial response was to amend several specific statutes to include provisions for impact assessment and to begin development of a comprehensive approach. The latter is of particular relevance here in that the initial approach of the newly created Environment Agency was a draft statute establishing a general legal requirement for impact statements for all significant projects. The initial 1975 Agency draft was considerably weaker than those proposed by the opposition parties and the Japan Federation of Bar Associations; nonetheless, it was too strong for industry, MITI, or the Ministries of Transportation or Construction to accept. The result was a series of revisions over the next several years, with each draft weaker than the last, until eventually the opposition parties, the Bar Federation, and environmentalists began to oppose the draft as being weaker than the preexisting judicially developed requirement.

The prime issue in this process was not the requirement of environmental assessment itself; all sides to the controversy agreed with its necessity. In fact the Japanese government, including those ministries opposed to the Environment Agency draft, has integrated a comprehensive system of assessment into its development planning process. The central issue was the legal nature of assessments, specifically whether the ministries were to retain discretion over when and how to conduct environmental assessments. Just as the Bar Federation, the Environment Agency, and the opposition parties had carefully studied the American statutory process, so had MITI, Transportation, Construction, and the Keidanren. The problem was that whereas the former had seen rational planning and environmental protection, the latter saw unnecessary delay and loss of bureaucratic control.

The end result of this process has been that, although Japanese and American impact assessments are similar in coverage and technique, they are radically different in legal effect. Both are conducted pursuant to elaborate guidelines and must satisfy certain criteria. But in the United States those guidelines and criteria are legally mandated by statute and enforceable in court; in Japan they are developed ministry by ministry in coordination with the Environment Agency and are of no legal force, at least in the sense of judicial review of an agency or a developer's compliance with them. In this sense they remain legally informal—legal non-events that do not increase the possibility of judicial intervention or ministerial loss of control.

It is important, however, not to leap from the datum of no legal enforceability to the conclusion either that the guidelines are meaningless or that the ministries have complete discretion in development planning. Local opposition can still force delay or cancellation of a particular project, and the government puts great emphasis on convincing the local residents that any given project is in their best interest and that the project sponsors have done everything necessary to minimize or eliminate environmental and social disruption. The mechanism for this persuasion is the public hearing or "explanatory meeting" (*setsumeikai*) modeled after the legislative hearing of the American Administrative Procedure Act. Such hearings can be traced directly to judicial language in several pollution opinions dealing with the construction of public facilities where the court in finding for the plaintiffs cited the failure of the government agency or contractor to follow "democratic procedures" not only in choosing the site but also in explaining that choice to the affected residents.

Explanatory hearings are now ubiquitous in development planning. Like Japanese impact assessments, however, they turn out to be different from what an observer familiar with American hearings might expect, as the example of nuclear power plant siting may suggest.[32] Both MITI and the Atomic Energy Safety Commission hold hearings for each new plant. The Commission hearing is administratively required and concerns reactor safety only; the MITI hearing is required by MITI's guidelines and deals with all other concerns from electricity discounts for local residents to thermal pollution. Both hearings follow the same format. Only residents of the affected area are allowed to attend or participate. Since nuclear plants are typically located in remote areas, this rule usually limits participation to farmers, fishermen, and merchants. Even if a nuclear physicist did live in the area, his participation might be of limited value because speakers are allotted only ten minutes each and permissible topics are carefully controlled. A transcript of each hearing is made and published, but there is no legal requirement to consider its content in decisions on the siting or design of the plant. In fact, these decisions have already been made, and the hearings give industry and government spokesmen an opportunity to explain and justify them and answer residents' questions. Because of the low level of technical sophistication of the residents, these questions sometimes focus on the possibility of nuclear explosions and ignore the more likely problems of radiation leaks, waste disposal and storage, thermal pollution, or evacuation planning.

Not incidentally, one effect of this form of hearing has been the radicalization and isolation of the antinuclear movement in Japan. Opponents of nuclear power consider such hearings a cynical manipulation of local residents and have refused to participate. Instead, segments of the movement conduct vigorous, frequently violent demonstrations at the site of the hearings, with the result that the participants in the hearing often need to be escorted into the building by riot police. The demonstrators are not typical of all opponents of nuclear power in Japan, but they have assumed greater prominence than their numbers or ideas would otherwise receive because more measured, independent opposition voices have been effectively excluded from the planning process by the form and legal nature of the hearings. The practical denial of an effective forum for serious opposition while simultaneously giving the appearance of following "democratic procedures" is of course precisely what the explanatory hearing is designed to accomplish. The end result is that the government can portray the process of environmental planning as responsive to citizen concerns and accessible to citizen participation, while remaining relatively immune from effective legal or political challenge.

The reestablishment of social peace was, if not the primary, at least a strong secondary motivation in the adoption of most of the measures discussed earlier: the dramatic turnabout in regulatory policy, the creation of extrajudicial avenues for compensation for pollution injuries and the resolution of pollution disputes, and the systematic inclusion of environmental concerns and limited citizen participation in government planning. By the early 1980s, a decade after the height of the antipollution movement and the implementation of most of these measures, social peace had returned to Japanese society, at least in the environmental area. Environmental litigation has largely disappeared as a major political or legal factor in national policy, and the central government has recaptured the initiative in environmental planning. Cases of local importance still occur, but plaintiffs are usually unsuccessful and even their occasional victories receive little attention beyond the immediate area. Similarly, citizens' movements have largely faded from the political scene. The national environmental movement is moribund, and even local quality-of-life groups are much less common. Commentators who ten years ago hailed citizens' movements as evidence of fundamental changes in the Japanese polity are once again discussing the resilience of the Japanese traditional style of government.

Identifying the causes of this development is extremely risky. Certainly the success of the government's pollution control efforts and the greater prominence of economic problems in the late seventies and early eighties would have meant a somewhat lower profile for environmental issues even had the government done nothing else. It seems unlikely, however, that these two factors constitute a complete explanation. The Japanese economy remains robust by international standards, and environmental protection policy, particularly if one looks beyond the indices of urban pollution to more general questions of ecological deterioration, still leaves a great deal to be desired. A third explanatory factor is the limited view of environmental problems shared by many Japanese. Even in its heyday, the Japanese environmental movement was less concerned with ecological issues than with human health problems, and these have been largely solved, at least for the short term. But this explanation overlooks the appearance in the early and mid-1970s of what have been called the second and third generations of Japanese environmental litigation, cases concerned more with quality of life and ecological issues than with human health per se. These cases were evidence of a movement toward a wider definition of environmental problems, but they too have largely disappeared.

A fourth possible reason for the decline in environmental activism is the legal nature of the second and third generation of pollution cases. There was an evolution from politically and morally charged cases like the Big Four, through more ambiguous cases that pitted substantial public benefit against significant private suffering, to quality-of-life cases involving narrower private interests with less appeal to the general public. The best example of the second generation was the *Osaka Airport* case, which pitted surrounding residents against the central government's operation of Japan's second largest airport.[33] The *Osaka Airport* plaintiffs were suffering from physical and psychological injuries resulting from aircraft noise, but their injuries did not approach those of the Big Four plaintiffs. Similarly, the airport authority, the defendant, while perhaps negligent in planning the airport, was serving a legitimate public need and, unlike Chisso or Shōwa Denkō, could not be portrayed as selfishly profiting from the plaintiffs' suffering.

The third-generation cases are even more morally ambiguous. In the *Biwa Lake* case, for example, plaintiffs are attempting to stop development surrounding Japan's largest lake.[34] Although alleging possible future health injuries, the plaintiffs' true concerns are ecological: the project was poorly planned and threatens to pollute irretrievably the entire lake. Against these sound but abstract ecological fears, the government could point to pressing needs for more water for downstream users and more industrial land for the continued economic prosperity of the region. The public's attitude toward the moral and social issues underlying such environmental litigation is simply too ambivalent to provide the broad and deep political support enjoyed by the Big Four plaintiffs. The legal nature of the cases likewise changed: what had been straightforward tort actions against private companies for compensation for past injuries became actions against public entities for prospective equitable relief, presenting plaintiffs with administrative law doctrines severely restricting injunctive relief against public entities.[35]

But even the combination of the political and legal nature of these cases cannot fully explain the decline of environmental litigation in Japan in the late seventies. Despite the doctrinal and political difficulties, second- and third-generation plaintiffs had achieved remarkable success in the early and mid-seventies: the line of environmental cases led by the Osaka High Court's 1975 opinion in the *Osaka Airport* case developed judicial exceptions or alternatives to many of the narrow doctrines of Japanese administrative law and led many lawyers and scholars to conclude that the doctrinal obstacles to effective environmental litigation would be overcome. That line of cases was eventually overruled by the Supreme Court in its 1981 reversal in *Osaka Airport* which, while upholding compensation for past harm, slammed the judicial door on most forms of equitable relief against government defendants.[36] But the Supreme Court opinion was really only the coup de grace for a movement that was already politically dead. The frequency and success rate of environmental cases had greatly declined by the late seventies, as had general interest in the question of pollution, even to the point where substantial projects attracted neither lawsuits nor citizens' movements despite clear evidence of poor or nonexistent environmental planning.

If the factors discussed above are unable to explain entirely the return of social peace, we can with some confidence turn to the role of the government measures described earlier in this section. On one level their contribution would seem irrefutable if one assumes that in the absence of government intervention, some percentage of the several hundred disputes handled by the prefectural and central mediation systems in the late seventies and early eighties might have become lawsuits. Similarly, one might assume that some portion of the hundreds of thousands of locally processed complaints would also have developed into major social conflict except for early intervention and resolution. Certainly every case mediated is not a lawsuit forgone, and the vast majority of citizen complaints were perhaps trivial enough to be discounted as sources of potentially serious confrontation. Nonetheless, the mediation and compensation schemes probably had a significant pretrial diversion effect. It is important, however, not to overlook less direct influences which, although perhaps even less provable in a statistical sense, are nevertheless significant.

Third-party intervention, particularly by a powerful government in a society with a tradition of submissiveness to authority, has a greater effect on conflict than just diverting it from judicial to bureaucratic channels. First, it particularizes potentially general issues and substitutes ad hoc decision making for the application of universal rules. In so doing it hinders the coalescence of many localized conflicts into generalized national ones. Each conflict is resolved on its own facts and circumstances, with little need to discover commonalities or invoke universal principles. Bargained and mediated resolutions need satisfy only the expectations of the immediate parties rather than the requirements of generality and universality inherent in legal rules or principles. Because of that flexibility and the consequent legitimacy of considering all relevant factors rather than solely those that are legally relevant, the diversity among conflicts is accentuated and the recognition of an identity of interests among participants in environmental conflicts is made less likely. The informality and confidentiality of mediation exacerbates these difficulties, since the very existence of similar problems may never be known by those similarly affected. This phenomenon is most clearly true of geographically separated incidents, but it is potentially true even for persons affected by the same pollution source.

A second effect of third-party intervention was well captured by the epithets applied to the group of Minamata patients that chose mediation, the "entrustment" or "leave it to the others" group. In the Japanese context, mediation usually means dependence. Although there have been no studies on the environmental mediators' role, the frequent imbalance in the strength of the parties means that the individual complainant will be relying on the government mediator to balance the scales for him. This structural bias strengthening the mediator's role is reinforced by the high status of Japanese officials and the tradition of reliance on the government for protection that many pollution victims fought so hard to overcome. This tendency is strengthened at the prefectural or central levels, where the mediators are largely retired judges, lawyers, and law professors—individuals of high prestige and authority. Although the resulting power of the mediators is potentially troublesome on a substantive level, the important point here is the psychological effect on the victims and complainants—the temptation to "leave it to the others"—and the increased social control given the government. A system of mediation may lead to fragmentation and isolation for potential litigants, but this need not be so for the internal apparatus of the mediation system itself. Because all the mediators are appointed, trained, and supported by the government and mediation itself is intrinsically ad hoc, the potential for subtle, hidden, or even unintentional manipulation toward preferred government outcomes and policies is undeniable.

The tendency toward dependence is reinforced by the "explanatory" form of public hearing exemplified by the nuclear power hearings. The aura of authority inherent in the official–citizen relationship is enhanced by the hearing format, which puts the citizen in the role of supplicant and the official in that of expert explainer. MITI officials see the hearings as a vehicle of reassurance that the government has considered and will continue to consider the local residents' interests. There is little expectation by any of the parties of equality in position or of the citizens' participating in making the decision in question.

A final key point, very different from third-party intervention but one that demands attention in light of the earlier review of the victims' motivation, is the settling of moral accounts implicit in the plaintiffs' victories in the Big Four, the dismissal of Kawamoto Teruo's indictment, and the eventual conviction of Chisso executives for homicide. Each policy response discussed here—the stringent pollution control measures, the mediation and compensation systems, the environmental planning with citizen participation—contributes to the popular belief that the government has ceased the mindless, unquestioning quest for economic growth characteristic of the 1950s and 1960s and has recognized its moral and political obligation to consider the well-being of all its citizens. But these legislative measures in themselves, though preconditions to the restoration of stability, might not have been sufficient to bring a psychological and political end to Japan's pollution episode without the dramatic judicial condemnations of government and business that were central to these three legal events.

Except for the indictment and prosecution of Chisso executives, it is difficult to describe these events as responses by the government or even as official, in the sense of bureaucratic, actions at all. Not only are Japanese courts independent of government manipulation in this sense, but it is also true that the Ministry of Justice prosecutors argued vigorously that the Supreme Court should reverse the *Kawamoto* decision and reinstate the District Court verdict. Nevertheless, in the eyes of the average Japanese, these opinions constituted official recognition not only of the legitimacy of the victims' demands but also of the moral culpability of the government's complicity in the pollution disasters. The *Kawamoto* High Court opinion is particularly important here because it both explicitly detailed the state's inaction and established Kawamoto himself as a martyr. With the Supreme Court's affirmance of this decision, the victims' moral vindication was complete.

Historical and Social Context of the Pollution Experience

Robert Bellah has described Japanese society in the Tokugawa Period (1603–1868) as animated by a deep sense of shared obligation that pervaded all relationships and provided meaning and structure to society.[37] This world view has been characterized by others as a "covenant" (or *ininkeiyaku*—"delegation" or "entrustment contract" in Japanese) and contrasted with the Western concept of a social contract. Under the covenant, the subject owed clear, minutely delineated duties to the lord, but the lord's obligation was not conceived of as specific duties owed in return.[38] His responsibility was not to his subjects per se but to the maintenance of the social structure on which everyone depended. The fundamental normative principle of that structure was benevolence, as embodied in the neo-Confucian concepts of the benevolent lord (*jinkun*) and benevolent rule (*jinsei*). This norm made reciprocal what was otherwise a relationship of unilateral obligation owed by the peasant to the lord. It both embodied an implicit bargain whereby obedience was traded for social stability and also limited what would otherwise have been totally discretionary power.

Under the covenant, collective action or protest (*hyakushō ikki* or "peasant rebellion") was legitimate not when a particular wrong was committed, but only when the underlying relationship was threatened. Since the substance of the lord's obligation was a matter of grace, there was no system for entertaining specific village complaints against domain officials. When official malfeasance or neglect threatened the destruction of the social structure, however, it had to be resisted. Illegal *ikki* aimed at the restoration of the covenant and benevolent rule were the result.

The popular stereotype has been that *ikki* were spontaneous and violent uprisings by groups of enraged, long-suffering peasants storming the official residences of the corrupt or incompetent domain bureaucrats. This vision is a romanticized view of exceptional *ikki* and neglects the vast majority of the approximately 7,500 *ikki* recorded in the Tokugawa and early Meiji periods.[39] The typical *ikki* was more in the nature of collective protest than rebellion and followed a recurrent, if not officially authorized, pattern. The usual sequence of events was quite predictable: an initial refusal by the village to follow prescribed procedures concerning the payment or assessment of taxes or corvée was followed by a petition for redress to the local official. If no appropriate response was forthcoming at that level, the petition would be directly presented to a higher official. Finally, a group would go to the domain office and stage a symbolic protest, such as a sit-in. By this point the local authorities would usually respond. On the one hand, the petition would be accepted and concessions made to village demands; on the other, as many participants in the *ikki* as possible would be punished. In the early Tokugawa punishment was typically severe, including execution of the leaders, in order to demonstrate to other villages that the concessions and the protest that achieved them were not to be considered a precedent and that attempts by other villages to negotiate tax rates or other economic matters remained illegal. As time went on, however, precedents accumulated and a pattern of technically illegal negotiations was established.

The essence of these negotiations was a struggle between conflicting normative systems. The peasants appealed to a rhetoric of natural law, embodied in the Confucian concept of *ri*, which acknowledged the unilateral nature of the lord-peasant relationship but which further recognized the peasants' right to rebel should the lord fail in his role as benevolent ruler. The lord relied on the myriad positive-law rules (*fa*) governing village life and prohibiting the very process by which the peasants appealed to *ri*. It was these legal prohibitions that justified the villagers' punishment even when their demands were acknowledged as just; for the lord recognized the continued force of positive law regardless of the obligations of *ri*. It was not inconsistent, therefore, for central authorities to confiscate the lands and castle of local lords in explicit recognition of the peasants' demands while simultaneously executing the village headmen responsible for the protest. Later, after harmony and benevolent rule had been restored, it was not uncommon for martyred headmen to be deified by the descendants of the very lord who had ordered their death. Although the typical *ikki*, particularly in the later part of the Tokugawa, did not end in execution, the continued illegality of direct petitions gave the whole process a sense of desperation and irregularity. Patterns developed, but an explicit common law of peasant protest could not. Natural-law justice could thus be satisfied without establishing a standard procedure for its realization or a specific set of criteria for its definition.

Tokugawa peasants assumed a stable set of social and moral norms that envisioned a strictly hierarchical society where each status group was clearly distinguished from the next. The virtuous man was rewarded both in this life and in the next, and the ideal of virtue was central to social stability. If the peasants were virtuous, their lord would be compassionate; and if the lord was virtuous, the domain would enjoy peace and prosperity. The *ikki* played a substantial symbolic role in this vision of society because by its nature and by the consciousness of the peasant participants, it reaffirmed the importance of personal virtue: the peasants demanded of the lord that he be virtuous and contended that they had the right to make such demands because they in turn had been virtuous. Peasant protests, therefore, became symbols only of rebellion and not of revolution; they stood for the celebration of the status quo, not its overthrow. As one village leader in 1820 put it, "High and low are like fathers and sons . . . when we complain of extreme difficulties to whom else but to the high should we go?"[40] This dependence of the peasants on the ideal of the lord even as they revolted against his person carried over and animated conflict well into the Meiji period (1868–1912), as is exemplified by the pattern of response in the Ashio copper mine incident, modern Japan's first experience with industrial pollution.[41]

The Ashio mine was one of the first technologically advanced enterprises in Meiji Japan and was of extreme importance to the nation's economic and industrial development in the late nineteenth century. Unfortunately, its ecological importance was equally dramatic. In 1890 the mine's deforestation of surrounding mountains began to cause periodic flooding that poisoned the rice paddies of whole prefectures in central Japan with the runoff of copper tailings. The peasants' reaction, once they understood the source of the poison, was somewhat different from the expected. As well as using the traditional device of petitioning the central government, they also resorted to constitutional and statutory rights created by the Western legal system introduced by Meiji leaders as part of Japan's response to the West. Their elected representative to the Imperial Diet, Tanaka Shōzō, argued that the flooding infringed his constituents' property rights under Article 27 of the Meiji Constitution and demanded that the government revoke the mining concession of the Ashio owners under Article 10, Paragraph 3, of the Mining Law, which provided for revocation whenever the mining injured the public interest. The government acknowledged Ashio as the source of the damage, but denied the severity of the problem and any legal obligation to invoke the Mining Law. To further requests for direct relief, the central government replied that it lacked legal jurisdiction to deal with local problems.

Meanwhile in the summer of 1892 Furukawa Ichibe, the owner of the Ashio mine, began efforts to defuse the peasants' movement by arranging indemnity settlements with the affected villages. Through the mediation of prefectural political leaders, he concluded a series of contracts that required Furukawa Mining to install certain pollution-control equipment by 1893 and to pay compensation, in return for which the peasants agreed to cease their protest until the summer of 1896. During the Sino-Japanese War (1894–1895), Furukawa agents, usually local or regional officials hired by the mine, circulated in the region persuading village leaders to make these agreements permanent. The course of pollution, however, overwhelmed their efforts. By the mid-1890s conditions had deteriorated dramatically, and in the spring of 1896 peasant conscripts returning from the war provided a new militancy to the villages, which now began to denounce the contracts as frauds. With the end of the war, Tanaka Shōzō recommenced his campaign in the Diet, vigorously denouncing Furukawa's close personal ties with government ministers and his alleged use of company bribes to gain official complicity in suppressing the issue. In the summer of 1896, after the most devastating flood to date, the affected villages sent a second formal petition to the government. But despite the growing rural unrest and the beginning of urban interest in the farmers' plight, the government steadfastly maintained that the problem had been privately solved by the indemnity contracts, that Furukawa was faithfully implementing suggested antipollution measures, and that, given the future importance of the decision for mining and agriculture, it was too early to decide whether Ashio's operation was injurious to the public interest. Meanwhile Tanaka's intensified efforts to push for governmental acceptance of responsibility in the Diet met with increasing contempt by fellow members and other political leaders.

The eventual break came in the spring of 1897, when a young college student from the afflicted area began to appeal personally to individual ministers. His efforts, rebuffed initially, bore fruit when his threat to commit suicide on the doorstep of an influential politician got the requested interview and eventually a personal visit to the stricken area, first by that politician, then by several ministers. As each went to the area, he was struck by the devastation and the total unreality of the official reports Tokyo had been receiving. Simultaneously, the farmers mounted a massive protest march on the capital, clashing frequently and violently with riot police en route. The march led to more journalistic attention and public support for the protesters and eventually to the government's decision in May 1897 to force Furukawa to take effective measures or close the mine. The eventual result was the development by Furukawa of some of the best antipollution technology of the time.

Ironically, the crisis actually worsened after 1897 because the mine's efforts had no immediate effect on the massive piles of copper tailings and the annual floods that spread their poison throughout the Kantō Plain. Of course the farmers were not willing to wait for future effects, and growing disillusionment and bitterness among the peasantry finally culminated in February 1900 in a march on Tokyo by 2,000 farmers. Local police efforts to arrest the leaders were overwhelmed, the police beaten, and their prisoners released. On February 13 the marchers reached the village of Kawamata on the banks of the Tone River, where they were met by more than 200 regular and military police. In the resulting skirmish 6 policemen and 15 farmers were seriously injured and more than 100 farmers were arrested, 51 of them on the serious charges of sedition and incitement to riot.

The resulting series of criminal trials are of the utmost interest here.[42] The trial court, in an opinion limited solely to the facts of the actual incident, found 29 of the farmers guilty and acquitted the rest. The Tokyo Court of Appeals took the opposite tack and opened up the trial to a thoroughgoing inquiry into the defendants' grievances. The ensuing inquiry into the origin and severity of the pollution and the neglect of the government became a media bonanza for the farmers, including a seven-day on-site inspection by the whole court and representatives of the leading newspapers. Under its investigative authority the court sponsored the first thorough scientific study of the region, but the trial's most important role was the greatly needed cathartic airing of the whole issue. The eventual acquittal on March 15, 1902, of all but three of the defendants vindicated society's sense of justice. The later repudiation of the appellate court's reasoning by the Court of Cassation, followed by the dismissal of the charges on remand on technical procedural grounds, served to maintain the purity of legal doctrine but left the political result intact in a process strikingly similar to the *Kawamoto* Supreme Court decision more than seventy years later.

It is evident even from this brief discussion of the Tokugawa *ikki* and the Ashio incident that useful parallels can be drawn both between these two phenomena and between them and the modern pollution episode. The clearest is a similarity in the pattern of conflict, particularly in the sequence of events and the types of actions and reactions of the participants. Less clear from the limited data are similarities in the nature of the conflict: its normative framework, the attitudes and goals of the parties, the roles of various individuals and institutions. Implicit in these comparisons is the question of continuity and change in social conflict: what is new in the experience of the 1960s and 1970s, and what does it portend for the future?

In each instance the initial response was appeal to local authorities through petitions or their equivalent. This was followed by mediation aimed primarily at combining minor concessions—the indemnity and solatium contracts in Ashio and Minamata—with social pressure for submission to authority in order to convince the victims to tolerate their condition. In Minamata this tactic was largely successful, primarily because of the isolated, powerless nature of the victims, but in Ashio whole villages and regions were similarly affected, and collective mobilization made mediation more difficult. Even so, Furukawa was initially successful in buying time. But in Ashio, as in the *ikki* where by necessity villages almost always acted as a unit, the initial mediation process quickly evolved into a process more akin to collective bargaining than mediation.

When the petition-mediation process failed, the next step was collective action. In situations where the collectivity predated the problem (the fishermen's union in Minamata and the agricultural village in the *ikki* and in Ashio), this stage occurred sooner rather than later and is difficult to distinguish from the mediation process. The form of collective action also varied widely but always involved some form of ex-

pressive protest—a sit-in, a protest march, the one-share movement—
where the appeal was emotional rather than logical and was aimed
initially at the personal sympathy of the public and the relevant officials rather than at any particular institutional measure. When the
particular act was perceived as radical—filing suit for the Minamata
victims or the residents of Isotsu—the collective (for example, the
victims' association or the village) sometimes split, but that merely
redefined the unit. As in most protests anywhere, the psychological
burden and institutional obstacles were simply too great to contem-
plate acting alone.

If the collective protest was successful in gaining public sympathy
and convincing the government of the reality of the problem, there was
an investigation followed by often dramatic remedial action by the
government. The confiscation of corrupt lords' lands, the threat to
close the Furukawa mine, and the government response to pollution in
the 1970s are all examples of quick, effective relief that occurred once
the grievances were perceived as legitimate. And if the government
neglect was considered grave enough, there was a final stage, which
one might call catharsis, where the government attempted to reestablish faith in its benevolence. The eventual deification of Tokugawa
village headmen, the appellate opinion in the Kawamata affair, the
dismissal of the Kawamoto indictment, and the provision of govern-
ment-sponsored compensation to pollution victims are strikingly similar examples of this phenomenon. In each instance the message to the
society was the same: a recognition of the justice of the protest, an
admission of the government's moral accountability, and a promise to
do better in the future.

Thus the common pattern of conflict may be described as consisting
of appeals to government benevolence followed by collective, often
violent, protest, and eventually resulting in effective government action. The overriding legal characteristic of such conflict, however, is
informality. As a pattern or style of protest is repeated, it can acquire a
certain degree of predictability and may even evolve into a ritualized,
customary style of bargaining, but as long as the participants' actions
remain illegal, the development of a set of formal procedures is impossible. Except in a stable, simple society with extremely few variations
in possible conflict, the absence of procedural rules to limit the permissible tactics and factual scope of conflict means that all facts that are
socially, morally, or personally relevant to the participants become
part of the context of each dispute, and each dispute will remain *sui*

generis. Although the very existence of a recognizable pattern and established sequence of events with continuity over time implies some restrictions on acceptable modes of conflict, those restrictions were too loose to constrain substantially the choice of tactics—note the success of the one-share movement—much less control the course or ultimate outcome of the dispute.

Another factor encouraging informality was the rhetoric of these conflicts. The Tokugawa appeal to neo-Confucian benevolence most clearly militated against formal rules of procedure or logically determined standards for decision. The appeal to natural law over the more specific provisions of positive law that was central in the rhetoric of the *ikki* necessarily substituted flexibility and ambiguity in result for specificity and certainty. This is not to say that natural-law rhetoric is incapable of specification or systemization; but the Tokugawa authorities not only did not attempt it, they actively resisted any such development by denying the validity or decisional force of any specific argument or fact situation. Even in the pollution trials of the 1970s, the rhetoric often remained more moral than legal. This was immediately apparent in the attitudes of plaintiffs and attorneys in the Big Four, and of course in Kawamoto's defense in his criminal trial. But it was also present in the rhetoric and reasoning of the judicial opinions themselves, not only in the Tokyo High Court's *Kawamoto* opinion but also in the civil tort decisions.

The elevation of natural over positive law, of fairness over legal rules, and of moral over legal justice in affecting the outcome of disputes has certain implications for the nature of the dispute itself. First, it will lead participants to favor the expressive language of symbols over the logical language of rules. Thus the scene of Hamamoto Fumio clutching the lapels of President Egashira of Chisso and pleading "You're a parent too!" may have meant more to the court than the plaintiffs' failure to produce the pathological evidence supposedly required for proof of causation. Second, the centrality of moral judgments in these disputes may mask an even more fundamental implication of informality: the retention of decisional control in the more powerful party. If each dispute stands by itself and the decisional criteria are no more precise than a vision of the moral sense of society, the authorities retain a great deal of discretion in evaluating the validity of any given claim or protest. The Tokugawa lord or the contemporary Tokyo bureaucrat can consider factors exogenous to the conflict at hand in choosing his response. Given the relatively homogeneous nature of Japanese society, it also means that to a certain extent he can manipulate the decisional criteria by manipulating the moral con- sciousness of society—hence the deification of village headmen and the conscious reaffirmation of the paternalistic ideal of the covenant that we saw throughout these conflicts.

Closely related to the government's retention of control is the vertical nature of the conflict. The underlying cause of the conflict is seen as governmental failure. In the case of the *ikki*, it is explicitly the failure of the lord to be benevolent. As urbanization and commercial- ization increased in the later half of the Tokugawa Period, the causes of peasant unrest became more complicated and there were numer- ous visible symbols of rural economic injustice in the persons of rich peasants, merchants, and usurers. With few exceptions, however, the focus of the *ikki* remained on the lord. Even in the Ashio and Big Four incidents, the initial emphasis was on the government and its political responsibility rather than on the polluting companies themselves. As that approach failed because the government refused to respond adequately, the focus of the antipollution movement shifted to litiga- tion and a horizontal struggle with the companies themselves. The desire to deal directly and personally with the companies is most sharply drawn in the tactics of the direct-negotiation faction, but even here there is reason to think that the companies were seen by many victims as surrogates for the government, which they saw as the real responsible party. Nor did the government or the companies dispute this attitude, at least after the former was forced to take the problem seriously. Again, despite the initial emphatic rejection of mediation by the direct-negotiation faction, the government played a central role in the later stages of the negotiations with Chisso. The victims may have remained independent in the sense of retaining the political and psychological power to resist government importuning, but even they did not spurn the government's assistance when it was offered on their own terms. And whatever those terms and however independent the victims may have felt, once the government entered the negotiations their social character changed, and to the Japanese public the familiar pattern of government intervention and paternal- ism was replayed in a new setting. The final confirmation of the importance of the government's role was the defense strategy in the *Kawamoto* trial, where the bilateral, ruler-subject relationship was reaffirmed to be the heart of the struggle by the leader of the most militant of the victim groups.

We may be tempted to dismiss the modern plaintiffs' attitudes toward litigation as indistinguishable from those of their ancestors toward traditional vertical forms of protest. We may also see contemporary legal norms as essentially indistinguishable from the neo-Confucian *ri* put forward by the Tokugawa peasants or the public-interest standard of the Mining Law relied on by Tanaka Shōzō. But the modern pollution episode was not a mere replay of the past, and the use of litigation, whatever the substantive values applied, directly challenges the informal and vertical nature of conflict and therefore weakens government control over both the internal dynamics and the outcome of disputes. The open process of proof and the requirement of a statement of reasons for a preferred result inherent in the legal process substantially constrain the freedom of action of the participants. No matter how indeterminate the underlying norm, the public statement and restatement of the arguments and the reasoned justifications for particular outcomes universalize the issues in ways that profoundly influence the public's perception of the justice of different possible outcomes under similar or analogous circumstances.

The loss of informality, however, may be less significant than the intervention of relatively independent third parties into what had been a bilateral, hierarchical relationship. Once substantial control of the process and content of decisions passes to the lawyers and the judiciary, the victims need no longer look to the government to bestow its grace; they may demand satisfaction as a matter of right. Even if that right remains vague and ambiguous, the perception that the courts give citizens an independent forum to claim their due against the government and others higher on the social hierarchy can quickly erode the informality and verticality that enabled the government to dominate these disputes even during periods of relative political weakness. Without that power over the direction of conflict, the government may well lose its ability to set the social agenda, so important in maintaining social control. To a certain extent any successful protest, whether it be a peasant *ikki* or contemporary litigation, will usurp this function, but litigation, because of its public, incremental nature and its relative independence from direct official manipulation, threatens loss of control much more dramatically than the other forms of conflict we have reviewed.

The second and third generations of pollution litigation provide an excellent illustration of this point. Although the Big Four represented a more immediate and dramatic challenge to conservative rule, the prospective and procedural orientation of later suits went beyond an appeal for government action to demand an independent role in the policy planning and implementation process. Although it is clear that this litigation did not present as immediate a political threat as the earlier cases, it threatened to open up the process of government and make it responsive to private citizens and groups not only in terms of substantive result—that was the Big Four's role—but also in terms of procedure. And to open up the administrative decision-making process to citizen participation and judicial scrutiny would have meant the dilution of the government's influence over the course of social change and its ability to contain and influence social conflict.

At present, the government's reaction to the Big Four—the regulatory measures and the mediation and compensation schemes—seems to have combined with the changing nature of the issues in later environmental cases to ensure that litigation whose purpose was consistent with traditional modes of conflict did not evolve into liberal legalistic litigation. It remains to be seen whether these and similar measures will hold in areas of conflict other than pollution, or whether the example of the Big Four will lead other potential plaintiffs to sue for less noble motives. To investigate this question and to test the theories of Japanese conflict based on the pollution example in other areas, we turn our attention to two other areas of contemporary conflict.

THREE

Instrumental Violence and the Struggle for Buraku Liberation

THE COMBINATION of forceful confrontation and litigation that marked the Big Four cases may have disappeared from the environmental area, but it has become and probably will remain an important means of social redress in some limited circumstances. Most clearly related to the Big Four are celebrated product-liability cases concerning substances such as thalidomide, SMON, chloroquine, and PCBs, cases that demonstrate the persistence of litigation as a paradigm of moral struggle in the relatively quiescent eighties.[1] But focusing solely on the aftermath of the pollution cases would result in an unnecessarily narrow picture of the role of law in social change in Japan. In this and the next chapter I shall look at ongoing conflict in two areas unrelated to the environment: discrimination against Burakumin and sex-based discrimination in employment.

My discussion of Buraku discrimination (Buraku is the adjective for Burakumin) will focus on the use by Burakumin and particularly by their mass organization, the Buraku Liberation League (BLL), of a tactic known as "denunciation struggle" (kyūdan tōsō).[2] Simply stated, denunciation is the attempt by a group of League members to convince one or more majority Japanese to adopt the BLL interpretation of a particular event, language, or policy that the BLL considers discriminatory. Although this tactic frequently consists of no more than two or three Burakumin explaining the BLL's wishes to a local bureaucrat, it differs from mere persuasion or the exercise of the freedom of expression in that implicit in all denunciation is the actual or threatened use of limited physical force by large groups of Burakumin.

Development of the Buraku Liberation Movement

Although there has been considerable in-migration since the Meiji Restoration of 1868, Burakumin are generally considered to be the descendants of Tokugawa Period outcastes and to constitute 1 to 3 percent of the Japanese population. Discrimination against various groups was present earlier, but a permanent and distinct outcaste group was a product of the Tokugawa Period. The more than 250 years of internal stability during this period rigidified a formerly somewhat fluid occupational and feudal hierarchy and led to the legal delineation of the outcastes as a separate segment of society, prohibited by legislative decrees and judicial decisions from participating in majority life. Outcastes were forbidden to marry commoners, to live outside their designated ghettos, or even to serve as commoner's servants. They could not eat, sit, or smoke in the company of commoners, dress their hair in the conventional manner, wear *geta* (wooden sandals), or cross a commoner's threshold.[3]

Although the various myths of their origin refer to racial differences, Burakumin are racially, linguistically, and culturally identical to other Japanese. Their outcaste status was largely based on occupation rather than ethnic or cultural differences, and although many were engaged at least marginally in agriculture,[4] they were chiefly limited to roles considered degrading (beggars, actors, or jugglers) or ritually unclean in a Buddhist society (butchers, tanners, executioners, or other occupations dealing with death). Although occupational segregation was hardly welcome, the monopolies it created did give the outcastes an economically stable base on which to build their own society, and large and complex Buraku societies developed in Tokugawa cities.

It would be inaccurate, however, to assume that Tokugawa outcastes were content with their condition. Recent research has shown that they constantly struggled against discrimination during the Tokugawa Period, particularly from the latter half of the eighteenth century. Their struggle took many forms and had various goals. At times, the Burakumin accepted their separate status and exploited it to gain a degree of political independence or lessen their economic burdens. At other times groups of Burakumin would make elaborate legal arguments claiming that, although certain sumptuary laws or economic restrictions might apply to some minority groups, their particular group was not included and they should be treated as commoners for those purposes. At yet other times, Burakumin variously argued that commoners or officials were illegally preventing them from exercising traditional rights, such as the entry into the village-owned commons; that particular strictures were so harsh as to deprive them of a reasonable livelihood and that, therefore, they should be repealed; or simply that all agriculturists—most Burakumin legally owned and farmed land—should be treated alike and should have to abide by the same status rules as all other peasants and nothing more. These arguments were made with the same rhetorical and analytical style as that used by majority peasants in other Tokugawa protests. Since the dispute frequently originated in conflict with majority farmers, the process often functioned as a form of two-party litigation. At other times, the process consisted of petitioning and repetitioning the authorities directly, frequently accompanied by the preliminary question of whether the Burakumin had the legal right to petition at all.[5]

Their success was limited but substantial enough to encourage others to continue to protest, and the process continued through the Meiji Restoration and up to the Emancipation Edict of 1871, which marked the formal liberation of the Burakumin from their feudal status as outcastes and "non-humans."[6] Legal emancipation, however, meant little. The government was at best indifferent to significant change, and although it provided loans to former samurai to help them adjust to the social turmoil of the period, it did nothing for the Burakumin. In fact, government policy directly contributed to continued discrimination by registering Burakumin as "new commoners" (shin heimin) in the family registries (koseki) maintained at each citizen's place of origin. The registries were open to the public, and it was thus simple for other Japanese to determine whether a potential spouse or employee was of outcaste origin. Since descent from a Tokugawa outcaste is the only distinguishing feature of Burakumin, the "new commoner" designation was indispensable to identifying and discriminating against Buraku individuals.[7]

The official indifference of the central government was accompanied by social hostility at the local level. There was a series of pogroms aimed at exterminating the new commoners in 1872 and 1873, and village governments moved to exclude them from all access to commonly held village land, a measure more vigorously supported by the Meiji courts than similar efforts had been by the Tokugawa authorities. Not even legal emancipation itself was a complete blessing: along with the formal but totally unrealized equality came the loss of feudal occupational monopolies. Although personal distaste for Burakumin remained strong, tradition did not prevent non-Buraku capital from moving into areas such as shoe manufacturing that had previously been outcaste monopolies. Thus, attempts by wealthy Burakumin to capitalize on former monopolies and raise the group's general economic level failed partially because of new competition. The end result of the emancipation, therefore, was enhanced legal status at the cost of intensified social discrimination and loss of economic privileges.

Government neglect and overt social discrimination continued through the first decade of the twentieth century, but by the end of World War I general social unrest had contributed to a growing militancy among Burakumin. In 1918 spiraling inflation and relatively stagnant wages led to a series of rice riots throughout Japan. Burakumin played a large, often leading role in the riots, and the experience strongly affected their attitude toward themselves, society, and the government. Up to this time Buraku leaders had tended to explain discrimination as the majority's reaction to the low standard of living of Burakumin and to stress self-improvement and adoption of upper-class mores as the road to equality. Participation in the rice riots, however, made Burakumin much less willing to blame themselves and much more aggressive in demanding immediate action from the government, in terms of both economic programs and the elimination of discrimination in schools, the military, official documents, and public employment.

The government response was prompt and not insubstantial, at least in terms of economic assistance.[8] Funds were allocated for physical improvement in urban Buraku ghettos, and various joint government–Buraku organizations were formed to deal with Buraku problems. These efforts, however, failed to prevent the alliance of Burakumin with the growing leftist movement of workers and tenant farmers, and in the early 1920s the Suiheisha (Levelers' Society) was founded by militant young Burakumin strongly influenced by Marxist and Christian philosophy. Despite hostility from the government and older Buraku leaders, the Suiheisha quickly became the dominant Burakumin organization, a position it retained until the triumph of militarism in the 1930s. Its leaders scorned the supplication and paternalism of the past and devised a new strategy called denunciation struggle (*kyūdan tōsō*) that would rely only on the strength of the Buraku movement itself.

The first denunciations followed shortly. In May of 1922, just three months after the founding of the Suiheisha, seven members of the

Nara branch were arrested and convicted for disturbing the peace after they had confronted a school principal for condoning discrimination and discriminatory language. That November Suiheisha members were arrested in Nagoya for forcefully demanding a public apology from an individual who had used discriminatory language. Similar denunciations followed over the next few years, usually directed at the use of offensive expressions and followed by prompt police intervention, arrest, and conviction.

The chief characteristics of these early denunciations were their spontaneity and anger. They were addressed to individuals with the goal of obtaining a public apology and a promise not to use discriminatory language in the future. Although they frequently succeeded in this limited aim, they did so at considerable cost. Denunciation sessions were hastily planned and sometimes deteriorated into violent confrontations with groups of commoners. The end result was often the suppression of overt discrimination, especially the use of derogatory language, but also increased hostility toward Burakumin among the majority population and a view of the Suiheisha as violent and frightening. In the late 1920s, realizing the futility of this approach and conscious of the need to unite with other elements of the Japanese left, the Suiheisha changed its strategy for denunciation. Instead of attacking all individuals indiscriminately, it made distinctions among different types and sources of discrimination. If the discriminator was of the working or lower class, he was to be considered himself a victim of oppression and educated rather than intimidated. If, on the other hand, the discrimination was institutional, the Suiheisha mounted a carefully orchestrated denunciation campaign to force its elimination.

This shift in strategy was formally adopted by the Suiheisha membership in 1930. The goal was to link the elimination of discrimination to the general class-based complaints of labor and tenant farmers. Targets of denunciation were portrayed not only as enemies of Burakumin but as enemies of all oppressed Japanese, and the tentative identification with the left of the early twenties was concretely developed by cooperation and joint action where possible. The result of this new approach was a series of campaigns in the thirties that stressed institutional change rather than individual apologies and targeted the judiciary, the military, the penal and educational systems, and cultural and economic practices.

Many of these campaigns were remarkably successful: individuals who practiced discrimination were often transferred and institutional policy frequently changed. A campaign against the criminal conviction of two Burakumin brothers, who had failed to disclose their origin to a majority woman to whom one of them became engaged, succeeded in the discharge of the presiding judge, the transfer of the prosecutor, and the release of the brothers. In educational campaigns, principals and teachers who practiced discrimination were removed and discriminatory practices such as segregation in the classroom eliminated. These and other successes provoked relatively little backlash among the majority. In fact, the Suiheisha was treated with increased respect, and by 1935 the movement was planning each denunciation campaign with great attention to its political significance and potential contribution to integration with the rest of society. One part of this sophisticated campaign was the decision that Burakumin candidates would run for public office; this process culminated in 1936 with the election of the chairman of the Suiheisha, Matsumoto Jiichiro, to the Imperial Diet with only a minority of his votes coming from Burakumin.

Perhaps because of the identification of the Suiheisha with leftist issues, the attitude of police authorities toward Burakumin remained consistently unsympathetic. The Nara police were typical. In 1923, in response to the earliest denunciations, the prefectural police office published guidelines entitled "The Control of Denunciation Behavior" in which it criticized denunciations as frequently using force and intimidation to coerce involuntary confessions and apologies and threatened that such denunciations would henceforth be dealt with through the criminal law. Instead of intimidation, the police urged that discrimination be settled by "friendly discussion without demands for public apologies."[9]

The courts were equally unsympathetic. Suspended sentences were the norm, as they were generally for minor offenses, but actual incarceration was not uncommon, even in cases where the underlying goal of the denunciation was eventually met and its justice acknowledged by the authorities. When denunciation sessions deteriorated into pitched battles with rightist or ultranationalist groups, the Burakumin were frequently treated with greater severity than majority defendants. Although research is scant, there appears to be little evidence of either courts, police, or prosecutors exhibiting the tolerance toward confrontational tactics that was shown in the *Kawamoto* case. On the contrary, the emphasis was on the maintenance of social order and the prevention of unauthorized interference with the functioning of official bureaucracies.

The police and judicial reaction, however, failed to discourage the use of denunciation. From the early twenties to the mid-thirties more sophisticated use of denunciation helped the Suiheisha enter the political mainstream, and the shift of denunciation targets from often hapless individuals to social institutions led to small but significant improvements in the life of Burakumin. These developments were finally cut short not by the conviction of participants in individual denunciations, but by the coming of World War II. But the foundation had been laid for the continuation and strengthening of denunciation tactics in the postwar period.

As soon as Japan's defeat and the promulgation of the Constitution of 1947 made it possible, the Suiheisha, now under the name of the Buraku Liberation League (BLL), renewed its political and social efforts for equality. It quickly forged close alliances with the Japanese Communist Party (JCP) and the Japanese Socialist Party (JSP), began demanding the revival and strengthening of prewar efforts by the central and local governments to improve Buraku conditions, and participated vigorously in leftist causes such as the 1960 riots protesting the extension of the U.S.–Japan Security Treaty. As with their participation in the 1918 rice riots, the Burakumin's identification with national issues enabled them to gain wider recognition of the existence and justice of their claims. The result was broader support for a series of successful mass demonstrations and protest marches organized by the League that came shortly after the 1960 treaty riots.[10]

The government's response was the creation in 1961 of the Deliberative Council for Buraku Assimilation to study the Buraku situation and recommend possible action. The Council's 1965 Report, four years in the making, was very close to what the BLL had desired. In the first section, it defined the problem and explained its causes clearly and straightforwardly. In the atmosphere of superstition and prejudice that surrounded majority Japanese beliefs about Burakumin, the candor and accuracy of the Report was of inestimable value, particularly because it came with the government's seal of approval.[11]

The 1965 Report emphatically denied the scientifically unsupported but widely held belief that Burakumin are racially or ethnically different from other Japanese and that their situation is related to, if not justified by, their origins. Nor did the Report characterize the problem as simply a remnant of feudalism that would inevitably disappear with the progress of advanced capitalism. On the contrary, it rejected the common idea that the best solution would be to ignore the problem on the assumption that calling attention to it would merely perpetuate it and delay its inevitable dissolution by economic and social change. It showed Buraku discrimination to be deeply rooted in Japanese society, a society which the Report saw as still premodern in many respects, where individual freedom of action is often shackled by irrational and superstitious traditions, customs, and beliefs, and where feudal concepts of social status, family background, and group orientation are still the basis of social order. Far from being peripheral or superficial, therefore, the condition of the Burakumin was identified as intrinsic to the very structure of society and caused not by sloth or inferiority but by social and economic discrimination denying Burakumin freedom of occupational choice, equal educational opportunities, freedom of movement, and freedom of marriage and social intercourse. The Report dismissed the Emancipation Edict as being purely formalistic and bringing no substantive change in the Buraku condition, and criticized later government efforts as incomplete, paternalistic, and limited to improvements in the physical environment.

The authors then turned to the question of the present situation of Burakumin. Relying on their own and previous government surveys, the Deliberative Council found that the physical environment was extremely poor. Ghettos were consistently located in the worst locations topographically and were often subject to periodic flooding. Public services—fire protection, sewers, water lines, streets, street lights, public offices—were often absent. The housing stock was poor; at best Burakumin lived in old wooden tenements with common baths, kitchens, and toilets, and often lacked indoor plumbing altogether. Educational levels were well below the national average: only 30 percent of Burakumin children, approximately half the national average, reached middle school. Employment opportunities were similarly limited, with most older workers in traditional small-scale outcaste occupations and most younger ones in day labor or service jobs. Very few were engaged in the modern sector of large firms or had permanent employment. Wages and income were low and job security poor. More than twice the national average of households were on relief, and many mothers were forced to work to supplement household income. Despite a relatively high degree of residential integration—the average ghetto was only 60 percent Burakumin—the survey indicated almost no exogamous marriage and very little social intercourse of any sort with majority Japanese. What little contact there was often involved incidents of overt discrimination.

Consistent with its earlier formulation of the problem as deeply rooted in majority society, the Report's conclusion attributed the Burakumin situation directly to discrimination and began with a statement of the state's duty to resolve the problem fundamentally and promptly, based on a correct understanding of its causes and structures. It then set forth basic recommendations for future government action, the first of which was the need for special legislation. Although there were many separate statutes affecting general Buraku conditions, they were part of general government welfare programs and did not include policies specifically formulated to end Buraku discrimination. What was needed was an enabling statute that allowed the government to take special measures directed solely at the Buraku problem.

The result was the passage in 1969 of the Special Measures Law for Assimilation Projects (SML).[12] As is the case with much Japanese legislation, especially that with programmatic goals, the SML gives broad authority for governmental action while mandating virtually nothing. Like the Basic Law for Environmental Pollution Control, the Equal Employment Opportunity Act, and the statutes providing the underlying legal authority for industrial policy, the language of the SML is extremely broad and aspirational; it creates no legal duties on the part of government agencies and no new legal rights for individuals, either in the form of private causes of action against other individuals or administrative causes of action against public entities. Instead the law is a continuation and political confirmation of the moral impetus of the 1965 Deliberative Council Report.

The SML, in other words, is better viewed as a political statement in statutory form than as a statutory framework mandating specific public and private conduct, in the manner of American antidiscrimination legislation. With minor exceptions, therefore, the legal context of the Buraku liberation movement remained unaffected by the SML's passage. But this was of little concern to the Buraku Liberation League at the time because it was concerned with the moral and political import of the law, not its legal effect, and as a statement of society's and government's political and moral responsibility to eliminate Buraku discrimination, the SML was of extreme importance and set the stage for a new wave of Buraku activism and militance. The vehicle for that activism has been denunciation.

The Yata Denunciation

The best way to present the tactic of denunciation is the description of a denunciation session itself. Although atypical in certain aspects, the incident that occurred on April 9, 1969, in Yata, an Osaka Buraku ghetto, provides a dramatic example of the BLL in action. Because of the controversial nature of this particular denunciation, perhaps the simplest approach to the incident is to excerpt the opinion of the Osaka District Court, which tried two officials of the League's Yata branch, Toda and Koizumi, for unlawful imprisonment.[13] Their victims were three middle-school teachers—Kanai, Okano, and Tamaishi—who had supported the Communist Party candidate in the March 1969 Osaka Teacher's Union election. These teachers were forcibly denounced because their candidate, Kinoshita, had issued an election pamphlet that the BLL considered discriminatory and because they had repeatedly reneged on promises to undergo denunciation voluntarily and to meet with BLL leaders to discuss these issues. Although the pamphlet focused on working conditions and hours and contained no directly derogatory language, the BLL considered it discriminatory in the context of a developing conflict between the Communist Party and the League over control of the Buraku liberation movement in general and specifically over the proper approach to Buraku education.[14]

As described in the court's opinion of June 3, 1975, the denunciation itself began on the morning of April 9:

> Shortly after 9:00 A.M. defendants Toda and Koizumi met 13 other BLL leaders in front of the Yata Citizens' Hall. Toda reported on negotiations with Okano and Kanai (teachers at Yata M.S.) conducted the previous day. Then Koizumi said, "Let's go to the middle school and find out why Okano and Kanai have broken their promises to come to our meetings. Then we'll bring them to the Hall and have a meeting." Everyone agreed and got in four cars and arrived at the school at about 9:30 A.M.
>
> The defendants met Okano and Kanai in the employees' lounge and pressed them, "Why haven't you come to meet us?" "Why didn't you come last night as you promised?" "We can't talk here, let's go to the Citizens' Hall." The teachers replied that denunciation was inappropriate, that they would talk only on a one to one basis, and that the BLL members should talk to their representative, another teacher named Tamaishi. At that time, two officials of the Teachers' Union and several other teachers happened to be in the room. After close to an hour, Koizumi went to the principal's office and persuaded him that their going

to the Hall would be related to the students' education. Then while the BLL cadres left the room, the principal and union officials tried to convince Okano and Kanai to go. They refused and asked the principal whether he was ordering them to go. He responded, "I am asking as a human being." This went on for about 20 or 30 minutes until about 10:50 A.M. when the defendants lost patience and reentered the room. Defendant Koizumi then ordered Okano and Kanai to come to the Hall. Whereupon two others grabbed Okano's arms and lifted him out of his chair, then walked and pushed him the 30 meters out the front door to the parked car. Koizumi then pushed him into the back seat and rode with him to the Hall. Okano initially refused, but once he was made to stand, he didn't put up any particular resistance and acquiesced in being pulled to the car.

Meanwhile defendant Toda and two others grabbed Kanai by his jacket and lifted him out of his chair while a third BLL member kicked away the chair. They then grabbed him by the arms and belt and dragged him out the front entrance where he was pushed into the car and driven to the Hall. Kanai complained about the violence and tried to plant his feet but to little effect. After he was brought to his feet, he more or less gave up.[15]

The court then turned to the atmosphere and events at the Citizens' Hall that morning, describing first the denunciation of Okano and Kanai by thirteen BLL members in a small second-floor room:

"Why didn't you come like you promised?" "If you don't think the pamphlet is discriminatory, then explain to us why it isn't!" Okano and Kanai, thinking that it was impossible to have a discussion having been brought against their will and in these circumstances, remained silent. Then Toda continued, "Why don't you answer? Say something. Bigot, if you don't self-criticize, we'll get to the bottom of this somehow!" Koizumi asked them, "If you admitted that it was discriminatory on the 18th, why do you deny it now?" Then, pounding the table with his fists five or six times, Koizumi continued the severe questioning in a loud voice: "You, you betrayed our children to the police!" "Our daughters have committed suicide because they were born as Yata children. That's your responsibility!" Then he said to Okano, "These are children who get into high school but then have to repeat a grade because their English grades are bad. As an English teacher, that's your responsibility. You just spend your time playing baseball and neglect the children's studies." Then he turned to Kanai, "You rat, you are like a reform school guard. You know everything about the Buraku, but when you get right down to it, you're just a fake! You're a social studies teacher but you never teach anything at all about the Buraku." Then to Okano again, "Say something, you bigot. Why don't you deny that it was discriminatory?"[16]

In the afternoon the BLL moved the teachers to a large meeting hall where Tamaishi, the third teacher, was brought in the same fashion to join them. The BLL also notified both the Teachers' Union and the Osaka City Education Committee of the denunciation and urged them to send representatives. By late afternoon, the crowd had grown to close to 100 people and included union members as well as League members and Yata residents. At no time were the police asked to come or intervene. The union, however, took an integral role in the process, including reports by union officials on their efforts to get the teachers to self-criticize.

Immediately after the union report, defendant Koizumi returned with Tamaishi, and the crowd's attention shifted to Tamaishi's relationship with Kinoshita, his view of the pamphlet, and his role in the Teachers' Union. The last topic was of particular importance; Koizumi grabbed a piece of chalk, drew a circle on the blackboard, and demanded that Tamaishi diagram his relationship to the union:

> When the latter refused to draw, Koizumi pushed him on the chest into the blackboard. When he still didn't draw, three or four BLL members seemed about to grab and beat him, but others intervened and prevented it. When the other teachers similarly refused, Toda turned to Tamaishi: "Do you understand the pain of being downtrodden that Burakumin experience? What if we trod on your feet?" With that Toda stamped hard right next to Tamaishi's feet; Tamaishi quickly moved his feet. Toda then said, "When I raised my foot, you immediately thought I was about to step on your feet. You prejudiced bastard, you think a Burakumin is always going to do something bad, don't you? I didn't step on your foot, but you moved it anyway. It's because you're afraid of Burakumin, isn't it?"[17]

When the three teachers remained silent, the crowd began screaming at them. Then the defendants started the sitting and standing game— calling them bigots (*sabetsusha*) and ordering them to stand, then telling them they were old and should sit. When they refused to stand, their seats were kicked out from under them. Then, when they remained standing after being told to sit, they were taunted by the crowd until finally one BLL member was about to push Tamaishi down to the floor but was stopped by Koizumi.

By 7:00 P.M. there were about 250 people in the hall, 150 of them teachers and the rest mainly Yata residents. At about 7:30, there was a break for dinner and the three teachers were fed and escorted to the rest room. The Vice-Chairman of the Osaka BLL then arrived and warned the teachers of the consequences should they continue to refuse to recant:

> "The BLL thoroughly denounces discriminators; no one has ever been able to escape. Frankly admit that you're one of them and self-criticize. No matter where in Japan discriminators may try to hide, we will run them down. Sometimes people who are denounced go crazy or are socially abandoned and useless. Think about it."[18]

At about 9:00 P.M. two representatives of the Osaka City Education Committee arrived and were immediately grilled by Koizumi:

> "Isn't the Kinoshita pamphlet discriminatory? What does the Education Committee think? These rats won't say anything. What are you going to do? These teachers are discriminators and won't even self-criticize. It's the Education Committee's fault that there are teachers who are so insensitive to assimilation education. What are you going to do?" While yelling at them this way, Koizumi was pounding the mike on the table until finally he broke the mike and dented the table. At that point Morita, one of the Education Committee representatives, said that he himself thought the language discriminatory and convinced the defendants to let him talk with the teachers in a room on the second floor. The teachers refused to recant, however, and they returned to the main hall after 20 minutes. Then Toda said to Okano and his colleagues, "No matter how long it takes, you're going to confess. You are determined discriminators, but we'll denounce you thoroughly; tomorrow, the next day, we'll keep it up."[19]

As the evening progressed, family, friends, and supporters of the teachers arrived. Among them were officials of the Communist Party, who refused an offer to negotiate the matter directly with the BLL. At about 2:00 A.M., after further efforts to get the teachers to talk proved fruitless, the Chairman of the Osaka BLL adjourned the meeting:

> "We've gotten as far as we can today so let's go home. I am now involved and will try to do what I can. But this is not the end of the denunciation; the Yata Branch and the Osaka BLL will thoroughly continue it. The Osaka BLL agrees with the Yata Branch that we must continue to denounce anyone who doesn't self-criticize. We are going to ask the City Education Committee to fire these prejudiced teachers."

Then the women's section brought out sushi and distributed it. At about
2:50 A.M., April 10, after they had each eaten one piece of sushi, Okano
and the other teachers left the Citizens' Hall.[20]

The theory and practice of denunciation will be discussed in detail
later in this chapter, but it should be noted here that although the Yata
denunciation is unusual in its scale, it is not otherwise unrepresenta-
tive. Struggle sessions rarely reach this pitch of emotion or involve this
many participants; more typical is a meeting of two or three League
representatives with an individual teacher, bureaucrat, or businessman
in which they try to convince him to change a policy, retract a statement, or prevent action that the BLL considers discriminatory or otherwise disadvantageous to Burakumin. Even in such small meetings,
however, the potential for escalation is present.

As the role of the Japanese Communist Party in the incident itself
indicates, the roots of the Yata denunciation go beyond the alleged
discriminatory language of the Kinoshita pamphlet to a virulent power
struggle between the JCP and the League. The BLL's alliance with the
JCP began to sour in the mid-1960s with the coincidence of two major
events.[21] First, the death in 1960 of Matsumoto Jiichiro, the Buraku
movement's leader since before the war and a prominent JCP member,
led to a change in leadership within the League and a shift in liberation
strategy. Second, the success of the movement in obtaining the Deliberative Council Report in 1965 and the Special Measures Law in 1969
fundamentally changed the relationship between the BLL and conservative governments on both the local and national levels. As League
leadership shifted, the possibility of working with the conservatives
became a reality at the same time that the Liberal Democratic Party
began responding to pressure to help the Burakumin. The result has
been a form of arm's-length cooperation between the ideologically
leftist BLL and the conservative LDP.

The Communist Party was initially and continues to be bitterly
critical of what they consider the co-opting of the liberation movement. One dimension of their opposition is ideological. Simply stated,
the JCP believes that Buraku liberation can only be completely
achieved through a transformation of Japanese society that will liberate
all oppressed Japanese. Although the Communists acknowledge the
special burden of Buraku discrimination, they characterize it as a remnant of feudalism currently exploited by monopoly capitalists which
will eventually be destroyed by the further development of Japanese

capitalism. Thus government aid solely for Burakumin, rather than for poor Japanese of all backgrounds, splits the proletarian movement. The JCP believes that affirmative action is intended by the conservatives to do just that—split the left and thereby preserve the status quo in Japan while simultaneously transforming the Burakumin, once reliable participants in leftist causes, into indolent dependents of the government.

The League's interpretation of the problem is fundamentally different; they believe that a proper understanding of Buraku discrimination requires a more sophisticated analysis than mechanical Marxism. They argue that discrimination is pervasive in Japanese society and present among members of the working class and the Communist Party itself. According to the BLL, the structure of the contemporary labor market that segregates the Burakumin into a distinct group supplying marginal, unskilled, low-wage labor is dependent on pervasive discrimination, and since that structure benefits working-class Japanese as well as those of other classes, all are guilty of discrimination. Until all majority Japanese recognize their own discriminatory attitudes, therefore, the split in the proletariat will remain a real one, more fundamental than the Communists' characterization of it as a feudal remnant or a cynical creation of the Liberal Democratic Party. Thus there are real differences between Burakumin and other poor Japanese that class consciousness alone can neither explain nor resolve. The BLL, therefore, can both accept affirmative-action efforts, even those of conservative governments, and justify limiting them to Burakumin.

The split became irreconcilable in 1969. That year marked the passage of the Special Measures Law, toward which the JCP had been only lukewarm, and the start of nationally subsidized affirmative action projects, toward which the JCP was extremely suspicious. It also saw the outbreak of many, often violent, confrontations between JCP and BLL supporters. Communist sympathizers within the League either withdrew or were purged, and the JCP organized a rival Burakumin organization. Since that time there has been unremitting hostility between the two groups, and one of the major areas of conflict has been education.[22]

The Yata incident, therefore, should be viewed as an integral part of a two-dimensional struggle for control of Buraku education in Osaka. Most fundamentally, it reflected ideologically different approaches to teaching about Buraku discrimination in all schools nationwide. But on a more concrete level, it concerned the quality of education in Osaka schools with large numbers of Burakumin students. As part of affirmative action programs, local school authorities had taken broad measures to increase the educational attainment of Burakumin students. Along with such improvements as increased staffing and equipment, remedial classes, and additional counseling, there was a decision in the late 1960s to prevent cross-district registration by students at schools outside their district. In a phenomenon analogous to "white flight" in American schools, the percentage of students attending schools outside their school district was highest in districts with a substantial Burakumin population. Prohibiting open enrollment, it was argued, not only would eliminate an overt manifestation of discrimination but also would improve the educational environment at Buraku schools, both because majority students generally had higher levels of achievement and also because superior teachers currently assigned to elite schools could be reassigned to Buraku schools.

Osaka teachers, although institutionally committed by their union to affirmative action in education, were ambivalent toward the panoply of specific affirmative measures urged on them, the net result of which was fewer jobs at elite schools and more at Buraku schools. According to the BLL, JCP teachers were particularly reluctant to fight hard for the prohibition of cross-district enrollment because they were over-represented at elite schools and faced transfers to arduous, less prestigious positions at Buraku schools. In this context, the Kinoshita pamphlet was easily interpreted by BLL leaders as hostile to affirmative action in education. Ostensibly complaining about working conditions, the pamphlet explicitly mentioned only the problems of cross-district registration, extra tutoring, and other affirmative action matters as making teaching "more difficult and distressing." Although its language might seem restrained and ambiguous to one not familiar with the growing JCP–BLL hostility over Buraku education, the pamphlet was straightforward enough to those involved to be judged a clear impediment to assimilation education and thus to Buraku liberation.

When the pamphlet first reached their hands, League leaders immediately determined that it was discriminatory and began the denunciation process with the following document, entitled "Denounce the Discriminators of the Kinoshita Faction":

> The pamphlet spreads Buraku discrimination, opposes the Buraku liberation movement, and exploits the teachers' outmoded consciousness as a foundation for opposing assimilation education. It slanders assimila-

tion education and impedes its progress. When read in conjunction with the other campaign material, its true purpose becomes clear. The cause of the teachers' difficulties and anguish is implied to be assimilation and grade promotion. The terrible conclusion is that the actual source of teachers' problems is the Buraku liberation movement. This hurts the struggle for the people's liberation, slanders and splits [the movement], obscures the real enemy, and encourages the continuation of discrimination. This person is truly nothing more than a bigot. We can not permit this kind of discrimination. This type of discriminatory thought and incitement must be resolutely denounced.[23]

The next step was a "fact confirmation meeting" on March 18 with Kinoshita and two supporters at the Citizens' Hall, where League cadres demanded and eventually received an admission that the pamphlet was discriminatory and an agreement to submit to a formal and public denunciation to be held March 24. Kinoshita promised to persuade all his supporters to attend and present written self-criticisms, and meanwhile to recall as many of the pamphlets as possible.

Between March 18 and 24 the BLL was able to get the Osaka Teachers' Union to agree that the pamphlet was discriminatory, albeit unintentionally so, and to urge Kinoshita and his supporters to attend the March 24 denunciation. Nonetheless the meeting did not take place because, according to the BLL, the JCP urged the teachers not to cooperate. Despite further urging from both the union and the BLL, the teachers remained firm until early on April 8, when Okano and Toda agreed to a meeting of eleven teachers and eleven BLL members. After discussion with fellow Kinoshita supporters, however, Okano canceled the meeting later that day and even refused to meet Toda personally as he had previously promised, pleading that he was "not feeling too good." The BLL response was the April 9 denunciation.

As the involvement of officials of the Teachers' Union and the Osaka City Education Committee in the events of April 9 indicates, the Buraku Liberation League was determined to use this denunciation as a vehicle for more than individual recantations by Kinoshita and his followers. Their first demand was the removal of teachers, virtually all Communist-Party-affiliated, who actively opposed their stance on assimilation, and they put great pressure on Education Committee representatives both on April 9 and thereafter to carry out their "administrative responsibilities." In response, the Committee announced in an official circular its agreement that the Kinoshita pamphlet was discriminatory and was "regrettable." Then in May, when school disruptions concerning the pamphlet and the JCP teachers' attitudes continued, the Committee removed Kinoshita, Okano, and Tamaishi from the classroom and ordered them to report to the Osaka Educational Research Institute, where they were "to study so that they may understand that the Kinoshita pamphlet is discriminatory." That September, after summer vacation, Kinoshita, Tamaishi, and four others were transferred to Buraku schools (Okano already taught at one) so that they "might wrestle with assimilation education while learning the reality of Buraku discrimination."[24]

The seven teachers, however, stood firm. Their transfer to Buraku schools led only to increased disruption as Burakumin students and parents protested their beliefs, and in early 1971 the Committee finally found a permanent solution. It retransferred eight teachers (the original seven plus Kanai, the third target of the April 9 denunciation) back to the Research Institute, this time for a full year of research and reflection. Thereafter, each year on the same day the Committee extended these teachers' research assignments for another year. This ritual was repeated until 1976 and 1977, when first one group and then the rest were finally allowed to return to teaching duties. By then, all eight had spent at least five full years assigned to a single room in the Research Institute where, surrounded by BLL publications on the correct approach to assimilation education, they were to reach an understanding of their past mistakes.

During those years the eight teachers, all leading supporters of the JCP approach to assimilation education, were isolated from their colleagues and students. They emerged in 1977 with their ideology intact, but their forced "sabbatical" effectively cowed other teachers sympathetic to their views and helped the BLL establish complete dominance over assimilation education policy in Osaka. That control continues despite a vigorous legal counterattack by the JCP that has eventually won every legal battle but has failed to reverse the decisive loss of the political war. This counterattack—its planning and execution by JCP lawyers, its legal success and political impotence—is itself worthy of detailed comparative analysis, and to the extent that it was part of the JCP's general resistance to the use of denunciation, it will be discussed briefly later in this chapter. But for now our focus remains on denunciation itself. We have already seen how the BLL used the denunciation process not only to intimidate and then neutralize the particular teachers opposed to them, but also to force the Teachers' Union and the Education Committee to take a position on whether the Kinoshita pamphlet was discriminatory and thus whether the BLL or the JCP approach to assimilation education would control educational policy. Now it is time to see whether the tactic fared as well in the legal arena as it did in the political.

Denunciation Tactics in Court

Most objects of BLL denunciation do not file a criminal complaint despite the clear violations of the criminal code involved in many sessions. JCP members and sympathizers are the exception: they do not hesitate to use the courts to protect their legal rights and further their political goals. After the Yata incident, therefore, the JCP encouraged the teachers to file a complaint and successfully persuaded the prosecution to indict.

The resulting trial became a key test of the legality of denunciation tactics. It was heavily covered in the JCP and BLL media and portrayed as an important political and moral struggle between the two organizations. It was, in other words, the continuation of the political struggle by other means, with both camps demanding the judicial imprimatur for their moral position. This view of the case was most eloquently stated by the teachers themselves, who, when asked why they did not file an action against the Education Committee early in their banishment, replied that a civil case would have detracted from the effectiveness of the struggle against the BLL being waged through the criminal case.[25]

Although condemning the indictment as the product of a JCP campaign to smear them as violent hoodlums, the BLL leadership immediately set out to turn it to their advantage. Like Minamata victim Kawamoto, the Yata defendants did not deny the facts of the indictment; rather, they upheld them as necessary and appropriate behavior. They did not use the trial to defend or excuse their own actions but to focus moral scrutiny, both the court's and the public's, on the acts of their oppressors. But in order to do so, they had to convince the court to extend its inquiry beyond the facts of April 9 to include the whole social and political context of Buraku discrimination. As we saw in the *Kawamoto* case, a broadened inquiry is not as difficult to obtain in Japanese criminal cases as it would be in an American case, and neither the District Court nor the High Court in the *Yata* case hesitated to consider evidence concerning the underlying social problem of discrimination. Nor is there any evidence that the prosecution objected.

Judicial openness to discussion of the social context, however, ensured neither an acquittal nor an opinion sympathetic to the BLL position. To accomplish these goals meant convincing the court, first, that the Kinoshita pamphlet and the JCP position that it represented were in fact discriminatory; second, that denunciation was a legitimate mode of redress for victims of discrimination; and finally, that the defendants' acts of April 9 were within the legally accepted scope of denunciation sessions. If all three issues were decided in the defendants' favor, there would be an acquittal. If the defense won only the first two, at least denunciation within certain limits would remain as a tool for future use. Since the BLL had definitively eschewed litigation in favor of denunciation and had predicated its political strategy on the use of denunciation, judicial recognition of the "right of denunciation" (*kyūdanken*) was of prime importance. Even if the court refused to recognize denunciation as a legal right, however, a conviction would still not represent a total disaster for the BLL if the court at least recognized the discriminatory nature of the Kinoshita pamphlet, for that would mean, or would be construed to mean politically, the judicial rejection of the Communist approach to assimilation education. Even this limited victory would help to consolidate BLL control over educational policy. Only if the court remained silent or—the worst case—found the pamphlet nondiscriminatory while condemning BLL violence would the case be a total JCP victory and of substantial help in their ongoing political struggle with the BLL.

The District Court's acquittal of June 3, 1975, was therefore a stunning political victory for the BLL. Even the subsequent reversal and conviction by the Osaka High Court almost six years later was a qualified victory. The passage of eleven years since the incident and almost a decade since the end of the underlying power struggle over educational policy greatly weakened the political impact of the High Court decision. Moreover, the High Court differed with the District Court only on the final question of the acceptable level of violence and affirmed the BLL position on both the nature of the pamphlet and the existence of an abstract right of denunciation.

After the recitation of the facts, the District Court went directly to what it termed the "heart of this dispute," the discriminatory nature of the election materials. In so doing, it implicitly adopted the BLL's interpretation of the case—that it was a dispute between the JCP and the BLL and that the court's role was to determine who was "right," that is, who had acted correctly in the course of that dispute. This approach meant that not only the nature of the pamphlet but also all the surrounding circumstances would become relevant. Hence, in evaluating whether the pamphlet was discriminatory, the court did not limit itself to the face of the document, to Kinoshita's subjective meaning, or even to what an objective reader might get from the language. Instead, it adopted the position of the Burakumin reader: it recounted the nature of Buraku discrimination, the affirmative action efforts in education in the Yata ghetto, the educational and socioeconomic conditions of most Yata residents, the discriminatory impact of cross-district registration, and the vital importance of educational attainment to Buraku liberation, and concluded that the pamphlet, whatever its author's subjective intent, could be interpreted as discriminatory and had become "an obstacle to the progress of assimilation education, which plays a central role in Buraku liberation."[26]

The court then turned immediately to the implications of a finding of discrimination:

> Legal remedies against discrimination are definitely limited. Their scope is narrow and frequently there is nothing that can be done. In light of these circumstances, it's justifiable for society to accept the process called denunciation against discrimination as long as the methods and tactics don't exceed reasonable limits. Furthermore, the question whether reasonable bounds were exceeded cannot be determined uniformly or abstractly. It should be determined by reference to all the circumstances: the content and degree of the discrimination targeted by the denunciation in question, the events leading up to the discrimination, the process of negotiations between the discriminator and the denouncers, the attitude of the discriminators, etc.[27]

Thus, according to the court, denunciation is not merely legitimate, it is indeterminant in the sense that permissible severity will vary according to the circumstances, including cooperation or lack thereof by the discriminating party. If the discrimination is extreme and the discriminators recalcitrant, the bounds of legitimate denunciation will be broader. Presumably the court will be the final arbiter of what those bounds are, but the opinion gives only a vague list of relevant circumstances and no criteria at all as to what will be considered excessive. Perhaps even more troubling, the courts give little guidance as to the permissible purposes of denunciation. Both opinions cite the inadequacy of legal redress for discrimination and imply that denunciation is justified when it supplements or replaces legal process. The High

Court further specifies that prior recourse to legal procedures is unnecessary, but the only direct mention of the purposes of denunciation is
the High Court's implication that direct demands on a perceived discriminator for an explanation, self-criticism, or a change in attitude are
one part of denunciation.[28] There is no indication that these are the
only permissible goals.

In addressing the events of April 9, the District Court first noted the
victims' bad faith during the preceding negotiations: they had repeatedly reneged on promises to cooperate and later denied initial admissions that the pamphlet was discriminatory. This behavior was
characterized by the court as "a betrayal of any relationship of mutual
trust."[29] Compounding the victims' bad faith was an obstinancy that
the court clearly felt was inappropriate and to some extent justified
their subsequent treatment:

> The victims were talked to three times by their colleagues, the school
> principal, and union officials who tried to convince them to meet with the
> BLL. The BLL also agreed to conduct the meeting on a one on one basis.
> Considering their position in society, they should have gone to the meet-
> ing and, even if you assume the language in question is not discrimina-
> tory, clarified their way of thinking and argument. Instead, there was no
> indication of a sincere intention to do so. Also, at the meeting in question,
> they remained almost entirely silent, citing the force used to bring them
> as the reason. It is undeniable that this was one cause of the length of the
> meeting and of their fatigue and exhaustion.[30]

After close scrutiny of the complainants' conduct the District Court
turned to that of the defendants, but even here it was reluctant to leave
the underlying context behind. After noting that the force used to bring
the teachers to the Citizens' Hall had been "limited to pulling and
pushing" and that the teachers had made no attempt to call the police
or ask their colleagues for assistance, the court began its characterization of the meeting itself by admitting that the teachers were not free to
leave the hall at will. But it quickly qualified that statement by noting
that although over half the audience consisted of union members and
other non-BLL observers, the teachers never indicated to them that
they wanted to leave. The court also noted that adequate rest periods
were given, food provided, and the rest room made available, and that
individual teachers were allowed to smoke and even make telephone
calls. Then the opinion returns to the question of the teachers' duty to
cooperate and the weight of the past discrimination:

Thus, although the denunciation itself was extremely tense and severe and they were overwhelmed with invective, this was almost entirely anger at their refusal to talk and expression of the residents' anger at the discrimination. When one tries to imagine the depth and enormity of the discrimination suffered by Burakumin in the past, these reactions can be seen to a certain degree as unavoidable after the discriminatory content of the language involved in this case.[31]

The court concludes that the defendants' actions of April 9, though "perhaps somewhat excessive and showing a need for prudence in the future," could not be judged as "deserving punishment."

The tone of this opinion is precisely what the defense had hoped for. Its focus is clearly on the Communist teachers and their own and society's obligation to cooperate with the League in eliminating discrimination. The defendants' actions are dealt with almost as an afterthought, and the teachers' rights not at all. What to a Westerner might be the most salient characteristic of the April 9 meeting—the total humiliation and domination, both psychological and physical, of an individual by a group—was simply not a matter of concern to the District Court. Indeed, the larger the group, the more varied and intense the pressure to recant, the less the court seems to have been inclined to adopt the individual's perspective in analyzing the case. As one reads the opinion, one has the constant impression that the court is about to praise the defendants for their patience and forbearance in the face of the teachers' clearly unreasonable behavior.

The High Court relied heavily on the more elaborately reasoned and factually detailed opinion of the District Court.[32] It agreed that "legal redress for discrimination is in reality limited" and that "direct demands by victims of discrimination for explanation and self criticism are to be permitted . . . whether one calls it 'denunciation' or not." The court noted that denunciation cannot exceed "the socially reasonable bounds as set by the legal order" but then admitted that "a certain level of severity is to be approved."[33] It then applied this standard to the defendants' conduct:

Even if one fully considers the justice of defendants' motive and purpose, their use of physical force to bring the victims against their will to a mass meeting where they were subjected to violent conduct and where leaving was made extremely difficult for a very long time must obviously be said to exceed reasonableness as determined by reference to the legal order. Furthermore, even if one considers the complementary [*hojū*] nature of their conduct, if the purpose was only to modify the so-called discriminators' viewpoint and to demand self-criticism, it is hard to conclude that a "mass denunciation" of this kind was the only conceivable means or that this conduct was truly unavoidable. Also, if denunciation is intended to provide a warning to others, so-called mass denunciation may well be an extremely effective method, but it is cruel and soon becomes a form of private punishment that can not receive the full approval of the law. In addition, the extremely long duration of the victims' loss of freedom and the insulting invective of the assembled BLL members reached the point of causing mental and physical illness and exhaustion. The infringement of the victims' legal interests, therefore, can not be simply dismissed as trivial. In sum ... defendants' conduct clearly exceeded socially reasonable bounds and it is impossible to deny that they deserve punishment from the point of view of the legal order. Nor was there sufficient evidence to establish that defendants' conduct was unavoidable so as to negate their criminal responsibility.[34]

The High Court sentenced Toda (Koizumi had died while the appeal was pending) to the minimum sentence, three months in jail, suspended, and excused him from payment of court costs.

While the District Court opinion had been a total victory for the BLL, both sides were able to declare victory after the High Court decision. The headline in the BLL weekly *Liberation News (Kaihō Shimbun)* of March 23, 1981, was "Discriminatory Language and Denunciation Right Recognized," referring to the High Court's agreement that the Kinoshita pamphlet was discriminatory and its recognition of denunciation in the abstract. Only in the subheadline was the "reactionary" guilty verdict mentioned. The equivalent JCP journal, *The Road to Liberation (Kaihō no Michi)*, chose "Teachers Vindicated—BLL Set Back in Guilty Verdict." The national and more neutral *Asahi Shimbun* headline was "Denunciation Right Recognized—'Language Discriminatory' in High Court Reversal."

As the headlines indicate, the BLL and the defense attorneys interpreted the opinion as giving them two-thirds of what they wished for. The *Asahi* reported that it was the first High Court opinion to recognize in principle the legitimacy of denunciation, and the lead defense attorney, while condemning the guilty verdict as evidence of a fundamental misunderstanding of the events of March and April, 1969, praised the opinion as part of a growing judicial and social acceptance of denunci-

ation.[35] As for the opinion's effect on the future of denunciation as a
BLL tactic, another defense attorney stated:

> What the JCP wanted most of all from this decision was a denial of the
> discriminatory nature of the pamphlet and a characterization of the BLL's
> motives in this denunciation as illegal. But on these important issues,
> they were largely disappointed. This opinion will certainly never become
> a weapon for the JCP. On the contrary, even with the fundamental errors
> in part of the opinion, it will henceforth be one of the BLL's theoretical
> weapons in its continuing campaign of denunciation against
> discrimination.[36]

The High Court's guilty verdict received relatively little attention from
BLL commentators; they generally either dismissed it as part of the
judiciary's general submissiveness to the state or explained it as a
result of the JCP's and the prosecutors' distortion and exaggeration of
the events of April 9.

The Communist analysis naturally stressed the court's unequivocal
condemnation of the level of violence used.[37] While ruefully admitting
that the High Court repeated the District Court's misinterpretation of
the pamphlet, the JCP media refuted the common assertion that the
opinion had recognized denunciation as a legitimate BLL tactic, even in
principle. The language of the opinion that ostensibly discusses the
propriety of denunciation is, according to JCP lawyers, no more than
the reassertion of the basic constitutional right of free expression. Of
course, they argue, one may demand explanations and self-criticism,
and educating the prejudiced is extremely important, but that is not
what the BLL means by denunciation. The JCP claims that BLL denunciation is based on violence and intimidation, and the High Court
opinion explicitly found any violence whatsoever to be illegal.

The opinion is ambivalent enough to support both interpretations,
and in private neither the JCP nor the BLL is quite as confident as their
public analysis would indicate. The JCP is pleased that in criminal
cases like *Yata* (there have been several others) it can usually count on
an eventual guilty verdict if the violence or injury is substantial. It is
also painfully aware that such verdicts, coming many years after the
event and accompanied by nominal suspended sentences and ambiguous opinions that are frequently cool to the complaining witnesses and
sympathetic to the defendants, will have little effect on the underlying
political struggle. BLL leaders, on the other hand, are bitter about the
fact that the courts would convict the victims of discrimination while

offering little help in combating discrimination itself. They also fear that continued guilty verdicts, even with nominal sentences, will give substance to the JCP campaign to portray the BLL as no more than a group of gangsters. I shall return to these issues later in the chapter, but first let us look more closely at the historical and intellectual evolution of the concept of denunciation.

The Theory and Effectiveness of Denunciation

The three themes of self-determination, martyrdom, and the realization of true humanity have dominated Buraku thinking about denunciation from the very beginning and are eloquently set out in the 1922 founding Declaration of the Suiheisha:

> Burakumin throughout the country unite!
> Long suffering brothers:
> In the past half century, reform undertakings on our behalf by many people in various ways have not yielded any appreciable results. This should be taken as divine punishment for permitting others as well as ourselves to debase our human dignity. Previous movements, though seemingly motivated by compassion, actually degraded many of our brothers. Therefore, it is necessary for us to organize a new collective movement through which we shall liberate ourselves by our own effort and self-respect.
> Brothers—our ancestors pursued liberty and equality, and practiced these principles. But they became the victims of a contemptible system developed by a despicable ruling class. They became the manly martyrs of industry. In recompense for their work in skinning animals, they were skinned alive. For tearing out the animals' hearts, their own warm hearts were ripped out. They were spat at with ridicule. Yet all through these cursed nights of evil dreams, their human blood has kept on flowing. We, who have been born of this blood, are trying to become divine. The time has come when the oppressed shall throw off the brand of martyrdom. The martyr's crown of thorns shall receive blessing.
> We, who know how cruel and cold it is to be discriminated against, must not use disrespectful words and cowardly behavior to retaliate against ordinary human beings. To do so would be to discredit our ancestors who died for freedom and to desecrate humanity. Therefore, we should work passionately for human rights and seek the light of true humanity.
> Let there be warmth in the hearts of people, and let there be light upon all mankind. From this, the Levelers Association is born.[38]

The determination to "liberate ourselves by our own effort and self-respect" was a reaction to earlier government efforts to improve ghetto conditions that were criticized by Burakumin because of their implicit premise that discrimination was caused by the Burakumin's poor conditions rather than the reverse and because they were perceived as intended to appease Burakumin and diffuse their militancy. The Burakumin feel that in order to avoid being co-opted by the majority, they must rely only on themselves and must understand that liberation can come only by the force of their own demands. Denunciation, because it is entirely within the control of Burakumin themselves, is considered much more conducive to maintaining this independence than either litigation or more informal types of third-party intervention.

The second theme, the sense of martyrdom, is embedded in the language of the Declaration itself, both in its mention of striving for divinity and the martyr's crown of thorns and in its overall apocalyptic tone. The Suiheisha flag is black, emblazoned only with a blood-red crown of thorns denoting the martyrdom of Christ. The flagpole is a bamboo spear, symbolizing the militance of traditional peasant *ikki*, a social phenomenon that is itself deeply identified with martyrdom and quasi-religious sacrifice. The Suiheisha is striving for a paradise where no discrimination will exist; its mission is an absolute one, and its members are willing to make any sacrifice necessary to reach it. With this consciousness of mission, it is almost inconceivable that either legal process or mediation would be as satisfying or appropriate as denunciation.

The third theme—the identification of the Suiheisha with the realization of true humanity, of warmth in the hearts of all people, and of light upon all mankind—links Buraku liberation with the struggle of all humanity. The disappearance of Buraku discrimination will not only liberate Burakumin but also allow former discriminators themselves to realize their own full humanity. True liberation is a prerequisite to human progress and means justice and a better life not only for Burakumin, but for all Japanese. Implicit in this sense of shared progress toward human perfection is the conviction that Buraku liberation depends on and contributes to human enlightenment. Hence, the process of liberation must also contribute to enlightenment; it must be educational in the most profound sense. The goal of Suiheisha and Buraku Liberation League activities, therefore, is not merely the eradication of overt discrimination, but also the transformation of the discriminator's consciousness from one that desecrates humanity to one that honors it. Again, the direct human contact inherent in the process of denunciation is much better suited to this goal than conventional forms of dispute resolution.

Japan's defeat at the end of World War II and the ensuing political reforms greatly increased the scope of Buraku liberation activities and eventually led to a more sophisticated and elaborate articulation of the concept of denunciation. Not only were the Burakumin free to associate openly with leftist parties and to benefit from the additional organizational and financial support that those parties now commanded, but the enactment of the new Constitution and the consolidation of liberal democracy in Japan completely transformed the intellectual context within which Buraku theorists and academics operated. In addition to Christian theology and Marxist theories of materialism and class structure, they began to use psychological and sociological theories to explain discrimination; in addition to the idea of the revolutionary proletariat and the united front, they could now draw on the ideology of liberal legalism and rights consciousness as strategies for liberation. By the 1970s, the BLL literature on discrimination and specifically on the meaning and justification of denunciation had combined these new ideas with prewar ones to create a series of elaborate arguments that attempt to explain and justify the content and use of denunciation.[39]

Law and legal institutions play a powerful role, albeit often a contradictory one, in the thinking of BLL theorists. On the one hand, the new Constitution is seen as guaranteeing Burakumin a whole series of human rights previously denied them. The rights to life, liberty, and the pursuit of happiness (Article 13), to equality before the law (Article 14), to free choice of occupation (Article 22) and marriage (Article 24), to work (Article 27), to a minimum standard of "wholesome and cultural living" (Article 25), and to an equal education correspondent to each person's ability (Article 26) are all cited by the BLL as supporting their aspirations and vision of a society free of discrimination. On the other hand, the BLL claims that the direct application of the Constitution only to governmental discrimination and the failure to provide clear statutory redress for discrimination make it impossible for the BLL to use the legal system to enforce the rights granted by the Constitution. The use of denunciation, therefore, is justified because it is the only means left to Burakumin to enforce preexisting constitutional rights.

In contemporary BLL publications there is a fairly clear separation between, on the one hand, the explanation of social structure and of the origin and nature of discrimination and, on the other, the strategy and tactics necessary to eliminate discrimination. The former continues to be dominated by Marxist analysis, but the latter is discussed predominantly in terms of legal rights and liberal legalism, with denunciation as the vehicle for realization of those rights. The rights theory of denunciation, however, remains inextricably interwoven with the themes first enunciated in the Suiheisha Declaration—the necessity of independence and autonomy in the movement, the Burakumin's apocalyptic view of their mission and their utopian vision of the future society, and the underlying need to educate and reform the majority to achieve true liberation for all Japanese—and a discussion of the quasi-legal argument alone would distort the BLL's perception of denunciation.

BLL theorists claim that the right to use denunciation is itself one of the fundamental human rights (*kihonteki jinken*) guaranteed by the Constitution. They reason that the several rights guaranteed by the Constitution can only be realized by denunciation since both private and public legal redress are assumed to be unavailable.[40] It follows that the denunciation right is implicit in the Constitution; without it, the situation of the Burakumin would be no better than it was under the prewar Constitution, which made no pretense of granting human rights. In this context the denunciation right is not only one of the fundamental human rights, but as part of the prewar struggle for equality, it preexisted and helped lay the foundation for the postwar rights enumerated in the Constitution.

Although the explicit substantive right—marriage, occupation, education, and so on—underlying specific denunciations varies with the factual context, two that are frequently given prominence in discussions of liberation strategy are the right to employment inherent in Articles 22 (freedom of occupation) and 27 (right to work) and the right to a minimum level of existence of Article 25. The latter has formed the legal basis for the BLL's postwar campaign of "administrative denunciation" against primarily local governments, which is aimed at the material improvement of Buraku ghettos. This campaign has been extremely successful in achieving dramatic improvement in Buraku conditions: housing, sewage, medical care, police and fire protection, education, and community facilities have all been substantially upgraded in the name of actualizing the Burakumin's Article 25 right to a minimal standard of living and in response to constant denunciation activity against local officials. Similarly, the right to employment was the justification for the announcement in 1975 of a major denunciation campaign for equal employment opportunity.

Most Japanese legal scholars consider both the rights to existence and to employment solely aspirational—as political promises rather than legal guarantees. BLL theorists reject this view,[41] arguing that the Constitution entitles Burakumin to a minimum level of employment and standard of living and to a society free of discrimination. But establishing an underlying right does not justify the means to attain it, and of course it is the limited use of force inherent in denunciation that distinguishes it from the simple exercise of freedom of expression and brings into question its legality. The BLL justifies such force by the failure of the legal system to protect these rights from criminal infringement by majority discrimination.

Translating this into specific legal terms, one leading BLL theorist, Yagi Kōsuke, has relied on Articles 35–37 of the Criminal Code and what is referred to as the "right of resistance" (*teikōken*). The underlying common thread in this series of arguments is the necessary defense of vital interests:

> Where one's existence as a human being is invaded, resistance is natural . . . Some elements in authority and in political parties try to equate denunciation with violence and intimidation. But think about it for a moment. Denunciation is an educational process, but it is between persons whose fundamental human rights have been denied and those who have denied them. It is not the Buraku masses lecturing the discriminators on algebra. Denunciation is urgent action designed to recover lost human rights. A certain amount of rough language is natural, even while trying to reform discriminators' thinking . . . No one is so superhuman that he can deal with life and death matters in a lightheartedly smiling way. For that reason, it is in denunciation's very nature that it be conducted in a tense atmosphere.[42]

Turning to the self-defense language of Article 36, Yagi argues that any incidental intimidation or violence associated with individual denunciation sessions should qualify as conduct "necessary to prevent the imminent, unjust infringement" of human rights and, therefore, as "legitimate self-defense."

Yagi also exploits Article 35's language justifying "conduct required by law or legitimate obligation" to find further legal basis for denunciation:

The Constitution scrupulously provides fundamental human rights as the rights of all citizens. It restricts and supersedes all other laws and guarantees humans their fundamental rights. But Buraku discrimination is an area where citizens' rights are incompletely protected. That is to say that the existence of discrimination itself indicates that there has been a violation of the Constitution. Therefore, denunciation struggles conducted by the Buraku masses constitute behavior undertaken to fulfill the Constitution by demanding the confirmation of fundamental human rights. Buraku liberation and its main pillar, denunciation, are no more than the realization of the language of the Constitution and should be considered as "conduct required by law," in this case by the Constitution. Thus, even if on occasion there are problems with denunciation and illegality [*ihōsei*] is theoretically present, that illegality will be nullified because denunciation is in reality a proxy for constitutional provisions.[43]

But the essence of the right of denunciation lies not in constitutional rights or statutory provisions for self-defense or justification. For the Burakumin, denunciation springs from the desperation of their existence; it is their only way out of what they describe as the "living hell" (*iki jigoku*) of discrimination. Charges that denunciation is intimidation are countered by the assertion that discrimination is intimidation, denunciation only its answer. To the BLL, the qualified recognition of denunciation by the Osaka District Court and High Court in the *Yata* case was recognition of the severe harm caused by discrimination and of the natural right to resist its imposition. To the extent that the courts limited this right, however, the BLL saw them as lapsing into a reactionary attitude:

Whenever human beings are totally denied their human rights, it is a universal tenet of humanity that they can resist, whatever the particular legal system. This is all the more true in a class society where law inevitably reflects class structure and is meaningless to protect the powerless whenever their interests conflict with those of the controlling class. Burakumin, who are at the bottom of the oppressed and exploited class, therefore, are almost totally excluded from the framework of legal protection. From that fact, it is even more appropriate for Burakumin to use the only tool of resistance open to them. Since denunciation is thus the only available method for Burakumin to protect themselves and their behavior in doing so is excused as justified, to put a limit on the exercise of that right clearly shows the class nature of the opinion.[44]

It does not follow, however, that denunciation cannot be abused or distorted or that every attack by Burakumin on majority Japanese is justified. To ensure that denunciation is not used for personal vengeance, BLL cadres, as they did in the Yata incident, hold preliminary "fact confirmation" meetings with the alleged discriminator to clarify not only the allegedly discriminatory word or deed but also to develop the context of the incident and thereby bring into relief its "true meaning." By this process the BLL can usually both convince the discriminator of the nature of his conduct and also prevent the abuse of denunciation as a tool for personal retribution or gain.[45] It is of the utmost importance to BLL theorists that denunciation remain a tool of the Buraku masses and not of any individuals; retaining its mass character lessens the possibility that denunciation will deteriorate into a personal weapon or lose its political character. Only if the political aspects are kept foremost can the clarification of responsibility for discrimination be achieved, and therefore it is against the interests of the BLL itself to allow violence or intimidation to enter a denunciation proceeding.

Although in theory violence, threats, and intimidation are not part of denunciation, even BLL apologists will admit that they occasionally occur in practice. To state that violence occurs and to condemn it does not, however, help identify it or help determine whether given behavior in a given setting is appropriate or not. The JCP and the Osaka High Court found the *Yata* defendants' conduct inappropriate, but the BLL and the District Court did not. All such decisions will remain indeterminate as long as they are discussed in general terms, but there is one instance of a more concrete debate that gives an idea of the standards and limitations the BLL is willing to accept. This debate arose in 1975 when the Governor of Hyōgō Prefecture announced a set of guidelines for the conduct of denunciation. The BLL reaction is instructive not only for what it shows about the BLL attitude toward the specific guidelines, but also for what it reveals about what denunciation means to the BLL.

The guidelines were a direct response to a particularly severe denunciation of school officials and urged that future denunciations retain their mutually educational character and be conducted in accordance with "democratic rules" (*ruuru*), including requirements that duration and location be mutually agreed upon beforehand, that the proceedings be open to the public and the participants free to leave, that violence or intimidation be banned, and that children and students not participate. The response of the Hyōgō Chapter of the BLL to these conditions was immediate:

> Every denunciation is a struggle to regain human dignity—a struggle by the totally powerless. For that reason, we can never relinquish the denunciation right. For discriminators who have from the beginning ignored their official responsibilities and promoted discrimination to declare denunciation "mutual education" and claim that therefore the first issue in denunciation is for the parties to decide jointly on the rules is to turn denunciation upside down. It is contemptible. Denunciation can only be mutually educational when the discriminator begins to stand in the shoes of a Burakumin, to think like a Burakumin. You can't reverse the process by putting the conclusion at the beginning and reversing form and substance.[46]

Making the object of denunciation think like a Burakumin requires a relationship between denouncer and denounced equivalent to that of discriminator and discriminated. This implies a deeply emotional involvement by the denounced, a feeling of powerlessness in the face of his tormentors, that is totally at odds with the equal, arms-length bargaining envisioned by the Governor's guidelines.

What offended the BLL was not the requirement of openness—all denunciations are open to the public, they assert; indeed, attendance is encouraged. Nor was it the requirement of voluntary attendance, although the League certainly would argue that there is an obligation to attend. The problem was the failure of the guidelines to understand the essence of both discrimination and denunciation. For the BLL, the requirement of mutually agreed terms confuses the victim with the assailant; it is like the burglar who becomes indignant when caught in the act. Discrimination cannot be the subject of negotiations—as one BLL theorist put it, when someone has you by the neck, you don't sit down to talk about it. The Hyōgō Governor's first mistake was not to realize that discrimination is indeed a life-and-death matter; his second was to misunderstand the goal and nature of the denunciation process. To Burakumin, discrimination is deeply embedded in the consciousness of the Japanese, so deeply that they often do not even realize that it exists. Without the realization both of the meaning of his own behavior and of what Burakumin endure, the discriminator cannot be reclaimed for humanity. This is what the BLL means when it characterizes denunciation as educational, not that the process can be conducted by the rules of a classroom. And this kind of experiential education cannot be accomplished through any means other than denunciation— not the debate of the Governor's guidelines, not mediation, and not litigation.

A central part of the BLL's justification for denunciation is the failure of political authority to provide through the legal system any alternative vehicle for their movement. From the strict treatment of Suiheisha leaders in the 1920s to the conviction of the *Yata* defendants, the BLL's view has been that judges would inevitably favor majority litigants over Burakumin in civil suits just as they discriminatorily convict BLL participants in denunciations. This view is complemented by the assumption that, even if the judges were to be fair, the private law doctrine necessary to attack discrimination simply does not exist.

There is considerable doubt about the truth of these assumptions. Although it may well be that Japanese judges are "prejudiced" in the sense of not fully agreeing with BLL interpretations of the necessity and nature of denunciation and therefore convicting BLL participants, there is no reason to assume they would be unsympathetic to civil litigation initiated by the BLL. Nor, as we shall see in detail in the next chapter, does it appear that there are insurmountable doctrinal obstacles to the effective use of litigation against discrimination. Indeed, recent judicial history seems to disprove both these assumptions. In those few cases where individual Burakumin have sued civilly, they have won.

Perhaps the most important legal case for Burakumin generally was brought in the 1960s against the authorities of the formerly rural village of Inoue in Nagano Prefecture for refusing to share with Burakumin villagers the proceeds from the sale of lumber in the village commons.[47] The court cut through various statutory and customary law defenses to find rather easily that the Burakumin were entitled to share in proceeds from the commons even though their hamlet had historically been administratively distinct from the majority hamlets that constituted the village of Inoue. Although empirical data are lacking, there is evidence that this legal victory contributed to changing commons policy vis-à-vis Burakumin throughout Japan.

A case of more limited immediate impact but one that was also significant in terms of judicial attitudes toward discrimination was a tort suit brought by the parents of a Burakumin woman against her common-law (*naien*) husband and his parents.[48] The allegation was that the defendants' conduct after they discovered that she was of Buraku origin had driven the wife to suicide. In a later case, a jilted fiancée sued her prospective parents-in-law for preventing her marriage because of her Buraku origin.[49] The courts found for the plaintiffs in both cases, as they have in other similar cases including tort actions against the detective agencies specifically hired to investigate prospective spouses for Buraku origin.[50]

These cases, in conjunction with the doctrinal success of women in employment discrimination litigation, make it clear that alternatives to denunciation do exist. The doctrinal breakthroughs that were needed for success in the women's litigation are virtually identical to those needed to attack Buraku discrimination in employment. Similarly, the village commons case and the individual tort actions indicate that legal redress for discrimination, or at least for its consequences, is available. What may not be available, however, is the programmatic approach to concrete problems possible through denunciation. Denunciation functions in some ways similarly to institutional litigation in the United States. In contrast to the dispute-resolution role of courts—the settlement of points of law and fact directly related to a dispute between two parties—denunciation and similar techniques such as direct negotiations can go beyond the bipolar, passive model of judicial decision making. As does multipolar litigation, denunciation can coerce the involvement of important third parties and force them to commit themselves on crucial issues outside of the narrow confines of a specific dispute. In the less spectacular, more common denunciation campaigns aimed directly at changes in bureaucratic policies and programs, these advantages of denunciation over litigation become even more conspicuous. The administrative denunciation campaign that followed the Yata incident, for example, succeeded in reshaping Buraku education in Osaka in a step-by-step series of denunciation/ negotiation sessions aimed at programmatic change.

The success of denunciation in Osaka City educational policy has been repeated over a wide variety of fields in many separate areas of Japan, a few of which deserve mention here.[51] One is the development of social programs for Burakumin in Osaka and elsewhere. These programs, generically known as *dōwa* projects, typically include urban renewal projects such as sewage systems, housing projects, and community facilities like the Yata Citizens' Hall, as well as welfare benefits for individual Burakumin including scholarships, rent subsidies, and cash payments at marriage or the birth of a child. Both the level of welfare benefits and the BLL role in their administration depend on the power and activism of the local BLL, but in Osaka City the transformation of the physical environment and the level of welfare benefits available to BLL members are dramatic proof of denunciation's effectiveness.

The welfare programs are especially interesting not only because they raise substantial constitutional equal-protection questions—in some areas Burakumin receive the benefits regardless of income or residence, whereas no non-Burakumin are eligible—but also because of the way they are sometimes administered. In order to determine eligibility, the applicant's status as a Burakumin must be determined, and in many localities the government has delegated this task to the local branch of the Buraku Liberation League. The result is that the BLL becomes the only channel for benefits; without BLL certification of status, no application to the government bureau is considered complete. The League has used this delegated power to reward its sympathizers and punish its enemies, the latter being primarily Burakumin sympathetic to the JCP. As a result, non-BLL Burakumin are regularly denied benefits, and at least passive support of BLL policies and activities is necessary not only to receive financial benefits such as scholarships, but also to enter newly built public housing.[52]

The effectiveness of denunciation in economic issues in Osaka is paralleled on a small scale on the national level in terms of leather and beef import restrictions. Even though restraints on both items have been highly visible irritants in the U.S.–Japan relationship, Japan has strongly resisted liberalization. One reason is the concentration of Burakumin in these sectors, particularly in leather working and beef butchering and wholesaling, and the BLL's strong opposition to any liberalization. To ensure the continuation of current policies, key officials in MITI and other ministries are regularly visited by BLL representatives.

A third area is academic and media self-censorship.[53] Of the popular media, few deal with Buraku issues at any length, and none, except house organs of the JCP, openly challenge the BLL line. The taboo against the subject, or at least against an analytical or critical approach to it, extends to academic writing as well. There are few Japanese academics writing about Buraku questions—whether this involves legal scholars analyzing the legal status of Burakumin or sociologists studying rates of intermarriage or assimilation—except for scholars associated with either the BLL or the JCP. Even foreign authors have found that most Japanese presses, including the most prestigious academic presses, refuse to include any mention of Burakumin in translations of Western works on Japan.[54] Although it is never discussed openly, one factor contributing to the taboo is simple: the BLL monitors the Japanese press closely for discriminatory references to Burakumin and immediately initiates denunciation campaigns against perceived discriminators, their institutions, and their publishers. Rather than taking the chance that something they publish may be considered discriminatory, the publishers prefer to avoid the entire issue.

Whether the media campaign is wise or not—it has not only prevented overtly discriminatory expression but also any dispassionate discussion of the issues involved, which may in the long run contribute to further misunderstanding—there is no question that it has been successful in allowing the BLL to dominate the rhetoric of the Buraku question just as conclusively as denunciation has contributed to the BLL's success in other fields. But not all of the BLL's denunciation campaigns have been so successful. Employment discrimination is perhaps the single most significant area of relative failure, both because of its intrinsic importance and because of the light it sheds on progress toward the ultimate goal of Buraku liberation, the elimination of all discrimination against Burakumin.

The most dramatic evidence of continued discrimination, especially in employment, has been the series of commercially published books known as Buraku lists (*chimei sōkan*) giving the place names of Buraku ghettos.[55] Because of the difficulty of determining who is of Buraku origin, persons or companies wishing to discriminate have for a long time hired private detectives to check on the background of prospective employees or marriage partners. Until recently detectives could simply inspect an individual's family registry, which was open to the public and which would indicate Buraku origin. Family registries are under the jurisdiction of the Ministry of Justice, and the BLL and its prewar predecessors have long wanted access limited. Although the Ministry promised action as early as the 1930s and again in the 1960s, it was not until the mid-1970s that access was effectively restricted.

The first Buraku list appeared shortly thereafter. With such a list, an educated guess can be made about a person's background from his address alone. The first list was quickly suppressed; its author, a private detective, roundly condemned; and his corporate and individual customers given a formal reprimand (*kankoku*) by the Osaka office of the Ministry of Justice. The reprimand termed the purchase an "exceedingly pernicious violation of human rights" and urged the purchasing firms to strive for a "fuller understanding of the Buraku problem." Nonetheless, the first list was quickly followed by a second, then a third, fourth, fifth, and so on, so that by 1979 there had appeared a total of at least eight separate Buraku lists, all of which have been bought by thousands of companies, individuals, and at least one university. These books are useful for only one purpose: discriminating against Burakumin. The persistence of their authors, reported to be mainly private detectives, is eloquent testimony to the potential market and indirectly to the remaining strength of discrimination.

A second and related indication of the strength of employment discrimination is the level and quality of employment. Burakumin are much more likely than average to be underemployed or in low-paying jobs with little or no job security. Precise statistics are unavailable, but the *Asahi Shimbun* has reported that unemployment among Osaka Burakumin ran as high as 28.5 percent in 1977.[36] Although there are no available government statistics on Burakumin unemployment, the government agrees that Burakumin employed in manufacturing remain concentrated in small firms engaged in the labor-intensive production of goods such as woven bamboo products, knitwear, leather shoes, and sandals. Since these industries are those for which Japan has already lost its international comparative advantage, employment in these sectors is generally shrinking, especially in the small handicraft firms where most Burakumin are employed.

The net result of supplemental welfare benefits and poor employment prospects is that, although government cash grants and subsidies give short-term financial relief, the long-term economic condition of most Burakumin remains as insecure as ever. The prized goal of most Japanese, permanent employment with a big company, is almost impossible for Burakumin who are unwilling to conceal their origin. Some of the blame can undoubtedly be placed on lower educational attainment and poor test-taking skills, but continued employment discrimination also plays a role. One source has indicated that "every large company" has purchased a Buraku list. Whether or not this report is true, it is undisputed that large companies were prime customers for the lists. Although reliable national statistics are again unavailable, many employment surveys of rural and urban Buraku ghettos have been done by the JCP and the BLL. Time and again the same story appears: the surveyed ghetto is near one or several large factories; Burakumin may be employed as temporary employees, but very few, if any, are regular employees. As we shall see in the sex discrimination cases, temporary employees are denied most benefits of regular employees, including job security and fringe benefits. Continued discrimination against Burakumin is therefore important to big companies not only to preserve the homogeneity of background and outlook of the "company family," but also because a large pool of temporary workers acts as an economic safety valve during times of economic stress.

The employment picture is not uniformly bleak.[57] Some villages report Burakumin entry into hitherto forbidden areas such as fishing, and there are some reports of increased permanent employment. But overall progress is painfully slow, as the government statistics on family income attest. More than 20 percent of Buraku households are either on relief or exempted from all taxes, whereas the figure for the majority is somewhere below 7 percent. Similarly, almost half (46 percent) of Buraku households are exempted from all but the uniform basic household tax, while the national figure is about 20 percent.

Given the importance of employment to overall social status in Japan and the flagrant nature of the discrimination, the specific response of both the BLL and the government to the Buraku lists deserves special attention. The BLL reaction was a series of "fact confirmation" hearings followed by denunciation sessions of progressively wider scope. Not only were the compilers and purchasers of the lists invited, but also the purchasing companies' unions and government officials as well. As the campaign proceeded, representatives of political parties, labor federations, and high officials of the relevant ministries (Justice, International Trade and Industry, Labor) also attended and were invited to comment on the nature of Buraku lists and the necessity of action to prevent their reappearance in the future. Without exception, confessions and apologies were forthcoming from publishers and purchasers, and government agencies issued harsh condemnations of both compilers and their customers and strongly stated their resolve to eliminate employment discrimination in the future.

The BLL did not, apparently, demand increased hiring of Burakumin for permanent positions, preferring to concentrate on admissions of wrongdoing and educating the companies' officials about the true nature and immorality of Buraku discrimination. Ironically, this attitude precisely coincided with that of the government. When pressed about the desirability of legislation prohibiting employment discrimination, the Minister of Justice, despite admitting that the legality of private discrimination severely hampered his investigation into the Buraku lists, stated that discrimination was a "matter of the heart," and not suitable for legal attention.[58] With the massive denunciation campaigns then in progress and the participation of the Ministry's personnel in them, it is hard not to interpret the Minister's statement as an endorsement of denunciation over law as the preferred mode of antidiscrimination activity. Despite this concentration of moral and social pressure, however, publication of the lists continued, and there was little immediate indication of increased hiring of Burakumin for responsible positions.

Before we leave the question of the effectiveness of denunciation, brief mention must be made of the JCP's vigorous legal counterattack against BLL control of Buraku programs.[59] The number of civil actions filed by the JCP challenging BLL control of Buraku education or the administration of affirmative action programs alone run to several dozen, and there are many others in related areas such as the BLL-instigated refusal by local officials to allow JCP-affiliated Burakumin to use public facilities. Most of these suits have been legally successful because in many the constitutional violations involved are obvious—denial of free speech or academic freedom in the education context, or state discrimination against certain political beliefs (JCP sympathizers) in the administration of affirmative action welfare benefits.

These victories have meant a great deal to the JCP in propaganda terms; its publications proclaim victory after victory. However, turning these legal victories into political ones that weaken the BLL's hold over Buraku communities and local administration of affirmative action programs has been very difficult for several reasons. One is the frequent ambiguity of the judges' attitudes. Often the opinion, while holding narrowly for the plaintiffs, notes the need for Buraku solidarity and explicitly leaves room for alternative modes of operation that will help sustain that solidarity, which it equates with the organizational strength of the BLL. Then there are the limitations which are inherent in all litigation but which are particularly pronounced in Japan: the legal process is excruciatingly slow, particularly in political cases; the Japanese judiciary's hesitation to challenge administrative action is remarkable; and legal doctrines covering equitable remedies are extremely restrictive. A third reason is the political motivation of many local officials, who, if not actually sympathetic to the League, are certainly willing to use it as a weapon against the Communists. Most cases are appealed, and when appeals are no longer possible, administrative arrangements are made that help preserve BLL political domination of the Buraku community. The exclusion of the JCP from its former influence in the ghetto can only help the other major parties, at least on the local level, whether it is the Liberal Democrats or the Socialists who are the temporary ally of the BLL.

Denunciation in Social and Political Context

In relating the pollution experience to the Tokugawa *ikki* and the Ashio incident in the preceding chapter, similarities could be discerned both in the patterns of conflict (the sequence of events and the types, actions, and reactions of the participants) and in their nature (the normative framework, the attitudes and goals of the parties, and the roles of various individuals and institutions). There are problems, however, in extending this comparison, particularly as it regards the pattern of conflict, to the BLL's use of denunciation. Unlike the other three situations, the Buraku movement is not conducive to analysis as a single instance of social conflict, and single instances of denunciation like Yata are too inextricably tied to the evolution of the Buraku movement as a whole to discuss separately. But if we treat the movement itself as the object of comparison, some useful parallels can be drawn.

The sequence of events common to the other three phenomena was as follows: a systems breakdown leading to severe social dislocation; appeals to official authority for relief; collective, illegal, and often violent protests designed to gain public and official attention; effective governmental response to the substantive problem; and often a cathartic admission or recognition of official neglect. The situation of the newly emancipated Burakumin in the early Meiji Period was of course not the result of a systems breakdown but the reverse: their social status was an integral part of the prior system, and its continuation was, if not desired, certainly completely acceptable to the Meiji government and society. Aside from this fundamental difference, which will be discussed further, the course of Buraku liberation can be portrayed as following this pattern.

The response of Meiji period Buraku leaders was to petition for governmental relief—the "reconciliationist" policy later condemned by the Suiheisha and BLL—and the government, particularly local governments, often responded with minor concessions. As these lost their appeal, individual Burakumin (and later the Suiheisha) turned to violent protest, first as participants in mass movements like the 1918 rice riots and later in denunciation campaigns. The central government's response was cut short by the war, but the pattern was repeated in the postwar period, with the BLL's role in the 1960 Security Treaty riots and the mass marches on Tokyo providing the political pressure. This time the government response under the Special Measures Law has been substantial in terms of urban renewal and transfer payments. The analogue of the ritual apology and the *Kawamata* and *Kawamoto* trials can be found in both the 1965 Deliberative Council Report, which recounts both the government's and society's responsibility for discrimination, and the 1976 opinion by the Osaka District Court acquitting the *Yata* defendants (and, albeit ambivalently, in the 1981 High Court opinion), which approached the trial of the BLL leaders in much the same way as did the courts in the trials associated with the Ashio and Minamata incidents. Further similarities include the intense emotion of the actors, the personalization of the conflict, and the utopian and messianic tone of the victims. The personal sacrifice of Tokugawa village leaders, the emotional response of government leaders to the Ashio farmers' desperation, and the willingness of modern executives to engage in ritual acts of contrition in the Minamata episode all recall the focus on particular individuals and their behavior implicit in denunciation.

There are also, however, significant differences between contemporary tactics such as denunciation or direct negotiations and their historical antecedents. First is the presence of legal avenues of redress; there were none in the Tokugawa Period and few in Meiji. There are such options now, as the civil tort victories of individual Burakumin, the Big Four cases, and the women employees' litigation have demonstrated. Resort to confrontational tactics is now by choice; not only does the litigation alternative exist, but the BLL has both the resources and the sophistication to use the courts if it chooses to do so. Second—and this is more true of denunciation than direct negotiations—is the relative lack of spontaneity in execution of the modern protests. There are emotion and anger, to be sure, but these events are more carefully planned on both a tactical and a strategic level than their antecedents. Targets for denunciation are chosen at least in large part not out of desperation or rage, but on the basis of how their denunciation will contribute to a particular campaign. The scope and type of violence in individual sessions are usually scrupulously controlled by BLL leaders, and instances of significant physical injury or property damage in formal denunciations are rare.[60] Third, denunciation has become an intellectual construct, with BLL and JCP academics arguing over questions of technique and justification. This is a far cry from the peasant *ikki* or the farmers' marches of Ashio, which, though part of a finely articulated Confucian world view, were relatively unselfconscious in their execution.

A fourth difference, again particularly relevant to BLL denunciation, is a shift in rhetorical emphasis toward a justification of denunciation as being legal as well as moral. Although Ashio and Minamata leaders referred to constitutional and statutory violations by Furukawa Mining, Chisso, and the government, reference to positive-law norms was not at the heart of their rhetoric.[61] The BLL agenda, on the other hand, cannot be analyzed in vague Confucian terms as an appeal to the "covenant" between ruler and subject. Instead, the rhetoric is one of rights, based on specific statutory and constitutional provisions giving Burakumin certain legal as well as moral rights that denunciation is intended to protect or fulfill. Denunciation and, more ambiguously, direct negotiations are seen, even by the courts and the government, as legitimate means of self-help and therefore as integrated into the concept of the legal system. Although the deification of rebellious village leaders by later feudal lords and the resignations and apologies of the Meiji officials in the Ashio incident also ratified the motivations of the actors in these events, the government stopped short of ratifying their methods. Peasant rebellions and mass protest marches might have eventually been officially condoned in those specific instances, but they remained illegal. What the courts by their legal reasoning and government bureaucrats by their participation have done with the denunciation model of direct confrontation is to legitimize it, when conducted within acceptable bounds, as a vehicle for resolving social conflict. It is available both for the realization of certain constitutional and statutory rights—(equality in education and employment, a certain standard of living, compensation for pollution injury, and so on—not adequately realized by legislation and for redress against discrimination. It exists parallel to, but distinct from, ordinary legal process.

A final difference between denunciation and the other examples of social conflict is the nature of the BLL's goals. In the other three examples, conflict arose from the breakdown of the systems supporting the status quo, and to a certain extent, the subsequent protests were demanding only the reestablishment of a supposedly preexisting ideal order explicitly endorsed by the government itself. The Burakumin, on the other hand, are demanding a new order through the elimination of the traditional hierarchy and the realization of the norm of legal, political, and social equality, a norm that has been given a good deal more lip service than vigorous enforcement in postwar Japan. In this fundamental sense the Buraku movement is substantially more threatening to long-term social stability than the other social movements discussed up to this point. The question then becomes, if it is so potentially destabilizing, why has the government been so tolerant of the BLL's denunciation tactics? And this in turn brings us to the nature of denunciation and its political implications.

Litigation has been characterized as an alienating, politically impotent method of pursuing social change.[62] According to this interpretation, the focus of political movements on litigation and legal rights diverts political power from the substantive political issues to meaningless battles over abstract legal concepts and dissipates rather than mobilizes political power. One plausible interpretation of the decline and disappearance of the Japanese environmental movement is that it ran itself into the sands of litigation, that political struggles became legal ones, and that the movement slowed to the pace of the courts, eventually dying quietly at the hands of the Supreme Court in the *Osaka Airport* decision. Why, then, has the Japanese government seemingly preferred the direct political action of denunciation to the drawn-out formalities of litigation? Why has it not encouraged the Burakumin to follow the environmentalists into the quagmire of litigation?

The most important reason may be the relative effectiveness of denunciation and litigation in influencing the social agenda and determining whether individual disputes become issues in the general political debate. By keeping these controversies out of the courts, the government can prevent the crystallization of the BLL's grievances into questions of equality, discrimination, and social structure that have universal normative appeal. As long as the issues are particularized to those involved in specific disputes, the BLL's actions and demands seem so idiosyncratic that the fundamental issue of equal treatment is obscured and substantial political appeal lost. Even if the dispute reaches the courts, it does so as a criminal trial where the opinion, however sweeping in its support of the BLL position, will apply directly only to the legality of particular incidents of denunciation and only vaguely and indirectly to the underlying issue of equality. Because the

BLL's normative successes (for example, the judicial recognition that the Kinoshita pamphlet was discriminatory) are not fully applicable or meaningful beyond their immediate context, such disputes cannot provide a basis for political alliances with potential allies such as working women, Koreans, mixed-blood Japanese (*konketsuji*), and other minorities. In sum, as long as the BLL's tactics remain legally informal and normatively particularistic, the government will likely be able to maintain substantial influence over the course and pace of social change.

A second limitation on the political effect of denunciation is its eventual dependence on governmental action. Although denunciation may be initially directed at private individuals like the JCP teachers, its ultimate goal is to force the government to grant concessions, provide benefits, or otherwise take responsibility for the resolution of the specific problem at hand. The Yata denunciation and the way it was used by the BLL to manipulate the Osaka City Education Committee is an excellent illustration of this tendency, as is the campaign for welfare benefits in Osaka, but perhaps the best example is the denunciation campaign concerning the Buraku lists. The problem was seen as one of governmental failure and responsibility. Although the authors, publishers, and their customers were denounced, the focus of the campaign was the Ministry of Justice and particularly the Civil Liberties Bureau. Instead of pursuing each individual company, perhaps through litigation, and demanding future quantitative proof of nondiscrimination in hiring, the BLL turned to the government as being somehow responsible for the appearance and purchase of the lists and for their eradication.

At times, this may be the most effective approach. One can make a strong argument that it was so in both Ashio and the antipollution struggle of the sixties and seventies. But in both of these cases the government eventually became sincerely committed to alleviating the substantive problem of pollution. The antipollution movement had succeeded in both mobilizing sufficient political pressure to threaten the political elites and in convincing those elites of the need for an effective response. There is little evidence, however, that the government is sincerely interested in equalizing employment opportunities for Burakumin. Certainly, it is highly unlikely that the government views equality in this context as sufficiently beneficial economically to counteract the damage to the ideal of the homogeneous, all-male, all-majority Japanese corporate family of permanent employees that is perceived as one of the pillars of Japanese economic and social success. Urban renewal and the provision of welfare benefits are acceptable to and perhaps even morally required of a paternalistic government, but social equality is quite a different matter.

Thus, as long as the BLL focuses on governmental responsibility as the ultimate key to liberation, the government will be able to set the agenda of liberation. There is little evidence to suggest that this agenda will ever include aggressive measures to ensure Burakumin access to permanent employment in large firms, which leaves them, whatever their individual educational attainment or employment qualifications, as a pool of low-wage temporary workers. Instead of liberating Burakumin to enter the economic and social mainstream, the government goal seems to be providing some level of economic security for the Burakumin as a group, while conniving in the denial of individual access to majority society. Far from preventing this cynical strategy, denunciation may ultimately foster the dependence that it was designed to avoid.

FOUR

Civil Rights Litigation and the Search for Equal Employment Opportunity

ALTHOUGH the denunciation tactics of the BLL exhibit fundamental differences from the other modes of social conflict studied thus far, they also have deep roots in Japanese history and strong connections with contemporary phenomena such as the direct-negotiation tactics of the Minamata pollution victims.[1] As a means of social protest, therefore, denunciation falls within the mainstream of Japanese society. It is unusual, but not aberrant; and as long as the government is able to deflect the BLL from its egalitarian goals of full social participation, denunciation should pose little threat to the status quo.

The series of employment discrimination cases are quite different, with little connection to either historical forms of conflict or other contemporary phenomena. Although the Equal Employment Opportunity Act (EEOA),[2] which followed the employment cases, strongly resembles the legislative responses to litigation in the other case studies, the cases themselves are fundamentally dissimilar to the Big Four pollution cases both in terms of their long-term goals and in the nature and meaning of the litigation itself. They represent a new approach to social change in Japan, and an analysis of the cases and the way in which they relate to the passage of the EEOA and its enforcement by the Ministry of Labor can give us another view of the role of law in the articulation of grievances and management of conflict within Japanese society.

The role of women in the Japanese economy has always been significant. Their contribution in agriculture and manfacturing was crucial to Japan's growth up to World War II, and their role in these sectors, particularly in small-scale agriculture and light assembly, remains strong today. In the last twenty-five years, however, there have been important shifts in the composition of Japan's female work force that parallel fundamental changes in both the structure of the Japanese economy and the lives and aspirations of Japanese women. How these changes have evolved, and which trends are encouraged and which impeded, are the fundamental issues involved in the women's litigation. The answers to these questions will determine the economic and social role women will play and the opportunities available to them in Japanese society over the next several decades.

The depth and scope of the changes in women's economic role are apparent in the shift in the demographics of female workers over the last two decades.[3] Up to 1960 the pattern was simple: Japanese women entered the labor force early, worked overwhelmingly in primary industry, and retired, usually for life, to marry by the age of 25. Consequently, the typical female worker was young and single with substantially fewer years of service than her older male co-workers. By the 1980s, dramatic changes had occurred. Young women (ages 20-24) are still heavily involved in the labor market and still generally withdraw on marriage, but they now usually reenter the labor market in their mid-thirties after several years of child raising, with the result that the graph of labor force participation resembles an "M" with peaks at ages 20-24 and 35-50. The typical female worker is now middle-aged and married, works in the service sector, and is considerably closer to her male counterpart in both age and years of service.

The reasons for this change are the familiar ones—higher education rates, fewer children, a longer life span, declining farm population—but one statistic captures the underlying social change particularly well: before World War II, Japanese women had only 7.6 years to live, on average, after completion of their child-care responsibilities; now the average is 43.8 years. Add to this additional time their increased level of educational attainment (95.4 percent graduated from senior high school in 1980 versus 36.7 percent in 1950), declining household responsibilities, and the rapid growth of the service sector since 1960, and the statistics become readily understandable.

Increasing labor force participation, educational attainment, age, and length of service have not meant corresponding increases in equality of treatment for female workers. In gross differential, for example, women received 53.8 percent of men's wages in 1980, up from 42.8 percent twenty years earlier, but the trend in recent years has been for the gap to widen. By 1982 the figure was down to 52.8 percent, the fourth straight yearly decline and lower than the figure of ten years earlier (53.4 percent).[4] Indeed, Japan was unique among advanced nations to show an increase in wage differentials during this decade.[5] If one controls for education, length of service, age, and employment status, however, women do much better. Female high school graduates receive over 90 percent of parity initially—over 95 percent for college and university graduates—and, although the degree of parity immediately begins to decline, it never dips below 70 percent. Furthermore, unlike gross differentials, controlled wage differentials have been narrowing gradually, indicating increasing adherence to the norm of equal pay for equal work.

The problem, however, is getting equal work. The explanation of widening gross differentials coupled with narrowing controlled differentials takes us back to the shifting pattern of female employment. When women enter the labor market, particularly in the service sector, they are usually on a par with male counterparts. As they rise slowly in the company hierarchy, varying types of wage supplements like family and housing allowances that are generally available only to men create a significant gap, but the gap remains relatively narrow as long as the women remain employed. Once they stop working for marriage or childbirth, however, they lose both seniority and their status as "regular" or "permanent" employees. When they return to the labor force, they do so without seniority and as "temporary" or "part-time" workers, with lower wages and less employment security than regular employees and few, if any, fringe benefits. Despite the labels, part-time and temporary employees often work full time and remain with the same employer indefinitely. Therefore, the increasing number of married women returning to work and the increasing proportion of them working part time mean that, unless current efforts under the Equal Employment Opportunity Act are successful, women are threatened with becoming, like the Burakumin, a distinct subgroup within the labor force with low status, wages, and benefits, despite increasing levels of education and experience.[6]

It does not require sophisticated economic analysis to speculate on the role these women are playing in Japan's economy.[7] As the service sector continues to expand more rapidly than the rest of the Japanese economy, particularly the banking, insurance, and retailing sectors where women have traditionally been heavily represented, the demand for skilled and semiskilled female clerical workers will remain substantial despite the effects of office automation. If Japanese companies can fill these positions with married women, costs can be minimized and efficiency enhanced. Because these women, despite doing the same work as their male colleagues, have a different employment status—temporary or part-time versus regular or permanent—and fewer years of service, they can be paid less without directly violating the principle of equal pay. Equally important, the managerial and supervisory positions, naturally reserved for full-time permanent employees, remain largely, if not totally, male. When we remember that female "part-time" workers in Japan often work the same hours as regular employees but receive only 45 percent of average male salaries, the picture becomes even clearer.[8] By structuring its wage and promotion system to stress continuity as well as duration of tenure, the typical Japanese company can cut its costs tremendously while plausibly maintaining that it treats its similarly situated male and female employees equally.

Statistics understate the degree of discrimination against Japanese women today, especially against those interested in pursuing managerial or professional careers and willing to make the necessary sacrifices to meet the requirements for permanent employment. It is in the area of recruitment and promotion of women for managerial positions that employment discrimination has been stark and uncompromising. Almost two decades of litigation against forced early retirement of women have made it potentially possible for female clerical or assembly-line workers, if willing to adjust their roles as wives and mothers, to remain on the job as permanent employees and gain the continuity and seniority necessary for relatively equal pay and advancement. As we shall see, in practice Japanese women rarely attain such equality, but it is theoretically possible. What has been largely impossible for women even in theory is to be hired for management track positions. Thus, promotion to supervisory positions—for example, high-level clerical positions—has long been possible, but becoming a member of the managerial elite has not.

As of the mid-eighties, 70 and 80 percent of Japanese companies refused to hire female graduates of four-year universities. As a consequence, female university graduates faced slim career prospects and constituted the only category of Japanese for whom employment openings were not increasing. Employers readily admit this practice to the government and the press. In a 1981 Ministry of Labor (MOL) survey, for example, 45 percent of companies polled responded that they did not promote women as high as supervisory [*kakarichō*] positions, and only 39 percent of those responding actually had employed a woman as a supervisor or above.[9] A full 71 percent of respondents indicated that they treated women differently.

Employers' reasons for excluding university women vary:

"[An equal number of male and female executives] would deprive men of jobs and cause social unrest. By nature, women are better suited for raising children and domestic responsibilities." —Ohtsuki Bunpei, President of the Japan Federation of Employers Associations.[10]

"If more women are added to the present male work force, the competition for jobs will only benefit the capitalists. Are career minded women really prepared to work as hard as men?" —Oikawa Kazuo, Vice-Chairperson of Sōhyō, Japan's largest labor union federation.[11]

"[Female university graduates] tend to stop work after a few years. And quite frankly, we find them rather headstrong." —Furuuchi Masaru, Personnel Director of Kinokuniya Shoten, one of Japan's largest bookstores.[12]

These comments encompass the three major justifications for limiting women to their current supplemental economic role: an ideological belief in a certain view of the ideal Japanese family; a belief that equal opportunities for working women will lead to male unemployment; and a fear that career women will not fit in smoothly with the corporate family.

The last justification requires amplification. The exclusion of women from careers is relevant to the corporate family ideal in two ways: first, their entry into elite management would dilute the single-minded loyalty to the job exhibited by most male workers. Dilution would occur because of the resulting decline in the homogeneity of views, backgrounds, and life goals now substantially attained in large corporate employment. This ideal of homogeneity may also explain the failure of Japanese companies to hire Burakumin and Koreans who are Japanese residents. Not only would the solidarity caricatured by early-morning calisthenics and late-night drinking be threatened, but the typical long hours of overtime could not realistically be expected of women because of both their usual family responsibilities and legal limitations on female overtime and other protective provisions in the Labor Standards Act.[13] The second, less obvious reason that continued discrimination is crucial to the corporate family is the role currently played by wives in the Japanese family. Without the wife at home taking the immediate responsibility not only for child raising but for all other aspects of family life (except provision of income), the devotion of the male-management employee to his job would have to change.[14]

Behind these public justifications lies an even more fundamental, if often denied, reason for the preference for the current situation: it has created a large pool of docile, well-educated, low-wage workers whose terms of employment can be easily manipulated in response to economic pressures and who can be substituted for more expensive and inflexible regular employees. This pool is part of the dual structure of the Japanese economy briefly mentioned in regard to the employment of Burakumin.[15] The duality operates on two dimensions: within the individual firm there is a division between the regular or permanent employees and part-time or temporary employees; and among vertically interdependent firms there is a division between the elite large corporations, the Mitsubishis and Toyotas, and the many levels of progressively smaller subcontractors that supply them. The regular employees of the former enjoy high wages and employment security. In varying degrees, employees of the latter enjoy less of either. This dual structure plays a large role in the ability of large Japanese corporations to manufacture products and provide services cheaply and to guarantee to its regular employees lifetime employment. As such, it receives a lot of credit for Japan's economic success. Not surprisingly, women and Burakumin (and all other "undesirables" such as Koreans or the handicapped) almost invariably find themselves in the lower half of one or both aspects of the dual structure.

The Litigation Campaign

Employment discrimination litigation can be divided into two periods.[16] The first began in the mid-1960s and concerned overt and explicit discrimination in wage, retirement, and reduction-in-force policies. In large part, the gradual disappearance of such practices by the late 1970s and the passage of the Equal Employment Opportunity Act (EEOA) in 1985 are the result of the plaintiffs' success in convincing the judiciary to declare illegal a wide range of explicitly discriminatory practices. If it is now theoretically possible for female employees to stay on and receive even remotely equal treatment, they have these cases to thank. The second period began in the mid-1970s and continues today. It challenges a broad range of employer practices, generally variants of discriminatory promotion, job rotation, and tracking that attempt to accomplish indirectly the goals of early retirement and unequal compensation attained directly by earlier practices. There are indications that the plaintiffs of the second period, like their predecessors, will be largely successful in specific cases, but employers have countered with further measures that have been successful in continuing the general exclusion of women from equal participation in the Japanese economy. Whether that exclusion will continue depends not only on the way in which the Ministry of Labor interprets and enforces the EEOA but also on doctrinal developments in second-generation litigation attacking the problem of discrimination on a more fundamental, structural level.

The statutory basis of sex-discrimination litigation is quite thin. The Constitution of Japan, Article 14, flatly prohibits sex discrimination, but the courts have read into its language both a reasonableness standard and a state action requirement. Other constitutional provisions, particularly the freedom of marriage and family law reforms of Article 24, reinforce the equality principle of Article 14,[17] but until the application of the EEOA in 1986, the only statute explicitly covering private sex discrimination was the Labor Standards Act (LSA), the basic law governing labor management relations. Article 4 of the LSA prohibits wage discrimination but does not directly deal with discrimination in other terms of employment. Indeed, Article 3 of the LSA, which prohibits discrimination on grounds of citizenship, religion, and social origin, does not mention sex, and other provisions of the LSA grant special protection and rights to female workers.[18]

This left the prospective plaintiff with the provisions of the Civil Code,[19] which governs legal relations among private parties not dealt with by specific statutes such as the LSA. Article 1–2 provides that the Code is to be interpreted "from the standpoint of the dignity of individuals and the essential equality of the sexes." This language was part of the postwar Occupation reforms and was consciously directed at the pervasive legal disability suffered by Japanese women up to that time. Article 1–2 is supplemented by Article 90, which provides that any "juristic act whose object is such as to be contrary to public order or good morals is null and void." Both these articles, however, are abstract provisions not generally understood to create substantive rights or even to apply directly to ordinary cases. Despite the frequent use of such general clauses, these provisions are hardly an obvious basis for a broad-based campaign against the overt employment discrimination universally practiced by Japanese companies up to the mid-1960s. Nonetheless, it is on this ambivalent basis that the whole series of cases has been built.

The major focus of this development is illustrated by the line of cases coming out of the *Sumitomo Cement* case decided by the Tokyo District Court on December 20, 1966.[20] The facts of *Sumitomo Cement* are straightforward. Plaintiff Suzuki Setsuko went to work for Sumitomo Cement in July 1960, two years after Sumitomo had adopted its then current employment regulations. Those regulations introduced five principles applicable to the defendant's women employees: (1) only high school graduates would be hired, and women with less or more education would not be considered; (2) all new women employees would enter at the lowest rank of regular employee; (3) they would be limited to support jobs "not requiring a high degree of judgment and suitable to workers with relatively little experience or skill," such as typists or switchboard operators; (4) they would retain that rank and job until retirement and would not be allowed to transfer jobs or locations; and (5) all women would be required to sign an agreement to retire upon marriage or the attainment of 30 years of age.[21] Three years later, Suzuki married and refused to resign. On March 17, 1964, she was fired.

The reasons cited by the defendant for its introduction of a marriage retirement system are set forth in the court's summary of the defendant's argument:

> Contrary to the general practice in Japan of different wages for men and women, particularly at higher age levels, the defendant has adopted the policy of equal compensation. Except for merit differentials, starting salaries and step raises are identical for males and females, regardless of age levels. This policy was adopted despite the fact that most female employees are limited to support jobs where their contribution to the defendant company is much less than that of male employees with much greater responsibilities. This discrepancy would justify paying female employees less, but the defendant, realizing that unmarried women are free from domestic worries and are therefore more productive than married women, has decided to maintain equal salary scales, partially as recognition of their female employees' work and partially as a gift in preparation for their marriage.

> However, even the support work done by female employees requires attentiveness, perseverance, and precision, but the efficiency of female workers declines after marriage. Because of the lack of daycare and other facilities necessary to the continuation of employment after marriage, women give their domestic responsibilities priority, absenteeism increases, and they lose the qualities necessary for their job. Because of the aforementioned salary structure, however, long-term female employees

had to be paid higher salaries than men with more responsible jobs (particularly university graduates). There were increasing demands from defendant's male employees to rectify this anomaly.

To deal with these demands and to realize substantive equality between the sexes, the defendant could have either introduced separate wage schedules and paid women less initially as do other firms or it could have adopted a marriage retirement system so that female employees would enjoy high wages for only a short period. For the sake of the efficient operation of the company, the defendant chose the latter.

This choice, because it grants them higher wages than women at other companies, is advantageous to the defendant's female employees as well.[22]

Sumitomo Cement's dilemma was a real one, and it was repeated in virtually every case of the first period.[23] As long as the company retained the principle of compensation by seniority rather than merit or job classification, wages of unproductive regular employees in menial positions would rise almost as fast as everyone else's. Since women entered the company as regular employees just like men, they were paid the same and enjoyed basically the same step increases each year. Because they were relegated to jobs where their productivity could not rise, however, they were soon making more than they were worth. The almost universal response by Japanese companies was a form of early retirement system similar to that of Sumitomo Cement. To them, sex discrimination seemed entirely natural and consistent with Japan's laws and customs.

The Tokyo District Court took a different view of both law and custom. Reviewing the plaintiff's claims, the court first noted the economic hardship imposed on women forced to retire upon marriage and concluded that such hardship was a substantial restriction of their freedom to marry. Since the constitutional guarantee of freedom of marriage (Article 24) is immediately applicable only to state action, the court then turned to Article 90 of the Civil Code and the definition of "public order and good morals" in the context of private employment discrimination. Sumitomo argued that similar practices were virtually universal in Japanese employment, that they were expected and accepted as natural and fair by workers, unions, and employers, and that they were consistent with Japanese values and traditions. The court rejected this invitation to ratify social practice and instead referred to the ideals embodied in the positive law: "The essential equality of the sexes must be realized. The prohibition of unreasonable discrimination not just in relationships between the state and private individuals, but also in relationships wholly within the private sector, is a fundamental principle of the law. This is directly and clearly indicated for relationships between the people and the state in Article 14 of the Constitution and for relationships between private persons in Article 1–2 of the Civil Code."[24] The court then noted that although the Labor Standards Act prohibits sex discrimination only in wages and requires protective measures for women in other areas, "the fundamental principle of equality requires that unreasonable discrimination be prohibited . . . [and] that any collective bargaining agreement, employment regulation, or employment contract that is unreasonably discriminatory is null and void as violative of Article 90."[25]

The court then applied this reasonableness standard to Sumitomo's argument that women were inherently inefficient and discrimination thus fair and reasonable. The court concluded that any alleged inefficiency of women was caused by the company's own personnel practices rather than any intrinsic qualities of women and that the defendant could deal individually with any post-marriage productivity declines if, in fact, any existed. On the specific question of a productivity drop upon marriage, the court set a strict standard of proof: "It must be shown that the productivity of women generally declines on marriage, that the level of that decline is greater than for males under similar circumstances, and, at the very least, that the decline is caused solely by the fact of marriage by a female employee and not by the employer or society in general."[26] The court could find no such proof and concluded that, in contrast to the shrine maidens of Shinto ritual of whom religious doctrines require virginity, there was no reason for requiring Sumitomo's female employees to be single. The fact that the seniority-based wage scale meant the company lost progressively more money on female employees as they grew older was to the court simply a problem of the company's own making and could not be resolved by discriminatorily burdening its female workers.[27]

The use of Article 90 to apply the standards of the Constitution and Code Article 1–2 to private behavior remains the fundamental doctrinal approach to private employment discrimination cases. Mandatory retirement of women upon pregnancy or childbirth,[28] retirement at a young age (often 30),[29] and retirement at a mature age lower than men (usually 50 versus 55)[30] have all been struck down, as has the singling out of married women for layoff during time of economic stress.[31] In more than twenty major cases[32] over the last two decades, Japanese courts have struck down such discrimination as unreasonable and in violation of Article 90. Although the practices attacked were virtually universal when the litigation campaign began in the 1960s, by 1980 they had almost disappeared. Those companies that still maintain explicit separate retirement systems are under pressure from the Ministry of Labor to eliminate them, and there is no question that if one of their employees should choose to sue, she would win. But litigation would most likely be unnecessary, since the Ministry of Labor, most unions, and public opinion have all shifted from supporting such practices as a natural part of Japanese society to condemning them as violating the norm of equality. To attribute this shift entirely to the *Sumitomo Cement* line of cases would be too simplistic, but the pressure generated by these cases, both legal pressure in terms of the threat of lawsuits and the payment of compensation and moral pressure as the judiciary repeatedly condemned sex discrimination, was certainly part of the process of attitude transformation.

Although there is little doubt that there now exists a strong judicial consensus that the traditional forms of discrimination are illegal, not every case was won. A brief review of one of the cases won by the employer will illustrate the inherent limitations of the *Sumitomo Cement* doctrine and show the difficulties plaintiffs are facing in the second generation of cases. In this case, *Watanabe v. Furukawa Mining Co.*,[33] the defendant is the same Furukawa Mining Company that we encountered earlier in the Ashio pollution incident. Here, one of its factories manufacturing coal-mining equipment was accused of singling out married women for discharge during a recession. Furukawa Mining admitted the basic facts, but unlike Sumitomo Cement, denied any discriminatory motives. The defendant, in an attempt to deal with genuine economic difficulties, determined that fifteen jobs within the factory were dispensable. Five were staff positions, all held by men; ten were non-staff, all held by women, eight of whom were married. Those eight were the only married women employed at the plant. Of the fifteen dispensable employees, only the ten women were "requested" to resign. The plaintiff refused and was fired.

The company's defense and the District Court opinion (eventually summarily affirmed by the Supreme Court) supporting it illustrate the logical morass created when the egalitarian ideals of the *Sumitomo Cement* doctrine encounter contradictory preconceptions about women's role in the family and workplace. The company first explained that the selection of the ten women (out of a total of thirty at the plant) was primarily caused by the concentration of women in non-production-line positions. Most of the jobs slated for elimination were occupied by women, and the types of products produced at that factory were such that there were no suitable production jobs to which these women could have been transferred. The company noted, for example, that there was only one female grinder employed in the production department at that time. As for why married women were selected, the company admitted that something more than chance was at work. Although remarking that "it happened" that most of the women in positions to be eliminated were married, the defendant also noted that in the past almost all female workers had resigned on marriage or shortly thereafter and that married women do not need the money as much as men or single women because they can rely on their husbands' income. There was no indication, however, that the defendant had investigated the actual economic situation of any of those discharged. Finally, the company argued that, once it had requested resignations from ten women and had received nine voluntarily, it would have "excited the emotions" of the nine and its remaining employees and "cast doubt on the sincerity of the defendant's attitude" if the tenth had not been fired.

The court took these arguments at face value. It noted that, indeed, the plaintiff's husband was employed and made almost twice her salary, and that therefore she would be disadvantaged less than single workers or those who were the sole support of their households. The court apparently felt no need for empirical verification of this assumption, merely noting that its truth was "obvious." It was equally sympathetic to the company's potential morale problem should it allow the plaintiff to stay on:

> According to the testimony [of six witnesses], the other seven married women, although dissatisfied, considered the company's point of view and resigned voluntarily when they learned from the executive committee of the union that the company was looking for resignations on good terms (i.e., with severance pay) with married women as the focus. If this fact is considered together with the fact that the plaintiff's discharge was approved at a general meeting of the union, it is easy to surmise that, had the plaintiff been allowed to remain, the general feeling of the seven who had accepted company policy as final and necessary and voluntarily resigned would have been affected in such a way as to lead to an unfortunate situation in future labor management relations. That is because

these various people would have come to mistrust the sincerity of the company for discharging the other seven without substantial reasons.[34]

It is as if the court were implicitly scolding the plaintiff for not doing her share for the good of the company, an offense considered particularly regrettable when the union has agreed that sacrifices are necessary. The court's implicit impatience with an individual egoistic enough to defy her union as well as her company is strongly reminiscent of the District Court's attitude toward the JCP teachers' recalcitrance during the Yata denunciation and may have little to do with the plaintiff's sex. But when this proclivity for individual sacrifice is coupled with this court's automatic assumption that married women are better situated to make sacrifices than men, the result is a view of the employment world that gives scant consideration to the reality of individual employees' circumstances, as the easy acceptance of the characterization of the other women's resignations as "voluntary" illustrates, and holds little hope for equality in discharge procedures.

Fortunately for women in Japan, the *Furukawa* opinion is atypical. Most courts have followed the lead of the *Sumitomo Cement* court and looked at defenses like Furukawa's skeptically. Even the *Furukawa* court felt constrained to distinguish its case from those that involve "any deliberate systematic firing of women" on the basis of age, marriage, and so forth rather than economic distress. Still, the case remains noteworthy because, although it may be unusual in terms of the first generation of employment cases and in its enthusiastic embrace of the company's rationale, it demonstrates the extreme importance of the court's perception of the facts—and its wide discretion in characterizing them—in the application of the *Sumitomo Cement* doctrine. The *Furukawa* court refused to acknowledge the existence of "systematic, deliberate firing of women" unless it was in the precise form already discredited by other courts. Since the reaction of many Japanese employers to the *Sumitomo Cement* line of cases has been to change the form of discrimination and disguise its continuation in a much more sophisticated manner than did the Furukawa Mining Company, the *Furukawa* case is a reminder of the broad discretion given courts under the "public order" language of Article 90 and the potential for a sharp change in direction should judges, for whatever reason, modify their sympathetic approach shown to women plaintiffs so far.

Ironically, while a substantial line of cases was being built on the tenuous basis of Article 90, there was only one case in this initial period, the 1975 Akita District Court decision in *Nawataya v. Akita Cooperative Bank*,[35] that was based on the explicit, unambiguous equal-wage provision of Article 4 of the Labor Standards Act. One reason is that, until the early retirement systems were eliminated, the issue of equal wages was a secondary one. *Akita Bank*, for example, was not filed until 1971. A related reason is that wage inequality in Japan is initially relatively narrow, only broadening to 30 percent after several years. Since women usually left regular employment after a few years, either voluntarily or otherwise, wage discrepancy remained a minor problem for most. This does not mean, however, that unequal pay was rare or even uncommon. The *Sumitomo Cement* court specifically rejected Sumitomo's assertion that it paid women equally,[36] and, though in many instances the discrepancy may have consisted only of various forms of male-only allowances, in other instances employers maintained two totally separate wage schedules, with substantial disparities in compensation.

The *Akita Bank* case combined both forms of wage inequality. Compensation consisted of two elements: the "personal wage," which was computed solely on age and length of service, and the "functional wage," which was based on job and ability. Until 1970, in calculating an employee's personal wage, the bank used two schedules, A for men and B for women. The differential between schedules was ostensibly calculated to equal the living costs of a standard dependent family and was given to all men whether married or not on the assumption that even presently unmarried men would someday have to support a family. In 1970 this pattern changed in response to administrative guidance from the Labor Standards Bureau of the Ministry of Labor, and the bank began to use schedule A only for men who actually had dependent families. To prevent any male employees from suffering an actual decline in compensation from 1969 to 1970, however, the bank gave all male employees without families an additional adjustment payment that brought their compensation up to the schedule A level.

The court had little difficulty with these facts and dismissed out of hand the defendant's clumsy attempt to disguise its two-track system; the plaintiffs were awarded back pay for both pre-1970 and post-1970 periods on an identical basis. Concurrently, the Labor Standards Bureau was successful in eliminating administratively many other employers' "special adjustments," such as living-expense allowances and family allowances, that were designed to give men additional compensation without the embarrassment of explicitly different wage schedules.[37]

Thus, by the mid-1970s the success of the plaintiffs in the first generation of cases had made it clear that explicit discrimination in the traditional forms was very risky. Not only were companies losing lawsuits and back pay to female employees, but the Ministry of Labor had also begun to use administrative measures to gain compliance with the *Sumitomo Cement* doctrine and Article 4 of the LSA. The declaration of 1975 as International Women's Year added international pressure. This legal and political pressure combined with economic developments to cause employers to devise a rearrangement in the legal nature of their employment practices that would enable them to retain the economic and psychological benefits of discrimination without incurring social or legal criticism.[38] One common measure has been shifting from compensation systems primarily based on seniority to those based on performance or function, and simultaneously limiting women to low-paying jobs. Companies have also changed their hiring patterns, refusing to hire highly educated women or hiring women only as part-time or temporary employees. Where such clear-cut arrangements are impossible, employers simply promote women at a slower rate than men or use other discretionary measures to discourage long tenure. The net result is that, despite the successes of women plaintiffs from 1965 to 1975, the wage discrepancy between males and females not controlled by length of tenure or job status has been increasing since the mid-1970s and was greater in 1982 than it had been in 1972.[39]

Although discriminatory hiring and tracking are hardly new, their systematization has presented potential plaintiffs with new doctrinal and practical difficulties. Such practices were in the background in the *Sumitomo Cement* line of cases, and in most instances the courts rejected the companies' arguments that sex-based job assignments necessitated early retirement. But there is a significant difference between telling the defendants that they cannot shift onto their female employees the entire economic cost of combining discriminatory job assignment with a seniority-based wage system and telling them that the job assignment itself is illegal. Attacking discriminatory hiring, not only the refusal to hire university graduates but also the attempt to hire only women who indicate in interviews a willingness to retire upon marriage, presents even tougher doctrinal questions, as does discrimination in individual discretionary decisions such as promotions.

These difficulties are well illustrated by litigation now in progress against the Iron and Steel Federation.[40] The Federation is an industry group representing the interests of Japan's steel industry to the bureaucracy, the political parties, and other industry groups. In the late seventies, the Federation realized that it had to stop using different wage scales for male and female employees. Its response was not to equalize wages, but to transfer to menial positions all women who had somehow gotten into responsible ones. They also stopped hiring female graduates of four-year universities altogether.

Seven women sued, and their suit is representative of the legal and practical problems of fighting such discrimination. The plaintiff has had to characterize the defendant's policies as wage and retirement discrimination because discriminatory tracking and transfer of job assignments do not fall into any of the previously developed doctrines. Moreover, the development of new doctrines faces what the plaintiffs' lawyers see as the substantial problem of the doctrine known as the right of free enterprise and private autonomy recognized by the Japanese Supreme Court.[41] It is the attorneys' belief that it would be politically and psychologically easier, at least initially, for a lower court to broaden the scope of the *Sumitomo Cement* doctrine rather than explicitly forging new ground.

As we shall see later in this section in the *Suzuka City* case, this approach holds some hope in challenging discriminatory promotion, training, and job assignment policies, at least in the private sector. In dealing with discriminatory hiring, however, it it useless. Once a woman is hired, it is possible to equate most discriminatory treatment with wage or retirement discrimination because such practices restrict women to low-paying jobs where they are encouraged to retire young, both explicitly by their male superiors and implicitly by the dead-end nature of their work. This logical connection with wages and retirement is more difficult in the case of a refusal to hire, and for this reason long-term success will require the development of doctrine that will attack sex discrimination at a much more fundamental and intrusive level than has the *Sumitomo Cement* doctrine.

The hiring question also presents problems having to do with plaintiffs, both legal and practical. Plaintiffs' attorneys doubt whether a court would grant standing to a rejected job applicant because of questions of proving causation and damage, even with the explicit discriminatory policies admittedly used by many companies. Second, many lawyers doubt whether plaintiffs could be found. Becoming such a plaintiff not only would depart radically from Japanese conceptions of femininity but also would effectively ruin the plaintiff's chances for other corporate employment.

In addition to these specific problems, there are the general problems inherent in Japanese litigation that so frustrated the Communist Party in its attempts to fight the Buraku Liberation League. The *Iron and Steel Federation* court convenes only once every three months, and a decision is not anticipated for several years. Meanwhile, the Federation has reportedly hired only women recommended by its male employees and assumed to be sympathetic to its position, so that peer support for the plaintiffs, already nonexistent among male colleagues because of the union's opposition, is steadily declining. Given the ethos of the Japanese workplace, the psychological effect of such isolation can be extremely difficult to withstand—suing one's own company while still a member is a radical, threatening act to fellow employees as well as to management—and is a severe limit on the number of available, willing plaintiffs. Even when a plaintiff is available, there remains the question of remedies. As in most other areas of Japanese law, Japanese jurists assume that tort damages and back pay are all a plaintiff can reasonably ask for in such circumstances. Judicial orders for equal hiring or promotion in the future are highly unlikely, and damages, at least in the short term, are likely to remain small enough for most employers to ignore.

Despite these formidable obstacles, there have already been legal challenges of discriminatory practices, and there is reason to believe that more will follow. The first case unequivocally attacking sex discrimination in promotions was *Yamamoto v. Suzuka City*, decided initially by the Tsu District Court on February 21, 1980.[42] Plaintiff Yamamoto Kazuko had been hired as an office worker by the city in 1948 and regularly promoted thereafter. At the time of suit in 1972 she had reached the 21st grade (of 25 possible) of class 5 (of seven, class 1 being highest). She alleged sex and marriage discrimination in promotions and training, in the practice of giving women employees the additional duties of serving tea and light custodial service, and in the granting of family allowances. She demanded back pay of ¥383,730 for the difference between her actual salary and what she would have received had she been promoted at the same rate as her similarly situated male colleagues, ¥1,000,000 in damages (*isharyō*) for mental suffering caused by the defendant's discrimination, and lawyers' fees of ¥400,000, for a total of ¥1,783,730 (approximately $9,000).

The underlying factual premise of the case was the plaintiff's assertion that, at least up to class 4, promotions were granted as a matter of course once the employee had a specified number of satisfactory years in grade. Promotions, in other words, were not determined on individual merit and were not discretionary decisions but automatic ones, with only individuals with disciplinary records or long leaves of absence excluded. The city denied that there existed, at least legally, such a clear-cut seniority system and cited language in its employment regulations to the contrary. It further argued that because these promotions were in fact discretionary, the court had no power to review them. The plaintiff supported her allegations with statistics demonstrating that the city promoted men from class 5 to class 4 much earlier and more frequently than women. Hence fewer than 2 percent of the class 4 employees were women, as opposed to over 40 percent of class 5 employees. To reach class 4 women had to proceed through most of the 25 grades within class 5, whereas virtually all men were promoted as soon as they reached grade 16. As a result, Kawamoto remained in class 5 while similarly situated men were in classes 4 or 3.

The plaintiff's proof convinced the Tsu District Court that systematic discrimination had taken place in promotion (with especial discrimination against married women) as well as in training, assignment of tea and cleaning chores, and family allowances. It concluded that such discrimination violated Article 13 of the Local Public Employees Law (LPEL) and awarded ¥26,150 in back pay (the court disagreed with the plaintiff about the date on which she should have been promoted), ¥1,000,000 for mental suffering, and ¥400,000 in legal fees for a total of ¥1,426,150 (approximately $7,100). Although the reasoning of the opinion was terse, the court clearly relied on the plaintiff's statistical evidence to conclude that the defendant had promoted employees automatically rather than selectively and that it promoted males more frequently and higher than females. From that point, it was just a question of when precisely the plaintiff would have been promoted had she been male.

The Nagoya High Court on appeal approached the case fundamentally differently.[43] Whereas the District Court placed primary emphasis on the statistical pattern of promotions, the High Court emphasized the defendant's discretion in making personnel decisions. While acknowledging the substantial discrepancy in promotion rates, the Court rejected the plaintiff's argument that the city had in effect waived that discretion by promoting male employees automatically upon their reaching grade 16 of class 5. The court admitted that such promotions had been granted "rather generously," but concluded that promotion had not been so regular as to be deemed automatic.[44] Once the High Court decided to treat the promotions as discretionary, it focused exclusively on the defendant's reasons for not promoting the plaintiff. The defendant, despite having previously commended the plaintiff for "over twenty years with an excellent work record," argued that she lacked a cooperative and enthusiastic personality and had difficulty with interpersonal relations. Reiterating the broad discretion granted to public entities in administrative personnel decisions, the High Court accepted this rationale and denied the plaintiff all relief implicitly concluding that the defendant had not acted with discriminatory intent despite the statistical pattern of male-female promotions.[45]

Although the High Court reversal and the plaintiff's pending appeal to the Supreme Court leave a great many areas of ambiguity in the *Suzuka City* case, the most fundamental question—whether discrimination in promotions can be legally attacked under the rubric of wage discrimination—appears to have been answered in the affirmative. Both *Suzuka City* opinions implicitly adopt the plaintiff's argument that the discrepancy in wages caused by discriminatory promotions gives the victim a cause of action for back pay sufficient to bring her compensation up to what she would have earned had she been promoted equally. Although the High Court's cavalier attitude toward the plaintiff's statistical evidence reminds one of the court's approach to the pattern of layoffs of married women in the *Furukawa Mining* case and of the evidentiary problems presented once defendants deny discriminatory intent, the doctrinal portions of the opinion represent a significant advance which other judges—and the plaintiffs' success in the *Sumitomo Cement* line of cases indicates that many judges will be more sympathetic to women in their evidentiary judgments than were those of the Nagoya High Court—will be able to use not only in subsequent promotion cases but also in actions attacking other forms of implicit discrimination. If so, such decisions will put pressure on the Ministry of Labor in its interpretation and enforcement of the ambiguous mandate of the EEOA, so that *Suzuka City* may eventually be seen as another step in the evolution of employment discrimination doctrine begun by *Sumitomo Cement.*[46]

But the successful equation of various discriminatory practices with wage discrimination has the inherent disadvantage of limiting plaintiffs' remedy to back pay. Like Yamamoto in *Suzuka City*, the plaintiffs in the *Iron and Steel Federation* case have requested only back pay and damages rather than reinstatement in their former positions. Just as public-employee plaintiffs want to avoid administrative law doctrines restricting injunctions against public entities, private-sector plaintiffs want to avoid the constitutional doctrine of free enterprise and economic autonomy that inhibits mandatory injunctions against private defendants. To accomplish this, the same artificial distinctions are made so that promotion litigation can fit into the well-worn tracks of the *Sumitomo Cement* doctrine. How long this approach can continue and what will happen if the courts eventually confront promotion and hiring policies directly are unclear, but the result need not be certain defeat for plaintiffs. The courts will have to balance the principles of equality and free enterprise, and it is not unlikely that equality will prevail.

For the present, litigation will most likely continue to attack varied forms of discrimination under the guise of equal pay. This raises the question of whether the damage remedy will be adequate; for as long as courts are not even asked to mandate equality in areas such as promotions and training, they will certainly limit themselves to monetary awards. Given the relatively small amount of such awards, there is the possibility that defendant companies will choose to pay the occasional plaintiff rather than grant equal treatment. Whether this occurs will depend on many factors, perhaps the most important of which is the position taken by the Ministry of Labor in its enforcement of the Equal Employment Opportunity Act, but there is initial evidence that compliance will ensue. In the *Suzuku City* case, for example, plaintiff Yamamoto was promoted to class 4 the year after she filed suit. In a case brought against the Shizuoka Bank for discrimination in promotion, training, and job assignment but requesting only back pay and damages, the defendant agreed to a judicially recommended settlement by which it not only granted back pay to more than 100 women, the vast majority non-plaintiffs, but also agreed to promote nine women to management track positions.[47]

Such cases remain rare as potential plaintiffs and their attorneys continue to be cautious in attacking the practices that characterize employment discrimination in the 1980s. But they do indicate that the prospects for women to surmount the numerous legal and practical obstacles associated with contemporary employment patterns are not as dismal as many of those involved in the litigation suppose. Given the doctrinal innovation we have seen in the Big Four pollution cases and in the *Kawamoto, Yata,* and *Sumitomo Cement* cases, it is not improbable that eventually even discrimination in hiring will be vulnerable to judicial attack. As we saw with the first generation of employment cases, however, legal victories alone do not necessarily have a positive effect on all women workers. The real test of these cases is not just whether they can be won, but whether the legal victories can be turned to political advantage and force the government to interpret and enforce the EEOA aggressively.

Impact of the Cases

It would be extremely difficult to argue that Japanese attitudes toward women's roles in society have liberalized greatly in the last two decades. On the contrary, many Japanese women feel that popular attitudes have become more "traditional" since the 1950s, when there was a surge of democratic feeling, especially among women themselves, and the late 1960s, when the antiwar and student movements created a climate of individualism and social freedom. Since then, the feminist movement, at least as defined by the handful of women who are self-proclaimed "libbers," has deteriorated into a politically irrelevant source of amusement and object of ridicule. One reason has been its own choice of tactics—one well-known group chose to attack the sexual double standard by donning pink helmets and raiding the offices of unfaithful husbands—a mistake exacerbated by the media's predictable preference for covering such events rather than less flamboyant efforts to bring about incremental change. Another reason, many women argue, has been a strengthening of pressures on women to conform to the current stereotypes of the model Japanese woman.

Such pressures come from employers, whose vision of the ideal Japanese family tends to coincide with their needs for intense devotion to the job by male employees and for large numbers of part-time female employees; and from the Liberal Democratic Party and the Prime Minister's Office in the form of paeans to the unique tradition of the Japanese family—a "tradition" that, like permanent employment or low litigation rates, dates from World War II—found in the Diet's proclamation of Family Day as a national holiday or the LDP's promotion of "Social Welfare on the Family Basis."[48] The latter, and particularly the related LDP plan announced in June 1979 called "Outline of Measures Related to the Fulfillment of the Family Basis," are seen by women's groups as attempts to reinforce the current hermetic division of roles within the family.[49] The LDP vision of the "social welfare society" of the future is premised on a vision of "three-generation households," where the care of aging parents and that of the sick and the handicapped, as well as child rearing, are all family rather than governmental responsibilities. Since survey results indicate that most Japanese husbands do "absolutely nothing" in regard to such household chores as child care, meals, or cleaning, it is not difficult to infer that the burdens of the "three-generation household" will fall on the wife.[50] This vision of the future does not mean fewer working wives, however. Although the government's New Economic and Social Seven Year Plan for Full Employment does explicitly call for preferential employment of heads of households, it also calls for increased opportunities for women to "develop their abilities in keeping with women's life cycle."[51] One can surmise that the latter means working until marriage or childbirth, reentry into the labor market at about age 35, and then return to the home at 45-50 to care for elderly parents and in-laws.

This vision of family, society, and work is largely shared by Japanese women themselves. In a 1981 poll of housewives, 69 percent reported they believe that women's happiness is found in marriage, and 68 percent agreed that women's role was to "preserve the family while the husband works outside." Child rearing and housework were seen as the main source of satisfaction, but 65 percent nonetheless expected to work after their children were out of the house, with only 25 percent expressing no desire to work at all. Of the 65 percent, three-quarters said they would work for economic reasons and 18 percent for personal development or satisfaction.[52] There is even a reluctance on the part of women to share housework should their husbands be willing to do so: in a 1975 Japan Broadcasting Corporation (NHK) opinion poll on working women's attitudes in ten countries, the percentage of women in favor of having husbands help with the housework (including work in the kitchen, cleaning, and laundry) was lowest in Japan at 51 percent.[53] By contrast, in the next lowest country, Thailand, the percentage was 69 percent, and in Sweden not a single respondent opposed the idea.

Against this background, one would not expect the cases discussed here to have had any dramatic effect on the way Japanese view working women, and though it is impossible to judge with certainty, it seems likely that they have not. However, their failure to bring about a revolution in social consciousness—as the Big Four cases did regarding urban pollution—does not mean that these cases have had no significant social and political impact. Although there are no public opinion polls directly addressing the question, it is likely that the first generation of cases contributed to a general consensus that similarly situated men and women doing the same work should be treated equally and that unequal pay, marriage retirement systems, and the like are unfair. Such an attitude is entirely consistent both with the attitudes toward family and job just discussed and with the current employment pattern of women, and, while it may inconvenience corporate personnel departments occasionally, it hardly strikes at the roots of employment discrimination. Nonetheless, given the state of women employees in the mid-1960s and the fact that most women and most female attorneys involved in these cases are more interested in incremental reforms for the majority than in expanding management track opportunities for a selected few, it is a considerable achievement.

There has even been some recent movement in the area of equal hiring and recruitment.[54] In July 1982, Takashimaya Department Stores announced that they would begin hiring male and female management trainees on a one-to-one ratio.[55] Takashimaya has long been a pioneer in hiring women, but in the early 1980s several other retail companies, financial institutions, and government agencies announced the hiring or promotion of female managers. And in 1983, the Faculty of Law of Tokyo University hired its first female faculty member. Such cases are still unusual enough to merit media coverage, but they do occur. Whether they are epiphenomenal or will accelerate with the implementation of the EEOA will depend on many factors, the most important perhaps being the dynamics of the Japanese labor market, but including as well the future course of women's litigation and the response of the government.

The Ministry of Labor has been active in two aspects of employment discrimination. The first has been the enforcement by the regional Labor Standards Bureaus of judicially developed antidiscrimination doctrine; the second has been the legislative activity of the Women and Minors Bureau in Tokyo, principally the drafting and eventual enactment in May 1985 of the Equal Employment Opportunity Act. These two activities are not only mutually dependent but also closely intertwined with the doctrinal evolution of the first and second generations of employment litigation and the prospects for continued plaintiffs' success in the courts.

Prior to the late seventies any bureaucratic attention to sex discrimination was focused on the equal wage provision of Article 4 of the Labor Standards Act, with little or no attention to separate retirement systems for men and women. Because the *Sumitomo Cement* line of cases developed outside the Act, the enforcement personnel of the Labor Standards Bureau denied any responsibility for enforcing its doctrines despite the argument from female bureaucrats within the Women and Minors Bureau that separate retirement ages violated not only the Civil Code but also general provisions of the Act. It was not until the late 1970s, when a survey disclosed that the great majority of Japanese companies had clearly illegal retirement policies, that the Ministry made the elimination of separate retirement systems a major priority and not until 1980 that it issued administrative guidance urging their replacement. Even then the Women and Minors Bureau chose to approach employers directly rather than going through the standard enforcement procedures of the Labor Standards Bureau. That activity has continued, with the result that as of 1983 90 percent of Japanese firms previously maintaining them had discontinued mandatory retirement systems upon marriage or pregnancy, and 70 percent had eliminated all forms of separate retirement systems.[56] Given the virtually universal presence of such systems twenty years previously, these figures represent a major accomplishment for which the Ministry and specifically the Women and Minors Bureau deserve credit.

The Ministry of Labor's enforcement activity, however, is limited to practices whose illegality is beyond peradventure, hence its late start on discriminatory retirement. The Ministry is generally ineffective in attacking legally ambiguous practices and has largely ignored the introduction of functionally based compensation schemes which, coupled with discriminatory job assignment and promotion policies, have contributed to the actual decline in women's relative wages since the *Akita Bank* decision. Similarly, in regard to the increasing employment of women as part-time employees and the refusal to hire university graduates, the Ministry's activity had until recently been limited to what it calls "enlightenment guidance," a diluted form of administrative guidance that consists, in the latter instance, of representatives from the Women and Minors Bureau addressing business groups on the desirability of hiring university women.

Although even the officials involved refer to enlightenment guidance as "very weak,"[57] the assertion of equal opportunity as a positive value by ministry representatives is significant in the current normative context of Japan. But its total lack of legally binding effect and the ambiguity of the EEOA's treatment of university women underline the tremendous importance of the plaintiffs' continued success in the second generation of employment discrimination litigation. Only if the District Court's approach in *Suzuka City* is elaborated, extended, and firmly established can one expect the Ministry to move effectively against the wide range of contemporary forms of discrimination. Even then, as long as the approach continues to rely on characterizing all discrimination as wage discrimination, current hiring practices will remain unaffected. Whether legal doctrine can be developed to attack discrimination at the recruitment and hiring stage is, however, intertwined with the history of the enactment of the Equal Employment Opportunity Act and with the Ministry's exercise of its mandate thereunder.

In the mid-1970s, inspired by the International Women's Year of 1975 and the United Nations declaration of 1976–1985 as the U.N. Decade for Women, the Japanese government committed itself to eliminating discrimination against women by 1985. Consistent with that pledge, the Headquarters for the Planning and Promotion of Policies Relating to Women was established in the Prime Minister's Office, and in 1977 the National Plan of Action and the priorities for the first half of the decade were announced. Then at the 1980 session of the U.N. General Assembly, Japan signed the Convention on the Elimination of All Forms of Discrimination against Women, formally committing the government to providing equal employment opportunity for women by 1985.

To fulfill these commitments, deliberation on antidiscrimination legislation began in 1979 with the appointment of an ad hoc advisory committee, known as the Experts Group on Equality between the Sexes,[58] made up of representatives from labor and management and neutral members chosen from among women's groups, lawyers, and university professors. Its task was to research and discuss the meaning of equality in the employment context and to develop standards for evaluating whether particular practices were legitimate. Out of this process was to come a consensus on the correct approach to future legislation. The committee's report, "Views on the Criteria for Determining Sexual Equality in Employment,"[59] was presented to the Minister of Labor in May of 1982, but instead of achieving a consensus on the form of future legislation, the group split on whether to retain certain existing statutory protections for female workers, including limitations on overtime, the prohibition of night work, menstrual leave, and restrictions on employment in various dangerous or undesirable occupations. The split was along labor-management lines, with the former contending that the latter were using the sex discrimination issue to cut back on necessary protections while the latter argued that many provisions were archaic and that equal opportunity was impossible without revision. This split reflects a similar division within the women's movement, with union women, including many of the leading lawyers involved in employment discrimination litigation, strongly opposed to any weakening of existing protection.

The task of achieving a consensus on proposed legislation then fell to the Subcommission on Women's Employment of the Advisory Commission on Women's and Minors' Problems, the standing Ministry of Labor *shingikai* (advisory group or deliberative council) for women's issues. As had the Experts Group, the Subcommission, which also consisted of labor, management, and neutral representatives, split along labor-management lines with both sides rejecting a compromise draft proposed by the neutral members. Finally in February 1984, with the 1985 deadline for enactment in sight, the neutral members of the Subcommission persuaded labor and management to acquiesce in the presentation to the Minister of Labor of a report that noted their three respective positions and made no attempt to disguise their fundamental differences. The Ministry declared the report a reasonable compromise, drafted a bill based on the neutral position, and presented it to the Diet in May, where it eventually passed one year later.

Within the various *shingikai*, where most members were reconciled to legislation of some form, debate focused on three aspects of the proposed statute. The first centered on the practices to be prohibited. Labor and most public representatives wanted to declare illegal all forms of discrimination, as apparently required by the U.N. Convention. Management representatives were willing to include a prohibition against unreasonable discrimination in retirement and layoffs, but insisted on excluding from coverage practices concerning recruitment, hiring, placement, and promotion. The second major issue was the nature of the obligation to be imposed on employers—basically whether to include sanctions for prohibited practices or to rely on the good faith of employers. Labor wanted explicit penalties for all violations and the creation of a new agency within the Ministry with the power to issue legally binding directives (*meirei*) to offending firms; management wanted to limit enforcement to voluntary conciliation by a tripartite conciliation system to be established within the Ministry. The third area of contention, and the issue on which labor and management diverged the most, was the necessity of repealing existing protective provisions of the Labor Standards Act. Management insisted that without repeal of all but maternity benefits, true equality of treatment was impossible. Labor argued that, given the refusal or inability of Japanese men to contribute to household or child-rearing tasks, repeal would force working women to resign permanent positions and be reclassified as part-time or temporary employees, resulting in a further decline in the relative position of female workers. Instead of forcing women into the "workaholic" world of male Japanese workers, the labor representatives argued, the new legislation should have the long-term aim of reducing hours and improving conditions for all employees.

Outside of the *shingikai* the debate was more wide ranging, and opponents of the bill raised fundamental objections to any form of legal equality. On the most mundane level, employers' representatives argued that equality in employment would mean the end of those pillars of postwar growth and social stability, permanent employment and seniority-based compensation.[60] Equality in training and job assignment, for example, would present employers with the choice of providing women the same intensive training now given men or abbreviating training for all employees. The former would be economically wasteful because most women retire before the company can recover its investment; the latter is unattractive because it implies a shift to skill-based wage systems and the eventual treatment of workers as mere providers of labor rather than members of the company family. Skill-based compensation would eventually, the argument goes, engender job mobility and the replacement of the loyal enterprise union, another institution of Japan's economic miracle, by industry-wide unions on the American model.

Other opponents pursued the cultural implications of this economic scenario and concluded that nothing less than the cultural survival of Japan was at stake. In articles with titles like "Equality of the Sexes Threatens Cultural Ecology" or " 'The Equal Employment Opportunity Act' Will Destroy Japan," male and female academics and political commentators argued that the existing differentiation in sex roles was not only necessary economically but also central to Japan's uniquely successful culture.[61] In contrast to Western societies where sex roles may be based on an inferior position for women, these commentators claim that sex differentiation in Japan is not a question of inferior and superior but of mutual cooperation and the recognition of the need for both roles. Japanese women, therefore, already have true quality, an equality that would be destroyed by the passage of the EEOA:

> Abandonment of role differentiation by sex would lead to the free choice of roles by the individual. The decisive factor in this choice would not be based on considerations of mutual dependence, or the need among both men and women for people performing complementary roles. Rather, people would rank roles according to their perceived worth, thus turning the choice into a question of superiority and inferiority. Those people obtaining the best work would be satisfied and look down on others; those people forced to do lesser work would be dissatisfied and envious. An environment of cooperation and friendship would turn into one of competition and hostility.[62]

According to this view, it is easily demonstrated that such conditions would be disadvantageous for both sexes by reference to the extreme individualism and family disintegration—the division of mankind into "mere units," in one commentator's words—in those Western countries like Sweden and the United States where legal equality, as contrasted to true equality, of the sexes is perceived to exist.[63]

A third objection to the EEOA focused on its origins rather than its content. Despite the dozens of cases brought and won by women since the *Sumitomo Cement* case, few critics or proponents of the EEOA saw it as a response to domestic legal or social developments. Instead, most general commentaries on the issue attributed the government's determination to enact an antidiscrimination statute solely to international pressure created by the U.N. declaration of 1976–1985 as the Decade of Women and Japan's subsequent pledge to ratify the Convention on the Elimination of All Forms of Discrimination against Women by 1985.[64] Part of the opposition to the bill, therefore, was a combination of the perception that the EEOA was yet another law imposed on Japan by the West and the growing conviction among Japanese that it is the West that should be learning from Japan, not the reverse.

But the fundamental objection of many critics who stressed the EEOA's international origin was not its foreignness; the real problem was that the EEOA was not perceived as the product of a social consensus. Instead of validating or declaring preexisting social norms and behavior, these critics argued, the EEOA tries to create or mandate them. The split among the *shingikai*, the dependence of Japanese employers on clearly differentiated sex roles, and survey data indicating that most Japanese women were happy with the existing division of labor convinced many opponents that the EEOA was woefully out of place in Japanese society. They argued that the passage of an equal employment opportunity law should await proper social conditions, and that the norms of any eventual statute should not be too greatly separated from the actuality of employment practices.

This sentiment was particularly strong on the issue of whether to provide sanctions for violations of the statute. As one *shingikai* member put it, "The purpose [of the law] is not to make criminals."[65] And an industry representative was quoted as saying, "It is only during times of foreign occupation or revolution that customs accepted as normal suddenly become criminal acts."[66] Underlying these dramatic statements was the conviction that legal rights and obligations should not be inconsistent with customary social behavior. If the society's ideals—and some opponents agreed that equality, even the legal equality of the EEOA, was ultimately desirable—conflicted with its practice, the answer was public education and enlightenment until all, or as close to all as possible, citizens agreed. Until that point, legal compulsion—"the making of criminals"—was inappropriate.[67]

The law that emerged from the Ministry of Labor in April 1984, and that was enacted in May 1985, was a major victory for management, at least if one focuses on its impact on the mutual legal rights and duties of women workers and their employers. Although subsequently moderated by ministerial ordinance (*shōrei*), the management victory was virtually complete in terms of the relaxation of statutory protections for women workers in the Labor Standards Act, perhaps the most divisive issue in the labor-management confrontation. Restrictions on overtime and holiday work were abolished for women in managerial positions and for women whose duties require "specialized knowledge or skills" (a phrase translated by the Japanese government as "professional").[68] Although precise standards were left to subsequent Ministry ordinances, the maximum number of hours of overtime for women in nonmanufacturing industries permitted under the LSA was doubled from 6 per week and 150 per year to 12 and 300 respectively; restrictions on night work were eliminated for relevant industries, such as food processing and taxi driving; and minor privileges such as guaranteed menstrual leave or special travel allowances were repealed. In return, the law lengthened maternity leaves from six to eight weeks, a measure unopposed by management.

Management also did well on the questions of coverage and sanctions. Discrimination in retirement and layoff policy (Article 11) and in fringe benefits such as housing, loans, or health benefits (Article 10) is flatly prohibited, and discrimination in training and education given for the "purpose of providing workers with the fundamental skills necessary to perform their duties" (Article 9) is to be prohibited in accordance with guidelines promulgated by the Ministry. In the areas of recruitment and hiring (Article 7) and placement and promotion (Article 8), on the other hand, the EEOA asks only that employers "strive" (*tsutomenakereba naranai*) to treat female workers equally. Furthermore, there are no sanctions for violations whatsoever, even in those areas where discrimination is prohibited.

The only provisions dealing even indirectly with violations are in Articles 13–21, which establish a system of bureaucratically controlled informal dispute resolution. Article 13 asks an employer who receives a discrimination complaint to "strive" to deal with it autonomously (*jishuteki*) by referring it to a labor-management body to be specially created within the firm to dispose of discrimination complaints. When requested by either or both sides, the director of a prefectural Women and Minors Office (*fujin shōnen shitsu chō*) may under Article 14 render necessary advice (*jogen*), guidance (*shidō*), or recommendations (*kankoku*) to parties to a sex discrimination dispute, and, when both sides agree, Article 15 gives the director the power to conduct mediation (*chōtei*) within the statutorily created (Article 16) Equal Opportunity Mediation Commission. This commission shall consist of three individuals appointed by the Minister of Labor from among "persons of learning and experience" (Article 17) and shall, when deemed necessary, hear the opinions of those designated as the parties' representatives by the principal labor or management organization within the jurisdiction of the regional bureau (Article 18). The Commission may also draft proposed settlements (Article 19) and recommend (*kankoku*) their acceptance by the parties.

If one focuses narrowly on its doctrinal content and impact on future litigation, the EEOA is certainly congenial to management interests and has been referred to by employers, off the record, as strengthening rather than weakening their prerogatives vis-à-vis female employees. Except for prohibiting discrimination in training, the EEOA grants women no legal rights that they had not already gained through litigation. Indeed, to the extent that the courts will view the intervention of the Ministry of Labor and the creation of the EOMC as a legislative signal to go more slowly or even to retrench or withdraw from the employment discrimination area, the passage of the EEOA may have weakened the legal position of future plaintiffs. The flat prohibition of discrimination in retirement and dismissals did little more than confirm doctrine developed in the first generation of employment litigation. It may encourage a court to look more skeptically at a defendant's justifications in cases like *Suzuka City*[69] and *Furukawa Mining*, where statistics establish a prima facie case of discrimination, but the pointed omission of any sanctions from the statute did little to strengthen the previous judicial determination that discrimination violated the Japanese conception of "public order and good morals" encoded in Article 90 of the Civil Code.

In second-generation litigation, on the other hand, the EEOA may be actively harmful to plaintiffs. Until the passage of the EEOA, the courts in giving meaning to Civil Code Article 90 were guided primarily by the egalitarian ideals of Article 14 of the Constitution. Those ideals are, however directly applicable only to public entities, and their role in the *Sumitomo Cement* line of cases was, strictly speaking, limited to what they could be interpreted to say about society's attitudes toward sex discrimination. As long as society remained silent, the propriety of discrimination in recruitment, hiring, placement, and promotion could be approached, putting doctrinal problems aside momentarily, from the same perspective as discrimination in retirement. That is to say, judges would have pushed the ideals of Article 14 at the pace they considered reasonable and appropriate, and female employees and their lawyers would have had a substantial input into judges' perceptions not only of legal rules but also of social values. Now, however, society has spoken, albeit ambiguously: it has stated that discrimination in these second-generation areas, whatever else it may be, is not a violation of any legal duty. For Japanese courts to continue to push forward and declare such discrimination illegal, even under the guise of wage discrimination as tentatively begun in *Suzuka City*, has been made much more difficult, though perhaps not impossible.

Analyzing the EEOA solely from the perspective of its impact on the legal rights and duties of the employer-employee relationship, however, would not only seriously understate the social and political impact of the EEOA but also misinterpret its fundamental legal nature. Although it may slow down the pace of women's litigation, the act need not mean a deterioration in the status of working women. As we have seen, the considerable doctrinal success of plaintiffs during the two decades before the passage of the EEOA did not translate into an equivalent improvement in the position of women workers. Even in the area of retirement, it was only after the Ministry of Labor began to enforce it administratively that the full impact of the *Sumitomo Cement* doctrine was felt by the vast majority of female employees, and in doctrinally ambiguous areas such as promotion, women's status actually deteriorated. Although the courts largely set the social agenda, the key to substantial improvement in women's status in the 1970s and early 1980s was the intervention of the bureaucracy, and the real meaning of the EEOA in the 1980s and 1990s will depend less on the rights and duties created or eliminated by the statute than on the attitude of the officials of the Ministry of Labor.

Rather than a victory for management, the EEOA really represents an attempt by the Ministry to regain the initiative in the area of women's rights in employment. While it is true that the EEOA eliminated many preexisting legal rights of working women without granting any new ones, it does not immediately follow that employers have gained rights in each area in which employees have lost them. In fact, employers gained few absolute rights under the statute. Even the provisions relaxing the protections for female employees under the Labor Standards Act, such as the doubling of overtime in the new Article 64–2, typically grant the bureaucracy broad discretion in their implementation. The EEOA's approach to discrimination is similar. The prohibitions of discrimination in Articles 10 (fringe benefits) and 11 (retirement age, resignation, and layoff) are unqualified, as presumably was necessary given the *Sumitomo Cement* doctrine, but the Article 9 prohibition against discrimination in training is subject to further official definition. And the exhortations in Articles 7 and 8 to "strive" for equality in hiring, promotion, and so on are totally dependent on Ministry definition and initiative to have any real effect on employment practices.

The temptation of Westerners, particularly those trained in law, may be to regard purely hortatory provisions like those in Articles 7 and 8 with a good deal of skepticism. Regardless of the eventual response of the Ministry of Labor, the legal effect of "equal opportunity" in this context will be identical to that of similar phrases in the Special Measures Law for Assimilation Projects that we examined in the Buraku liberation context—that is to say, none whatsoever if one defines legal effect narrowly to include only directly and judicially enforceable rights and duties. As we saw with the SML, however, a lack of binding legal force does not mean legal irrelevance, much less political or social irrelevance, and in this instance there is further reason to take the rhetoric of the EEOA seriously. Unlike the Special Measures Law, Article 12 of the EEOA legally empowers (which in the context of employment discrimination is the equivalent of requiring) the Ministry of Labor to draft guidelines (*shishin*) setting forth measures that "should be taken by employers" (*kōzuru yō ni tsutomeru beki*) to secure equal treatment and opportunity for women workers in hiring, promotion, recruitment, and placement. Ministry bureaucrats will take the rhetoric of Articles 7 and 8 seriously, and the administrative guidance that they issue under Article 12 will influence employment practices in the future despite their legally nonbinding nature. What those guidelines will look like will depend on a variety of legal, social, and political factors, one of which, however, will certainly be the course of sex discrimination litigation.

The Social and Political Role of Civil Rights Litigation

In one sense, the plaintiffs and lawyers involved in the women employees' litigation perceive it as similar to the Big Four, that is, the cases are seen as part of a larger movement and the legal struggle as subordinate and auxiliary to the political one. The plaintiffs are acting not to secure individual rights to back pay or promotion, but as the vanguard of all women in an attempt to fashion major social reform. The litigation is not seen as protecting an oppressed segment of society by forcing the powerful to respect their legal rights but rather as helping to create a new moral and political consensus in Japan. This perspective is at least partially due to the character of the lawyers and others involved. Unlike some American activist lawyers, the Japanese lawyers lack a devotion to the "rule of law" as a description of an ideal legal system. The latter are much more political in the sense that they view these cases as contributing to social change rather than as correcting flaws in the legal order.

In reality, however, the cases have developed in a fundamentally different direction from that of the Big Four. Although the intended role of the suits may have been as an adjunct to advance the movement, their actual relationship to the movement has been substantially reversed. In comparison to the Big Four, the women's lawyers appear to be more concerned with the evolution of legal doctrine and to have a greater awareness of each case as building on the one before it. The social and political activities such as rallies and petitions are clearly adjuncts of the litigation rather than the reverse. The goals of the cases are also different, both in the short term in specific cases and in the long-term goal of the litigation in general. The former is simply a legal victory. The moral and emotional intensity characteristic of the Big Four and subsequent product-liability cases is here greatly muted; conventional legal reasoning has largely replaced morally based appeals for radically new doctrine in lawyers' arguments; and the measure of victory is more in the incremental doctrinal advance than in the condemnation of the defendant for morally repugnant acts. There is no expectation or demand that defendant companies' officials should personally apologize. Similarly, the long-term aim of these lawyers has always been legislation that will make further litigation more effective. The apocalyptic views of the Big Four plaintiffs or the participants in Buraku Liberation League denunciations are absent, replaced by a reformist rights consciousness that is much closer to American litigation than to Tokugawa *ikki*.

There are many reasons for the decline in the relative importance of political action in the movement against sex discrimination. The social and economic background of the plaintiffs is one. The Big Four victims were generally poorly educated and relatively unsophisticated, whereas the female plaintiffs in the women's employment cases are generally more urban, better educated, and more sophisticated about the legal system. The latter are also differently situated socially. Unlike the pollution victims, they are part of the company they are suing, and, except in the relatively rare cases where union support is available, this has meant little peer support, even from fellow victims of discrimination. In contrast to the intensely cohesive groups, factions, and counterfactions of pollution victims that eventually formed in places such as Minamata and Yokkaichi, working women are in an ambiguous position because of the fundamentally different way in which the two issues are perceived both by society in general and by the participants themselves.

It is clear that in the late sixties and early seventies the Japanese perceived pollution as a threat to their society. The equities were clear at all levels of discourse, and the polluters and the government were seen as wrongdoers not only by reformers and modernists but by conservatives and nativists as well. The Japanese are much more ambivalent about discrimination, particularly sex discrimination. Social conservatives see distinct sex roles as traditionally Japanese, and many unionists and businessmen view equality in employment as a threat to Japan's economic well-being. The women's movement itself is deeply divided on the issue of continued special protection for female workers, and although this division has not yet directly affected the conduct of many cases, it greatly influenced the shape of equal opportunity legislation and has inhibited the mobilization of a vigorous women's movement. Failing the creation of an energetic movement, the plaintiffs' and lawyers' attention naturally focuses on the cases and, given the lack of moral intensity, on the legal issues. Without a strong consensus even on the basic issues, the safest course is to focus on the specific cases of clear discrimination where there is general agreement. Similar splits exist in every social movement—the myriad factions of Minamata patients bear eloquent testimony to their presence among pollution activists—but in the women's instance these splits seem to have coincided with a failure to mobilize the political allies who could transform this series of legal cases into a political movement with the independent power to withstand the intervention and manipulation of the government represented by the passage of the EEOA.

In light of this failure, how do the women's cases relate to the litigation and direct negotiations of the Big Four, on the one hand, and the denunciation sessions of the BLL, on the other? It is important not to overlook the social complexity and mixture of motives present in the pollution phenomena, but if we understand that in general pollution victims considered litigation as a desperate appeal to the government to restore the status quo ante under which all citizens could trust the government to protect them, we can recognize fundamental departures in both the women's use of litigation and the Burakumin's use of denunciation. First, neither group is desperate in the sense of the literal destruction of life and community that faced pollution victims. Second, although the ultimate goals of both movements encompass fundamental social change, neither individual instances of denunciation nor those of employment litigation are in practice immediately concerned with the fundamental relationships or structure of society. Instead, they are concerned with incremental gains and the realization of specific interests through a particular tactic—denunciation for the BLL, litigation for the women. Despite the apocalyptic rhetoric of BLL theorists, these attitudes come very close to a reformist rights consciousness that is quite different from the consciousness generally motivating the pollution victims. The two post-pollution phenomena begin to look very similar in impetus, though not in choice of tactics, and very different from the pollution case.

But before we conclude that BLL denunciation and women's litigation play a fundamentally different role in social conflict from that of the superficially similar tactics of the pollution victims, let us look at their long-term social influence and particularly at the government's reaction. In the pollution case we saw that the eventual government response to the social upheaval symbolized by the Big Four and direct negotiations was an attempt to reassert its control over the mechanisms of social change. But it did so not by continuing its blind opposition to the antipollution movement but by accepting it, albeit belatedly, and admitting publicly that the protesters' demands were just and then acting on those demands quickly and effectively. This approach was not only politically imperative, given the broad and deep support of the movement, but clearly good policy in economic terms as well. Thus the government acted not just to placate forces beyond its control, but also because the Liberal Democratic Party, the bureaucracy, and their business allies were convinced that antipollution measures were in their own interests, even narrowly defined.

The crisis facing the political and economic elite went beyond the technical question of how to deal with pollution, however. The political disruption accompanying the pollution litigation of 1967–1974 showed Japanese leaders that social changes were occurring that threatened the stability of their control over the social and political agenda in Japan. The discrediting of both nationalistic government and military expansionism by World War II had combined with postwar economic conditions to create a strong national consensus in favor of economic growth. By 1970, it was clear that this consensus was disintegrating. Feelings about the corporations and the economic ministries, the postwar heroes of Japan, were changing dramatically, and the tragic side effects of industrial success were combining with increasing affluence to lead to a more diverse society that threatened to destroy forever the postwar consensus. And even though the antipollution movement was itself much more akin to historical forms of protest than the role of litigation made it appear, the very disruption it caused and its use of the courts to defy business and government threatened to open the courts generally to this type of socially charged litigation. If this had happened, the loss of social control would have been significant.

The aspect of the government's response of greatest significance here was its effort to reconstruct the pre-pollution consensus or, failing a genuine consensus, at least to prevent the continued use of the judiciary as an alternative to the more easily controlled extrajudicial modes of dispute resolution. This meant reestablishing the dependence on government that is implicit in the concept of verticality and the neo-Confucian world view. There are two ways to foster dependence: to eliminate all other means of redress and sources of support, or to grant as a matter of grace what the supplicants might get through independent means. The Japanese government used both. It vigorously fought the potentially decisive doctrinal development represented by the success of the second-generation environmental cases in the lower courts, and its success in convincing the Supreme Court to reverse the plaintiffs' High Court victory in *Osaka Airport* effectively closed the door to many emerging forms of environmental litigation. Simultaneously, the establishment of a publicly financed mediation/conciliation apparatus, although voluntary, greatly increased the disincentives for litigation. The system for administrative compensation of pollution victims also played an important role. First, it transformed a conflict that had potentially threatened the social fabric into a narrow struggle for government benefits and the victims from independent actors into government dependents. Second, along with the dismissal of the Kawamoto indictment and the criminal conviction of the Chisso executives, it served as an admission of the government's moral complicity in the tragedy and a reaffirmation of the central values of the covenant relationship—trust and benevolence.

With the pollution experience as background, we can now turn to the response of the government to the activities of the Burakumin and women employees. For even if I am correct in evaluating the latter phenomena as characterized by rights consciousness, this may mean little if the government or corporations can isolate these groups socially or direct their energies into acceptable channels. I shall begin with a reevaluation of the relative merits of denunciation and litigation.

One way to prevent individual conflict from becoming social conflict is to prevent the issues from moving from the particular to the general. Despite the considerable shortcomings of litigation, if the BLL had relied on a series of test cases based on Article 90 and the Constitution, it is highly likely that they would have been at least as successful as the women in achieving individual legal victories and probably considerably more successful in mobilizing general sympathy for their cause. They would have universalized their antidiscrimination struggle in a way that clearly identified the major villains not as individual JCP teachers or prejudiced bureaucrats, but as the social and economic system itself and its major supporters, large firms and the central government. Job discrimination could have been targeted and exposed, not behind the doors of a ghetto assembly hall with the BLL themselves as moral arbiters, but in the open forum of a courtroom where the considerable moral authority of the Japanese judiciary could have put discrimination in its proper place in the constellation of moral values embodied in the Japanese Constitution. A well-written, morally powerful opinion exposing the efforts of Japanese corporations to avoid hiring Burakumin would have presented the issue to the Japanese public in a vastly different way than the BLL's tactics have done.

This does not mean that denunciation is futile; dramatic gains have been made in the Burakumin's immediate economic and environmental condition. In terms of integration into the economic or social mainstream, however, relatively little has been accomplished, and many argue that denunciation leads toward further isolation rather than social integration. In this sense the Japanese government and large corporations have crafted the ideal situation: the moral issue of discrimination can be dealt with by pointing to the substantial affirmative action programs while the underlying social and economic structure is left unaffected. The BLL is kept, if not happy, at least preoccupied with socially marginal activities and programs. As long as it can continue to use denunciation successfully—and the government has done little to discourage its use or deny its legitimacy—the BLL will be able to achieve its local, particular goals. But the very strengths of denunciation in building organizational and group solidarity become weaknesses when the BLL confronts its broader aim of full integration into Japanese society. To reach this goal, Buraku solidarity will be relatively less crucial and political allies more important. To combat the widespread conviction that Japan is a strict meritocracy requires much more than isolated denunciations of purchasers of Buraku lists; it requires both the clear acknowledgment of discrimination by the courts and the forceful articulation of the widely held norm of equality. Only through the simultaneous exposure of existing practices by a seemingly objective arbiter and the convincing demonstration of the violation of norms valued by majority Japanese as basic to their society can the BLL forge the enduring political alliances needed to overcome the current impasse, in which a series of incremental victories lead to little ultimate change.

Clearly the direct-confrontation tactics that worked for pollution victims in mobilizing political support will not work equally well for Burakumin. One main reason is the social context. Whereas fear and awareness of pollution were shared by all Japanese in the 1960s, many Japanese in the 1980s deny that Buraku discrimination even exists. A second reason is the nature of denunciation as a tactic and the reasons for its appeal to the Japanese. To the extent that expressive violent protest has long and honorable roots in Japanese history, denunciation has legitimacy as part of Japan's social tradition. This is one reason that it has fared relatively well before Japanese courts. But in the pollution instance the tactic was traditional not only in form but also in the way it was used. The pollution victims eventually succeeded in portraying themselves as demanding not the realization of selfish interests but the preservation of the traditional structure of Japanese society; and the government reacted accordingly, steering the movement toward a comfortable dependence on government while discouraging alternative avenues of redress and change. The BLL, however, is asking for something quite different. Equality of treatment and opportunity is a radically modern value, but the government's response to denunciation so far has been remarkably consistent with its earlier reaction to the pollution movement: it has ignored the liberal, universalistic aims of the BLL while responding to its traditional tactics and immediate demands. Certainly the government is best served by taking this tack—its public works projects and grants to individual Burakumin once again render them dependent at little cost to the government or its corporate allies.

For several reasons, this strategy will be more difficult with the women's litigation campaign. Unlike the BLL, the women have directly and clearly challenged the social and economic foundation of contemporary Japan. They have already established an enviable record in the courts, and there is nothing traditional in goals or methods on which the government can focus its response. Therefore, despite its ambiguous record so far in achieving general change, the women's litigation campaign is potentially very threatening to the status quo. Whether that potential can be realized and real change can continue for women workers depends partially on the women's ability to continue to put legal pressure on the Ministry of Labor. It is true that the legal nature of the Equal Employment Opportunity Act gives cautious bureaucrats within the Ministry a basis for maintaining only a "soft" posture in its administrative guidance, and even if legal pressure continues, it is unlikely that the Ministry will vigorously pursue each new judicial doctrine favoring female employees. It is nonetheless also true that a consistently successful campaign to push the judiciary to declare discriminatory hiring and promotion practices illegal will strengthen women's allies within the Ministry of Labor and make it difficult both for the Ministry to issue only "enlightenment guidance" in these areas and for employers to resist whatever stronger guidance might be issued.

Whether or not continuing litigation is successful will in turn depend in part on the impact of the EEOA and its mediation scheme on judicial developments. There seems little doubt that the EEOA is part of a government attempt to follow the time-honored Japanese pattern of dealing with social conflict by simultaneously ameliorating its causes and incorporating the antagonists into government-controlled mediation machinery. This was the essence of Tokugawa mediation; it was the early twentieth century government's response to tenant–landlord disputes; and it was the reaction to the pollution problems of the sixties and seventies. Mediation in itself, of course, need not inhibit ongoing litigation. Title VII of the American Civil Rights Act of 1964 went even further than the EEOA in encouraging mediation of discrimination complaints:[70] it requires all grievants to file their complaint with the statutorily created Equal Employment Opportunity Commission and to wait until the EEOC has either taken action or issued a "right-to-sue" letter before the grievant can pursue independent legal options. Far from inhibiting private litigation, however, the passage of Title VII and the creation of the EEOC established a partnership between private litigants and EEOC officials that accelerated the pace and significance of private antidiscrimination litigation. The difference between Title VII and Japan's EEOA is not in their approach to mediation itself, but in their approach to independent private litigation. Not only did Title VII establish a private cause of action for employment discrimination, it also provided for injunctive relief and attorney's fees for the winning party. In contrast, the EEOA approaches the achievement of equality as primarily a bureaucratic responsibility and creates no new private rights or remedies, much less providing for attorney's fees for successful plaintiffs.

Given the history of the Ministry of Labor's enforcement activities, it is likely that the Ministry will approach sex discrimination as the

Ministry of Justice approached the continuing publication of Buraku lists and employment discrimination against Burakumin—as a "matter of the heart, not the law." If so, one suspects that just as the Special Measures Law was a political and moral victory for the BLL but left the Burakumin legally just as dependent as before, the major role of the EEOA, despite its egalitarian rhetoric and prohibition of some forms of discrimination, may be to engender such legal dependence among potential female plaintiffs and thereby to reassert bureaucratic control over the social agenda.

In this scenario, the regional Women and Minors Offices will mediate discrimination claims in a "fair and reasonable" manner, "fair and reasonable" being determined by bureaucratic criteria. As they are to current environmentalists, the courts will be open to dissatisfied women (as required by Article 89 of the Constitution), and it is possible that an American EEOC-style partnership between private litigants and the Japanese Equal Opportunity Mediation Commission will develop; but it is more likely that sex-discrimination litigation in Japan will meet the fate suffered by environmental litigation. Japanese courts, although admirably independent of direct government pressure, are sensitive to perceived social needs. If they perceive that women are getting "fair and reasonable" treatment—and judges' criteria are likely to resemble those of the bureaucracy—their enthusiasm for doctrinal innovation will doubtless weaken as it did in the environmental cases. We may even see the doctrinal equivalent of the *Osaka Airport* case in the next decade in the women's field. But if the government has been successful in regaining the initiative, no one will even notice. The force of the movement will have disappeared with the isolation of its leaders, the absence of popular support, and the capture of the core of the movement within the administrative machinery of mediation, conciliation, and compromise. This is not to say that women will not have succeeded in bringing about significant change; the reassertion of state control certainly need not mean regressive measures—in the environmental area, it meant the implementation of substantial structural reforms; in the Buraku situation, it meant a significant increase in living standards; and for women, it may mean a dramatic opening of employment opportunities at all levels. But the change will be on the government's terms and at the government's pace.

Should this capture of the women's movement actually take place, what will have been the effect of the employment cases? First, their central place in this instance of social change is further evidence for the political importance of litigation in modern Japan. In this sense they resemble the early pollution cases, but closer inspection reveals a fundamentally different political and social role. The primary effect of the Big Four cases was to shock the nation and its leaders into the realization of the extent of environmental deterioration and to provide a focus for the previously inchoate antipollution movement. The doctrinal content of these cases was less important than their political impact, and the plaintiffs' eventual victories were as much political as legal. In the women's movement, however, the plaintiffs have been less successful in galvanizing political support. The primary importance of these cases has been doctrinal, and their role has been to apply legal, not political, pressure to their opponents in government and industry. However, if my speculations about the eventual denouement of the women's litigation are correct, this transformation in the role of litigation in social change will have had little effect on the eventual result—the incorporation of the forces of social conflict and change into the machinery of the state bureaucracy.

FIVE

Legal Informality and Industrial Policy

THE PRECEDING three case studies have demonstrated that so-cial conflict in Japan is characterized by informality and verti-cality. Both attributes contribute to the government's ability to control the pace and direction of social change: informality limits the participants and significance of a specific dispute by stressing its par-ticular issues rather than the underlying universal principles involved; verticality engenders dependence on government resolution of conflict by involving it in most disputes at every level. We now turn to the question of whether these same attributes characterize Japanese law in an area where open conflict is rare: the formulation and implementa-tion of industrial policy by the Ministry of International Trade and Industry (MITI). The presence of these attributes would be partial confirmation of the view that informality and verticality are character-istics of Japanese law at all times, not just during times of crisis.

Industrial policy is appropriate in this context because it is an area where one would expect a great deal more conflict than now reaches the surface. This is particularly true in industrial policy that allocates shares of a static or shrinking pie, whether this involves setting prices or production quotas in a temporary recession cartel, export quotas in a voluntary restraint agreement, or quotas for the permanent elimination of capacity in a structurally declining indus-try. Other forms of industrial policy, such as promoting certain sectors, industries, or firms rather than others, have distributional impact that is theoretically as great, but the potential conflict is much less since the losers face only the loss of prospective growth rather than a decline in current levels of production, employment, or profits. For this reason, we will look most closely at industrial policy that demands sacrifice on the part of private parties in order to cope with economic difficulty.[1]

Before we do so, however, some introduction to the bureaucrats who staff the Ministry of International Trade and Industry is necessary.[2] This is particularly important for those accustomed to the American bureaucracy, for there are substantial differences in status, structure, and role between the American and Japanese bureaucracies. The most significant is that the Japanese government attracts and retains the very best university graduates. Unlike the American bureaucracy, which loses many of its best young officials to the private sector just as they become effective bureaucrats, elite Japanese bureaucrats stay with the same ministry until retirement in their early fifties. This personnel stability enables the ministry to train young bureaucrats both broadly in the full scope of ministry functions and deeply in a particular area of expertise. The result is a stable, experienced bureaucracy that is both extremely talented and thoroughly trained.

These attributes are part of a political and social context that is conducive to cooperative government–business relations. The economic bureaucrats and their business counterparts come from similar educational backgrounds, advance at approximately similar speeds, and rotate in and out of jobs having direct contact with each other's institutions. This contact is furthered by an informal, consultative policymaking process that encourages the formation of personal relationships across institutional boundaries.

What cements the relationship is a congruence of interests among public and private elites. When Japanese bureaucrats retire, most take positions in the private sector, many in the very firms they have been dealing with during their bureaucratic career—a process known as *amakudari*, or "descending from heaven." Whether they secure such a position on retirement is dependent not only on ability but also on whether the retiree has been sympathetic to industry concerns during his period of power in MITI. This potential leverage over individual bureaucrats is balanced somewhat by MITI's institutional leverage over individual firms and industries and by the history of the industry–ministry relationship. The point is not that individual officials are likely to compromise the public interest to ensure a favorable *amakudari* position; even if an occasional individual were to attempt such a deal, the diffusion of decision-making power inherent in the collective process of Japanese bureaucracies would make this extremely difficult. What is more likely is an identity of views between government and business that arises imperceptibly not only from the bureaucrats' self-interest, but also from the fact that the Ministry views some industries as partially its own creation. It is rare that MITI or at least the bureau of MITI directly concerned with a given industry takes a position antithetical to the industry's best interest. This attitude is mirrored in some industries by a history of dependence on MITI that dates from the fifties and sixties, when MITI used its power to foster growth in selected industries.[3]

The underlying precondition for this state of cooperative interdependence of government and business in Japan is the informal and bipolar nature of the process of industrial policy. Policy is set and then implemented with the constant participation of and consultation with the private sector. The major institutionalized form of participation is the *shingikai* or deliberative council, which we have already encountered in the setting of environmental, Buraku, and equal employment policy. As with the Ministry of Labor *shingikai* that considered legislative responses to employment discrimination, MITI often asks a *shingikai* to investigate a problem and suggest possible courses of action or draft needed legislation. MITI appoints council members from "knowledgeable and experienced persons," and MITI bureaucrats constitute the council's staff.[4] In addition to industry representatives, there are to an increasing extent representatives of labor, academe (usually economists), the media, and consumer groups, but dominance by industry and MITI remains the general rule. In the past and in many instances today the *shingikai* and the industry trade association are interchangeable, and the latter plays the role titularly given to the former. In the weeks between formal meetings of the council, Ministry bureaucrats and trade association members are in constant contact in order to ensure that, by the time the council formally convenes, the substantive questions will have been settled.

Informality does not end with the formulation of policy; it continues throughout its implementation. Even in areas where it has specific legal power, MITI rarely exercises it formally. Instead it prefers to use various informal, legally voluntary modes of persuasion, generically known as administrative guidance, to convince individual firms or groups of firms to comply with Ministry policy. Where MITI's informal persuasion is backed by specific statutory authority, compliance is to be expected. What is interesting about Japanese industrial policy is the degree to which MITI gains compliance in areas where it has broad, jurisdictional competence but no specific statutory authority. Part of the explanation lies in the interlocking interests of the government–business relationship, but the legal environment within which administrative guidance is used is also crucial to MITI's success.

The Legal Framework of Industrial Policy

The legal framework within which the *shingikai* process and administrative guidance operate consists of the statutory basis of MITI's authority and the administrative law doctrines that define its limits. The former delineates the areas in which MITI can exercise its discretion; the latter determine by whom, when, and in what forum that exercise can be challenged.

At the foundation of MITI's authority is the MITI Establishment Act, which defines MITI's jurisdiction, goals, and structure. On the next level are statutes like the Foreign Exchange and Foreign Trade Control Law (FECL) that give MITI responsibility for broad areas of economic policy. At a third level of specificity are statutes like the Petroleum Industry Law (PIL) that give MITI general authority to promote particular industries, and statutes like the Depressed Industries Law (DIL) that give MITI specific authority to deal with economic conditions affecting a number of industries.[5]

Overriding characteristics of all statutes are the wide scope of authority delegated to MITI and the vagueness of the standards by which MITI is to exercise that authority. Statutory provisions do not provide clear guidelines for the Ministry to use in carrying out the legislative intent of the Diet. As with the EEOA in the employment discrimination area, economic statutes are better viewed as identifying an area (such as the promotion of industry and international trade) or a problem (for example, the decline in competitiveness of Japanese industries after the oil shocks of the 1970s) and delegating legal authority to MITI to deal with it as it sees fit. When it comes to how, when, or toward what end that legal power should be used, most economic statutes are so broad as to be virtually meaningless.

The Foreign Exchange and Foreign Trade Control Law, as it was throughout the sixties and seventies, is a good example. It has been described as "the single most important instrument of industrial guidance and control that MITI [has] ever possessed," and an understanding of its structure is indispensable to understanding the continuity exhibited by the more specific statutes that followed.[6] Its first article reads: "Article 1 (*Purpose*).   The purpose of this Law is to provide for the control of foreign exchange, foreign trade and other foreign transactions, necessary for the proper development of foreign trade and for the safeguarding of the balance of international payments and the stability of the currency, as well as the most economic and beneficial use of foreign currency funds, for the sake of the rehabilitation and the expansion of the national economy." The criteria of Article 1 were the only guide for the bureaucracy's exercise of many of the specific powers granted by the statute. Article 52, for example, granted the Ministry the power to regulate imports: "For the purpose of sound development of foreign trade and the national economy, a person wishing to import goods may be required as stipulated by Cabinet Order [seirei] to obtain approval therefor." By simply putting goods on the Cabinet Order's proscribed list, MITI could control foreign transactions completely. In theory, official policy had to be consistent with the purposes of the statute as stated in Article 1—the "proper development of foreign trade," the "safeguarding of the balance of international payments," the "stability of the currency," the "most economic and beneficial use of foreign currency funds," and the "rehabilitation and the expansion of the national economy." But these goals are so broad and potentially internally inconsistent as to make them legally useless in limiting official discretion to implement Article 52 or any of the other statutory powers. The end result, which will become clearer when we look at how the Ministry has used the FECL in practice, was virtually no statutory restrictions on the government's regulation of foreign trade.

The FECL is typical of statutes dealing with industrial policy. Even the relatively specific statutes such as the Depressed Industries Law or the Petroleum Industry Law provide only broad and vague limits on administrative discretion. This is not by chance. Bureaucrats draft most statutes in Japan, and they do so with the goals of maximum discretion and broadest scope of authority foremost in their minds. Nor is it in any way remarkable or surprising in itself; equally broad delegations of power are common in U.S. economic legislation.[7] What distinguishes MITI's position from similarly situated American agencies is more the doctrinal matrix that restricts judicial review of administrative action in Japan, particularly the doctrines of justiciability, standing, and scope of discretion, than it is the lack of statutory standards.[8]

Plaintiffs seeking judicial review of administrative action face the initial problem of whether the challenged agency behavior constitutes an "administrative disposition [shobun] or other exercise of public power" as required by Article 3 of the Administrative Case Litigation Law (ACLL).[9] If so, the action is justiciable, and the inquiry shifts to whether the plaintiff is an appropriate person to challenge it. If not, the case is dismissed. The Japanese Supreme Court has limited Article 3 to administrative acts that immediately and directly create or delimit private rights and duties.[10]

Under this definition, most of industrial policy is beyond judicial review. MITI almost invariably acts informally in a legal sense, and only a final and legally formal act directly creates legal rights and duties. Thus in allocating quotas for the elimination of capacity in declining industries, MITI does not issue legally binding orders prohibiting production above a certain level. Instead, informal discussion among the members of the industry is encouraged until consensus is reached, with forceful arm twisting by the bureaucrats if necessary. Nothing in the process has immediate legal effect; it is only when the process breaks down that MITI relies on its statutory authority, and then often by way of a threat of collateral future action, such as the decline of required approvals for plant expansion or foreign exchange transactions. Such threats remain informal and thus are not administrative dispositions.

It is not just informal actions that escape judicial scrutiny. Supervisory orders, permissions, approvals, or regulations within an agency or even among agencies and public bodies like *shingikai*, no matter how formal or final, are not reviewable because they are considered internal government behavior that does not directly affect the legal rights or duties of private citizens. Furthermore, administrative acts with general effect, such as agency plans or regulations, are not judicially cognizable unless they immediately and concretely affect a specific person's legal rights or obligations. Thus, even a final *shingikai* report that recommends specific criteria for a production or price cartel would not be reviewable until its provisions were formally implemented, and then only if they legally restrained private action. Since MITI prefers to act informally even when possessing formal power, such occasions are rare, and even then the courts are liable to restrict standing to only the most directly affected parties.

Article 9 of the Administrative Case Litigation Law limits standing to persons having a "legal interest" in an administrative disposition. The requirement that the prospective plaintiff's injury be to a *legal* interest implies that injury to a nonlegal or "factual" interest will not give the injured party standing, and Japanese courts and scholars have historically limited standing to individual interests that an administrative agency has been specially charged by statute with protecting. Where an agency acts for the general public interest, therefore, personal interests injured by the government action are merely factual interests.

The leading case applying this standard is the 1962 Supreme Court case of *Sakamoto v. Japan*.[11] In *Sakamoto*, a bathhouse proprietor challenged a license granted to a competitor whose premises would have been closer to the plaintiff's than allowed by the Public Bathhouse Law. The lower court denied standing on the grounds that the statute was intended to protect the public health, not the economic interests of competitors. The Supreme Court took a broader view. Citing the possibility that excessive competition might eventually have undesirable public-health consequences, the court concluded that the statute was also intended to prevent "excessive competition" and that therefore the plaintiff had a legal as well as a factual interest in the integrity of the licensing system. This decision marked a widening of the standing doctrine, but it still relied on a direct and specific statutory connection between the administrative disposition and the plaintiff's harm. Neighborhood residents or consumers would not have had standing under *Sakamoto*, even though they were part of the public whose welfare the statute was enacted to protect, because their legal interests were general and indirect.

In the fifteen years that followed *Sakamoto*, the lower courts appeared to loosen standing requirements somewhat, particularly in the second-generation environmental suits that followed the Big Four. Those cases have not been overruled, and it may be that neighborhood residents alleging environmental harm would now be granted standing by the Supreme Court as well. But a 1978 Supreme Court case made it quite clear that any liberalization did not extend to the type of economic issues involved in industrial policy.[12] The case, *Federation of Housewives v. Fair Trade Commission*, was brought by a consumer group against the Fair Trade Commission's approval of labeling standards for the fruit juice industry. The plaintiffs argued that the Fair Labeling Law required greater disclosure of ingredients than had been required by the FTC. The court, however, never reached that question because it concluded that the consumers' injury was to "an abstract, general interest held equally by all citizens" incidentally created in the course of protecting the public interest. As such, it did not constitute the individual and direct interest required for administrative standing.

The *Sakamoto* doctrine applied to economic regulation as in the *Federation of Housewives* case severely limits judicial attack on industrial policy. *Sakamoto* may apply to grant competitors standing to contest, for example, the administrative allocation of production quotas, but it will not apply to consumers, labor unions, environmentalists, or even customer or supplier industries. The result is the elimination of most potential plaintiffs, since the constant consultation with industry representatives characteristic of industrial policy means that decisions are rarely finalized until everyone's acquiescence is obtained.

Even if a plaintiff were able to overcome the obstacles of justiciability and standing, he would then be faced with convincing the court that the agency's action was illegal—that is, not within that agency's scope of discretion. As the dismissal of the indictment in *Kawamoto* makes clear, Japanese courts are not afraid to move decisively when the government has acted unjustly. But the moral culpability of the government's conduct in *Kawamoto* was clear and is unlikely to be equaled in cases against MITI. Industrial policy litigation would instead involve variants of the less dramatic allegations that the administrative agency used incorrect criteria or procedures in making the challenged decision or reached a decision inconsistent with the statute on which it was based. Such allegations require the judiciary to evaluate agency action in terms of the scope of discretion granted the agency by the relevant statute. If the statute is detailed and unambiguous, this task can be simple, but such statutes are rare in the economic area. The court will more likely be faced with standards as vague as "the healthy development of the national economy" as in Article 52 of the FECL, or as internally contradictory as the various purposes listed in Article 1 of the FECL. Although Japanese courts have narrowed bureaucratic discretion in environmental cases by interpreting such statutes to require administrative agencies to use additional procedures or to give greater weight to environmental factors, the courts' approach in other substantive areas has had the effect of expanding the scope of discretion rather than narrowing it.[13] How this result has come about and its implications for industrial policy illustrate the importance of legal doctrine to the maintenance of informality in industrial policy.

While the formulation of industrial policy is invariably legally informal, its implementation cannot always be successful without recourse to formal powers under specific statutory provisions. If, for example, a petroleum company resists MITI's recommendations concerning production quotas during a period of oversupply, MITI need only remind the company of its powers in other areas, whether this involves controlling import of petroleum under the Foreign Exchange Control Law or approving plant expansion under the Petroleum Industry Law. If the company does not accede to the Ministry's demands, it faces the prospect of being rejected the next time it needs approval for an entirely different matter. Even when MITI does not have direct statutory power over the relevant industry, a recalcitrant company can be reminded of indirect sanctions such as the denial of government benefits or retaliation against allied companies in industries over which MITI has direct control.[14]

The danger for MITI in using unrelated collateral powers to coerce compliance with its policy is that it may one day have to invoke those powers, and if it does, judicial review becomes much more plausible. Such an exercise of MITI's formal power, for example to deny an import permit or a plant expansion application, would be an administrative disposition, and the rejected company would have standing. The question then would be whether MITI could legally exercise specific statutory powers to achieve unrelated policy goals. Most American courts would require that an agency's power under a particular statutory provision be exercised according to the standards set out in that statute for that provision; to ignore the statutory criteria and make a decision on the basis of whether the company or individual had cooperated with the agency in an unrelated incident would be considered an abuse of discretion. In Japan it is not so clear. There are no cases that bear directly on this point in the industrial policy context, but there are cases in other contexts that indicate that the range of permissible criteria is much greater in Japan than in the United States.

Most instructive is a series of land use planning cases where local governments have tried to control development by withholding necessary permits until developers have complied with a series of requirements that usually include gaining the approval of surrounding residents for the project and donating land for parks and schools. What makes this procedure relevant to this study of industrial policy is its legal nature. Instead of formally enacting its land use policy as a local ordinance, the local government merely announces it as administrative policy. As such, it has no binding legal effect on the developers to whom it is directed.[15]

Several developers have challenged this practice in the courts, arguing that it is illegal to refuse to issue a construction permit or to supply water on the ground that the developer has not complied with the informal policy devised by the city planning department. If the city wishes to require a certain act before issuing a permit, according to this argument, the city must formally enact such a requirement as a local ordinance, and the requirement must be consistent with the statute that grants the permit power (that is, the Construction Standards Law or the Water Supply Law), which means that it must relate to construction standards or to the supply of water. The plaintiffs contended that requiring the developer to donate land for a school or to reach an agreement with local residents on the height of the building or the number of units before issuing a water permit was nothing more than administrative blackmail and abuse of the local governments' clear legal power to require compliance with technical construction or hydrology standards in order to gain compliance with something they had no right to demand.

The courts have agreed with the developers' legal argument that their refusal to follow informal administrative policy cannot justify formal legal action such as refusing to issue or denying necessary permits. They have not said, however, that the city is required to issue or deny permit applications solely on grounds directly related to the technical aspects of construction specifications or water and sewage systems. The courts instead looked to the fundamental jurisdictional mandate of local government to safeguard the general well-being of its citizens. Controlling urban development is a legitimate concern of local government, and though it may not be permissible to use the failure to follow informal administrative guidance to deny a permit, the local authority may withhold the permit while it attempts to encourage the developer to negotiate with neighborhood residents on these issues.

The courts have not given the cities a completely free hand. In the first place, denial of a permit is treated more strictly than delay. More important, the authorities may withhold a permit only as long as necessary to engender compromise between the developer and the residents. Once it becomes clear that compromise is impossible, the city must act on the application. In return, the developer must bargain reasonably and in good faith. The net result is the creation of a vaguely defined sphere of action—one judicial opinion would define it by the "common sense of society"—within which the city can operate to "encourage" developer compliance with land use policy that is without any specific legal basis. A court will step in to protect the developer's rights only when it finds "encouragement" to have become compulsion.

The relevance of these cases to industrial policy will become apparent later in the chapter. For now it suffices to note that if an agency is legally permitted to invoke specific statutory powers to pursue broad social policy for which it has no statutory authority, that agency's discretion will be virtually unfettered. The Japanese courts have not gone quite this far, but they have given local governments extremely broad discretion in invoking what appear to be ministerial rather than discretionary bureaucratic functions such as connecting water or sewage systems or inspecting building plans. When this relaxed judicial approach to administrative discretion is combined with the narrow doctrines of standing and justiciability, the effect is to insulate almost entirely from judicial review many forms of bureaucratic activity in Japan. As we have just seen, this is true even in land use cases, where potential plaintiffs can usually satisfy the requirements of both standing and justiciability. The situation is even more extreme in the industrial policy context, where outsiders with conflicting interests are excluded and the procedure minimizes the need for formal administrative action.

Informality in Industrial Policy in the 1960s: The Sumitomo Metals Incident

MITI's legal powers were at their height in the 1960s before the liberalization of Japan's economy. The Ministry's statutory authority over imports under the Foreign Exchange and Foreign Trade Control Law and the direct control of industrial development given by its permit approval authority under statutes like the Petroleum Industry Law gave it enormous power over individual firms and whole industries, power that because of the doctrines governing judicial review of administrative action was virtually unrestrained legally. Given this concentrated power, it is not surprising that direct challenges to MITI's authority were rare in the 1950s and 1960s, particularly in those industries in which MITI was heavily involved. An examination of the most famous exception, the Sumitomo Metals incident, will illustrate how MITI's abstract legal powers were employed in practice to maintain industrial peace and ensure compliance with the views worked out by MITI and the management of an industry. It will also serve to highlight the close working relationship between the private sector and MITI that helps make these types of incidents so rare.[16]

The Sumitomo Metals incident arose out of a 1965–1966 steel cartel, but its roots lie deep in the structure of the steel industry and in MITI's role in its postwar development. Of all of Japan's basic industries, steel has long been considered the most fundamental, and its relationship with government has been particularly intimate. The two largest post-war firms, Yawata and Fuji, were the successors of the prewar state-owned Japan Steel, and retired MITI personnel were well placed in all of the top six steel companies except for Osaka-based Sumitomo Metals, which refused on principle to hire retired bureaucrats. But the real foundation of the relationship was neither the Japan Steel legacy nor the *amakudari* bureaucrats; it was the extraordinarily close coopera-tion between MITI and the industry throughout the postwar period in coordinating investment in steelmaking capacity. Since the early post-war period, the macroeconomic importance of steel and the uncer-tainty in the world market have convinced government and management alike that coordination of the rate of expansion and, in times of slack demand, the rate of production is in the interests of both.

The Sumitomo Metals incident provides a vivid illustration of the nature and intensity of this government–business cooperation. The story begins in the spring of 1965, against the backdrop of a severe decline in the demand for steel that combined with domestic over-capacity to threaten bankruptcy for some of the nation's largest firms. In response, the industry trade association, the Iron and Steel Federa-tion, created a committee to develop strategies for dealing with present and future market fluctuations. By May 26 the committee decided that a reduction in production was necessary to maintain appropriate prices, and on June 30 Bureau Chief Kawade of MITI's Heavy Indus-tries Bureau requested that the Federation immediately organize a production cartel to carry out the May 26 agreement. At a press confer-ence on June 30 Inayama Yoshiro, President of Yawata Steel and Chairman of the Federation, echoed Kawade's urgency and announced a meeting of the presidents of the six leading companies on July 12:

> I plan to meet all day if necessary, and if agreement isn't possible in one day, we'll meet again on the 13th. I have asked the presidents to set aside adequate time.
>
> This meeting will start with a completely clean slate, unencumbered by what has occurred up to now, and I am sure that a breakdown in the discussions can be avoided. This is imperative given the central economic role of the steel industry. I, at least, am firmly convinced that the presi-dents will be able to reach some sort of resolution.[17]

Inayama was correct. They agreed to cut production by 10 percent for the second quarter (July–September) of fiscal year 1965 (FY65) and directed Inayama to request MITI to administer the cartel.

These arrangements formed the basis of a workable system. MITI and the steel producers convinced the Fair Trade Commission, which has jurisdiction over the Antimonopoly Law (AML),[18] that the proposed cartel would not violate the AML because it would be supervised by MITI through informal administrative oversight and guidance. A formal depression cartel available under Article 24–3 of the AML, MITI argued, would take too long to establish, and speed was essential. When the Fair Trade Commission informed MITI on July 20 that it would not oppose the cartel, the outstanding legal obstacle was eliminated. On July 26 Kawade officially notified [*tsūkoku*] some seventy steel producers that they were to reduce production by 10 percent for the next quarter, that a committee was to be formed to regulate exports, and that MITI would work to arrange loans at favorable rates to cover related expenses incurred by cartel members.

On September 1, 1965, the Federation and MITI announced that the cartel would be continued into the third quarter (October–December) of FY65, but beneath surface unanimity, all was not well. Sumitomo Metals, a producer from Osaka in the Kansai region, enjoyed a growing market share and was dissatisfied with the reference period for the 10 percent production cut. President Hyūga Hōsai resented what he perceived as an alliance of Tokyo bureaucrats and businessmen to protect the market shares of the firms that sheltered the most ex-bureaucrats, particularly Yawata and Fuji, by setting the reference period as early as possible. But the rest of the industry, led by Federation Chair and Yawata President Inayama, fiercely resisted any changes. Throughout September and October, MITI arranged several meetings between Inayama and Hyūga but was unable to mediate a compromise. Finally, on November 9, MITI announced an alternative later reference period that resulted in a total production figure 30,000 tons higher, much of which would go to Sumitomo. Hyūga remained dissatisfied, however, and on November 13 announced that Sumitomo could not abide by MITI's guidance and would follow its own production plans.

MITI's response was swift, harsh, and public. On the afternoon of November 19, Vice-Minister Sahashi Shigeru announced that MITI would use its formal legal power under the FECL to limit Sumitomo's import of coking coal to the amount needed to produce Sumitomo's cartel allotment. This was the first instance in which the Ministry had publicly threatened a private firm with official retaliation for violating its informal administrative guidance. Sumitomo responded that such public coercion violated its right as a private company to manage its own affairs and threatened to take legal action should MITI's threats become reality. For Sahashi, the threat of legal action was a virtual declaration of war and a threat not only to economic stability but also to the credibility of MITI's general method of industrial policy:

> We will take whatever measures necessary to prevent the situation from worsening, not just restricting coking coal imports but any effective means. Sumitomo complains about its management responsibilities, but what about the other steel companies that are cooperating even though they may be dissatisfied? If Sumitomo sues, we can handle it. We would like the industry to abide by administrative guidance voluntarily, but in situations like these, it is natural to use force whenever the policy is in the best interests of the national economy.[19]

Meanwhile, the other top steelmakers announced their resolve to maintain the cartel and urged MITI to take immediate action to bring Sumitomo into line. For them, Sumitomo's choice of reference period for the 10 percent cut was dictated not by abstract principle, but by a selfish desire to expand its market share at their expense. Sumitomo's determination to go it alone was treated as a declaration of economic war: by leaving the system of industrial cooperation, Sumitomo had become a pariah and had to be totally boycotted by the other firms. Only by such extreme action could the solidarity of the remaining steelmakers be maintained, and the "worst case"—a total breakdown in the cartel and resort to destructive competition in a depressed market—be avoided.

In the weeks following the November confrontation, both camps began forging alliances within the financial and economic community. First, MITI Minister Miki Takeo asked the President of Sumitomo Bank to intercede with Hyūga; then Hyūga, Inayama, and Kawade of MITI made the rounds of business federations, the Liberal Democratic Party, and the Fair Trade Commission to present their respective views of the situation. The goal of MITI and the steel industry was "consensus building" within Japan's economic and political elites to isolate Sumitomo Metals and force it back into the fold.

In this contest for elite opinion, Sumitomo was at a serious disadvantage. Although Hyūga had some success in convincing Kansai area business leaders and the FTC to criticize MITI's "excessive" use of administrative guidance, he had little chance of countering the entrenched influence of the other steel companies and MITI officials in the national arena. A good illustration of what Sumitomo was up against is provided by a December 2, 1965, meeting of the Japan Committee for Economic Development (*Keizai Dōyūkai*), an important business association that convened to hear the Iron and Steel Federation's explanation of the problem. Presiding over the meeting was the chair of the Policy Committee, who incidentally was also a vice-president of Yawata Steel. The Federation delegation consisted of vice-presidents from Fuji Steel and Kawasaki Steel and directors of Yawata Steel and NKK (*Nihon Kōkan*). Not surprisingly, the sense of the meeting was strongly supportive of the Federation position. At the subsequent press conference, the chair explained the reaction of the members of the Committee for Economic Development:

> The Japan Committee for Economic Development has for some time been attempting to maintain economic order through internal adjustments, but just as the steel industry and related industries were at the point of stabilizing the market by setting up a system for cooperation, the Sumitomo Metals problem has arisen and caused cracks in the system. At today's meeting we did not hear about the infringement of Sumitomo's market share by Yawata, Fuji, etc.; we heard quite the opposite. In the near future, we will be hearing from Sumitomo President Hyūga, but we expect that President Hyūga, as an official of the Kansai branch of the Committee, will respect the underlying and fundamental principle of industrial cooperation and cooperative economic adjustment that the Committee stands for.[20]

This scene was repeated to a degree when the Federation delegation appeared before a Keidanren (Federation of Economic Organizations) group on December 4 that included another Yawata Steel official. Although in this instance there was also a representative of Sumitomo Chemical, it was clear that Sumitomo Metals could not amass the forces to counter the combined power of the entire rest of the industry and their allies in other industries.

Nor was Sumitomo successful in gaining bureaucratic support. On December 9 Chairman Kitajima announced the FTC's perspective on the dispute publicly for the first time, and, given the Commission's status as MITI's prime bureaucratic rival in industrial policy matters, it was not good news for Sumitomo. Kitajima agreed with Sumitomo that MITI's use of import restrictions to enforce an informal cartel posed serious legal questions and reiterated the position that such cartels were best organized formally under Article 24–3 of the Antimonopoly Law. But a formal depression cartel was not possible in this instance and, according to Kitajima, MITI clearly has the authority to provide guidance and leadership to the private sector. As long as the initiative remained with MITI and bureaucratic involvement did not become a mere cover for a private cartel, Kitajima saw no antitrust problem since the AML is only concerned with collusion within the private sector and cannot reach public-private cooperation directly. Thus, according to Kitajima, even though the indirect coercion of compliance with supposedly voluntary MITI suggestions raised serious doubts as to the legality of MITI's action, these were not the FTC's concerns.

By the middle of December, pressure mounted on Sumitomo as economic conditions continued to deteriorate and anxiety within financial circles grew. This pressure peaked on December 23, when the president of the Industrial Bank of Japan, Japan's most influential private bank, met with Hyūga and "strongly urged" that he compromise to avoid severe and imminent economic distress. The next day it was announced that Hyūga and Inayama would meet within the week, and on December 26 Hyūga visited MITI Minister Miki and agreed to abide by the FY65 quota in return for MITI's promise that it would "fundamentally reconsider" cartel allocations for FY66. After the meeting Hyūga stated that, although it was "regrettable" (*zannen*) that Sumitomo's demands had not been met, deteriorating conditions made it imperative that MITI be able to stabilize the situation and increase the fruits of industrial cooperation. On December 28 MITI formally announced Sumitomo's return to the fold, and Hyūga individually visited the presidents of the major steelmakers to pledge his future cooperation.[21]

Despite the charges and countercharges of Hyūga and Inayama, the substantive norm that underlay the resolution of the Sumitomo incident was not greed, but stability. The primary reason that the production quota formula was disadvantageous to Sumitomo Metals was not that Sumitomo was a Kansai firm in an industry dominated by Tokyo or that its refusal to hire *amakudari* bureaucrats had angered MITI officials. These factors may have influenced the choice of reference period, but the primary reason for Sumitomo's general condemnation was that its actions had threatened to disrupt the steel industry. To a young, aggressive, and relatively low cost company like Sumitomo, the recession offered opportunities as well as risks, but Sumitomo's taking advantage of those opportunities not only would have meant trouble for its rivals but also would have increased the risk of a general economic shakeout in the vast number of smaller suppliers and sub-contractors that surround the large steelmakers. This in turn would have influenced the general economy, and though some observers might see such influence as the healthy result of free-market competition, to MITI, the steel industry, and Japanese business leaders it meant only disruption and chaos.[22] Sumitomo Metals' refusal to cooperate thus threatened not only Yawata's market share but the "orderly competition" that is the preeminent norm of the Japanese steel industry, an industry that allows and welcomes growth and change but only on the terms and at the pace set by the MITI–industry consensus. It was the violation of that consensus that provoked MITI's unprecedented public response and that dramatically revealed for the first time the potential conflict inherent in the industrial policy process.

If we analyze the legal nature of that process in relation to the broader concerns of this book, we find the same two themes of informality and verticality that were present in varying degrees in the other case studies. Unlike a formal Antimonopoly Law depression cartel, the 1965–1966 steel cartel had no legal basis, and MITI's quarterly calculation and notification of production quotas were legally mere suggestions that the individual producers were free to ignore without fear of legal sanction. But far from weakening the cartel, such informality strengthened it. As long as there were no enforceable legal norms, industry and MITI were free to organize and operate the cartel as they saw fit, which in practice meant that the Iron and Steel Federation was in day-to-day control with the Heavy Industries Bureau in the background in case direct intervention became necessary. Given the structure of the Japanese steel industry in the mid-1960s—Yawata, Fuji, and NKK controlled more than 50 percent of the market—and MITI's particularly close relationship with the top firms, Federation control inevitably meant control by the top firms and an allocation policy that protected historical market share and minimized recent gains by smaller firms. The result was an industry "consensus" that was extremely difficult to resist even for a large, well-connected company like Sumitomo Metals. For the myriad smaller firms, direct opposition was impossible.

That this intra-industry bargaining is uncontrolled by legal norms does not mean that it is immune to other forms of external influence: the intervention of the banks and the economic federations in the late stages of the Sumitomo incident illustrates the interconnected nature of the Japanese business world and the influence of the banks in times of crisis. But external control is usually exercised not by the private sector but by MITI. Although the bureaucrats may say that the resolution of intra-industry disputes is up to the industry members themselves, it is the relevant MITI bureau that sets limits, facilitates coordination, and approves and enforces the final agreement. This oversight role includes not only protecting the weaker industry members from unfair domination, but also ensuring that the final outcome is consistent with MITI's perception of the national interest. In the latter role, the supervising bureau is influenced by the other divisions of MITI, which represent the interests of their own constituent industries and to an extent those of the general public. Informality, therefore, need not mean an industrial policy that either is unfair to weaker firms or ignores the broader national interest, but it does limit the ability of parties with divergent views to challenge that policy legally, as analysis of Hyūga's threat to sue demonstrates.[23]

At the initial stages of the dispute, Sumitomo would have lacked both standing and justiciability. Not a single action during the entire incident had the nature of an administrative disposition. The original decision to organize the cartel, the FTC's decision not to intervene, the MITI–industry agreement on the allocation formula, and MITI's quarterly notifications of each firm's allocation were all either "factual" or "internal" behavior that did not directly create or modify Sumitomo's individual legal rights or obligations. It would not have been until MITI denied or unreasonably delayed action on its import application that Sumitomo would have had its day in court. At that point, it would have had to prove that MITI had used illegal criteria or violated statutory standards in withholding Sumitomo's import permit. Given the lack of clear standards in the FECL or the Establishment Act, such a showing would have been difficult indeed.

What would seemingly have been Sumitomo's prime argument—that MITI was using its Article 52 power to coerce compliance with an unrelated bureaucratic activity for which it had no specific authority whatsoever—is considerably weaker in the Japanese context than it might first appear. Although there is nothing in any relevant statute authorizing MITI to create or administer cartels, economic policy and leadership are clearly within MITI's jurisdiction, and, if the land use planning cases are indicative, this broad mandate may be enough to give MITI authority to use its specific legal powers, even those not directly related to the particular dispute, to encourage compromise among private parties whose dispute is within MITI's jurisdiction. Although a court might eventually require MITI to act on Sumitomo's application and might even find a denial illegal, the delay would render any eventual victory by Sumitomo a Pyrrhic one indeed. The result is a dependence on industry consensus and MITI benevolence that echoes the verticality and dependence on government that we have seen in the other three case studies.

The Oil Cartel Cases: A Challenge to Informality in Industrial Policy

Aside from Hyūga's threat to sue MITI, the major legal question in the Sumitomo Metals incident was whether MITI's supervisory role made the cartel immune from civil or criminal liability under the Antimonopoly Law. Given the practical limitations on private antitrust actions, the Fair Trade Commission's early agreement not to intervene virtually eliminated this possibility in the Sumitomo incident, but the underlying question of the legality of informal MITI cartels remained and was eventually addressed by a series of civil and criminal cases known collectively as the Oil Cartel cases. These cases arose from MITI-orchestrated price and production cartels in the petroleum industry during the 1973 oil shock; they include two private damage actions[24] brought by consumers and two criminal actions[25] brought by the FTC against the industry trade association, private companies, and their executives. The courts in all four cases, most importantly the 1980 Tokyo High Court in the criminal cases, initially concluded that MITI's informal industrial policy has no legal effect in most circumstances and that cartel behavior taken pursuant thereto will usually constitute a crime. Although somewhat softened by comments in a Supreme Court decision four years later, the Tokyo High Court's condemnation of MITI's role in the formation of the cartels came at the height of an FTC–MITI battle over the shape of policy for declining industries and posed a direct and dramatic threat to MITI's accustomed mode of industrial policy.

The first case, *Japan v. Sekiyu Renmei*, involved production restrictions enforced by the Petroleum Federation (*Sekiyu Renmei*); the second, *Japan v. Idemitsu Kōsan K.K.*, involved price fixing by the firms themselves. The primary defense in both cases was that the defendants had acted with MITI's approval and in accord with its administrative guidance. The cases thus posed the often discussed but hitherto hypothetical question of whether a firm following government instructions was thereby immune from antitrust liability. The answer was a qualified no: the Fair Trade Commission initially and the courts ultimately will appraise the legality of any such arrangement independently, and firms involved in questionable activity cannot rely uncritically on ministry approval or acceptance to legalize otherwise illegal behavior. MITI's involvement was nonetheless not entirely irrelevant. In *Sekiyu Renmei*, the court held that the defendants lacked criminal intent because they had reasonably believed that they were acting legally in following MITI's instructions and establishing the production cartel. In the price fixing case, however, the court rejected the same defense because it found that the defendants had in fact known that their actions were illegal. Even the acquittal in the production case is of little significance, because these cases put future defendants on notice that MITI's imprimatur is not enough.

Holding individuals criminally liable for actions undertaken with the explicit approval and even urging of a government entity is quite remarkable in terms of criminal law doctrine, but what is of interest here is the courts' appraisal of the legal consequences of MITI's role. In both opinions the High Court found MITI's administrative guidance to have induced illegal private behavior. In the production case, MITI had initiated the production cartel during consultation with the industry and had requested that the Federation enforce it. The court found such activity by MITI to have led to violations of the Antimonopoly Law. In the price fixing case, MITI had issued guidance which the court characterized as resembling price controls. The defendants' price fixing went beyond strict compliance with MITI guidance, however, and MITI's general involvement and after-the-fact acknowledgment of cooperative price increases did not make them immune from the AML.

That legally informal MITI policy does not necessarily shield anticompetitive or otherwise illegal behavior from judicial scrutiny was not unexpected. MITI had claimed that its Establishment Law gave it general authority to issue administrative guidance in situations like the Sumitomo Metals incident, but first academics and later the FTC had taken the opposite position. Even MITI had long recognized the need for more explicit authority to back up its guidance. In the early sixties when MITI was facing the inevitability of the liberalization of international trade, Vice-Minister Sahashi attempted to persuade the Diet to enact legislation explicitly granting MITI the authority to promote specific industries, and in the aftermath of the Sumitomo incident, industry leaders called for a specific steel industry statute to prevent a repetition of the disorder and confusion of the Sumitomo episode.[26]

None of those legislative efforts bore fruit, in part because business and political leaders feared they would give MITI too much formal legal power. The surprising message of the Oil Cartel opinions is that such statutes may not have made any legal difference. MITI's involvement in the oil cartels was based not on the Establishment Law but on the Petroleum Industry Law (PIL), which was the type of industry-specific statute that MITI had assumed gave it the authority to intervene in precisely the manner involved in these cases. The PIL was enacted in 1962 with the purpose of fostering the development of the domestic petroleum industry and in anticipation of the decline in MITI's power following the international liberalization of Japan's economy. It was the model for the later proposed steel industry statute and was, in a single industry, what Sahashi had wanted across a wide range of industries. It gives MITI clear authority to monitor the petroleum industry and implies MITI involvement beyond mere observation. Article 3 requires the Ministry to issue an annual five-year supply plan which then becomes the basis for MITI review of individual refineries' production plans (Article 10). Based on that review, MITI decides whether to approve new refineries (Article 4), advises individual firms to restrict output (Article 10), or proposes resale price guidelines for petroleum products (Article 15). As do many economic statutes, however, the PIL frequently stops short of granting MITI the formal legal authority to carry out the role that in other sections it has implied MITI is to play. This ambiguity has significant advantages in day-to-day application, but in the Oil Cartel cases it became a liability. The High Court noted MITI's authority in the industry and acknowledged that it was meant to be implemented through administrative guidance, but concluded nonetheless that the lack of explicit legal authority in the law meant that MITI's informal involvement in production and pricing decisions did not legitimate the cartels that often resulted therefrom.

The High Court opinions stopped short of endorsing the Fair Trade Commission's position that all anticompetitive arrangements between government and business will violate the Antimonopoly Law unless they are specifically exempted by statute. The courts left open the possibility that a specific statute could justify anticompetitive conduct when such conduct is indispensable to the ministry's execution of its statutory mandate and the ministry approves the conduct.[27] But the statutory intent of the Petroleum Industry Law was to the contrary—that any petroleum industry cartel would have to go through the normal procedures for depression cartels under the Antimonopoly Law. Nor did the court find the defendants' actions indispensable to MITI's duties under the statute.

The High Court's treatment of administrative guidance left many legal questions unanswered. Who is to judge when a particular anticompetitive act is "indispensable" to the implementation of a ministry's duties pursuant to a particular statute? If MITI accompanied its guidance with a statement of its necessity, would that end the question? Both MITI and the FTC issued post-judgment statements approaching these and similar questions from contrasting perspectives, but what appeared clear in 1980 was that the PIL was an inadequate basis for guidance that induced behavior that infringed other public law rules. Given that the statutory basis for MITI's authority in the PIL is relatively strong, the legal fate of guidance based solely on the MITI Establishment Law or the broad terms of a statute like the Foreign Exchange and Foreign Trade Control Law seemed even shakier.

In evaluating the impact of these cases, it is important to clarify the nature of MITI's role. In both the production and price cartels, MITI largely delegated control to the trade association and the companies themselves. The degree of delegation was particularly strong in *Idemitsu*, the price fixing case, but MITI's involvement in *Sekiyu Renmei*'s production cartel represented the usual pattern of postwar industrial policy. MITI's close relationship with the Petroleum Federation was very similar to its relationship with many trade associations including the Iron and Steel Federation and was a necessary feature of industrial policy as long as the ministry preferred to control firm behavior voluntarily, that is, without recourse to an administrative disposition that threatened to "legalize" industrial policy and give individual firms the power to challenge MITI in court.

To get compliance without a disposition, MITI had to develop an acceptable uniform plan or allotment formula and convince each firm that the entire industry would comply. The simplest way to do so was to delegate to the trade association the task of formulating a plan that was both within the limits set by MITI and consistent with industry consensus. Similarly, the most effective mode of implementation was to rely on the trade association for routine matters, with MITI involvement occurring only when the consensus process failed. At that point the Ministry could intervene and use its considerable informal power to enforce either the original formula or a modified version that MITI considered fairer to the dissenting firms. And in those rare occasions when a firm was truly recalcitrant, MITI could threaten to use its formal power under the Foreign Exchange and Foreign Trade Control Law to cripple the firm economically.

By 1980, however, this method of industrial policy had been severely shaken by shifts in MITI's legal power. First, trade liberalization progressively weakened MITI's formal power over foreign exchange and trade until it became virtually impossible to use it in the traditional manner to bring dissidents like Sumitomo Metals into line. Then the Oil Cartel cases, particularly *Japan v. Sekiyu Renmei*, threatened the very foundation of the historical model by discrediting the informal cooperation among industry members, their trade association, and MITI that was at its core. After 1980, MITI's efforts to persuade or coerce reluctant firms to follow the consensus developed by the Ministry and industry leaders faced the potential argument that compliance might mean criminal prosecution. There were, for example, rumors after the Oil Cartel opinions that members of the paper pulp industry resisted MITI's attempts to "rationalize"—Japanese industrial-policy jargon for "shrink"—on antitrust grounds. Although such excuses are frequently merely a pretext for resisting unpalatable policy, they were plausible enough to provide regulated firms with another weapon to resist MITI direction.

Industrial Policy in the 1980s: The Legislation of Informality

The impact of these legal developments on MITI was exacerbated by economic trends in the late seventies and early eighties that added a new and more difficult dimension to the substance of industrial policy. With notable exceptions, MITI's efforts up to the mid-seventies had centered on promoting growth and controlling trade. It had used informal cartel and merger policy to foster growth in emerging sectors, to counter cyclical downturns in mature sectors, and to restrain exports in response to foreign pressure. In the 1970s, however, increasing competition from newly industrializing countries together with the dramatic rise in energy costs put many of Japan's hitherto successful industries at a severe competitive disadvantage. Just as its legal power was at its nadir, MITI had to worry not only about fostering the industries of the future and easing fundamentally sound industries through temporary difficulties, but also about devising and implementing policies to deal with a broad range of industries facing permanent decline. As we saw in the Sumitomo Metals incident, the establishment of production cartels to ease cyclical pressures has always been more difficult than emerging industry policy because the former more frequently requires sacrifices by particular firms as opposed to simply providing opportunities and incentives for future growth. But even in recession or export cartels, dissatisfied firms could console themselves with the assurance that any sacrifice would be temporary, presumably to be followed by another period of growth. Members of a structurally depressed industry cartel, on the other hand, are asked to eliminate permanently large proportions of their productive capacity. In an era of slow growth, such adjustments are even more painful since surplus labor cannot readily be shifted to other growing sectors of the same company or company family (*keiretsu*). The tensions underlying the question of allocation that are present in all MITI-inspired cartels become much harder to resolve in this environment, and the combination of trade liberalization and the Oil Cartel decisions meant that MITI would have to resolve them with substantially reduced legal authority.

One response to MITI's situation might have been legislation explicitly granting MITI the legal authority to establish and enforce compulsory cartels in specified industries. Such legislation would have avoided the problem of statutes like the Petroleum Industry Law that grant MITI broad responsibility but withhold the legal power to exercise it, but it might also have sacrificed the informality that made the PIL model attractive in the first place. What MITI and its industrial policy allies required was a statute that would give MITI the legal authority to intervene aggressively in declining sectors but without formalizing and rigidifying the cooperative relationship that had historically been the foundation of industrial policy. Complicating the drafting process was an increase in the power and prestige of the Fair Trade Commission over the last half of the 1970s, which meant that blanket exemptions from the Antimonopoly Law would be difficult to achieve. Despite these difficulties, MITI was able in 1983 to enact the Structurally Depressed Industries Law (SDIL), which to a remarkable extent satisfies the conflicting goals of MITI, the FTC, and industry without substantially departing from the established pattern of industrial policy.

The history of the SDIL begins in 1978 with the passage of the five-year Depressed Industries Law (DIL), MITI's initial legislative response to the first oil shock.[28] The DIL was conceived as a temporary measure to meet transitory economic difficulties in industries particularly affected by increased energy costs. International competitiveness was to be regained through the elimination of excess capacity in accordance with Basic Stabilization Plans drafted by the industry and MITI. When industry members were unable to meet a plan's goals on their own initiative, MITI had explicit authority to establish voluntary cartels, which would be exempt from AML attack, for the sole purpose of capacity elimination. Designation as a depressed industry was at the initiative of the industry and participation in subsequent cartels was voluntary, but the availability of antitrust immunity and loan guarantees from the statutorily created Depressed Industries Credit Fund made staying out difficult.

By 1982 the Depressed Industries Law had engendered substantial capacity reduction in the fourteen designated industries, but it had failed to restore the financial health of most of the firms in these industries.[29] The second oil shock of 1979 had vitiated the economic forecasts on which the DIL stabilization plans were based and plunged these industries into an even deeper depression. As a result, the consensus within MITI and among industry leaders was that some continuation of governmental assistance was necessary beyond 1983. The issue was what form government intervention should take. It was apparent by the early 1980s that many of Japan's basic industries were no longer facing temporary difficulties caused by cyclical market fluctuations, but permanent structural decline which the 1978 law with its narrow focus on capacity elimination was incapable of dealing with. Any revision of the law, therefore, had to extend MITI's powers to include the orchestration of mergers and other joint activities by members of designated industries. Some proposals envisioned substantially strengthening MITI's legal ability to control designated sectors, including the authority to exempt diverse cartels from the Antimonopoly Law to restrict imports, and to designate additional industries as eligible under the law beyond the DIL's one-year period. There was also discussion of the necessity of "outsider control." Under the DIL, capacity elimination cartels were legally voluntary; individual firms that chose not to participate—the "outsiders"—were not legally constrained by the agreements made by the cartel participants or by any recommendations MITI might make. To increase the effectiveness of the new law, the argument went, the legal voluntarism of the DIL would have to be revised so that MITI would have legal control over both outsiders and imports.

The call for greater support for these ailing industries and the apparent willingness of many sectors of society to grant MITI the sweeping powers necessary to implement such support elicited a broad public debate. This debate went beyond the particular statute involved to more basic questions of economic and political philosophy in a way reminiscent of the earlier debate over the DIL's passage and the debate over the controversial legislation proposed by MITI Vice-Minister Sahashi in the early sixties.[30] In fact, parallels were also drawn—perhaps overdrawn—to the forceful bureaucratic intervention in the prewar and wartime economies.[31] Labor, as well as the opposition parties, allied with MITI and the concerned industries in the debate. Against this broad coalition were mainly the Fair Trade Commission and neoclassical economists. As the debate developed, it became clear that MITI envisaged something less than the import restrictions and draconian powers that others wished for, while the FTC and the economists argued for no extension of the Depressed Industries Law at all. The law, they argued, had failed to accomplish its fundamental goal of revitalization, and its extension would lead only to further inefficiency and indefinite protectionism.[32]

The Structurally Depressed Industry Law that emerged is a classic political compromise. The FTC was able to prevent a second antitrust exemption and any control over outsiders or imports whatsoever, and to limit the extension of time for designating new industries to 18 months. MITI, on the other hand, succeeded in greatly extending the reach of the law. The SDIL's goal shifted from its predecessor's aim of overcoming temporary market difficulties to the "structural reform of designated industries." To meet this goal, MITI's jurisdiction and responsibility were extended from helping firms eliminate excess capacity to reach virtually every aspect of their operation. Appropriately, the plans to be jointly prepared by MITI and industry became "Structural Reform Plans" rather than Stabilization Plans and provide for (1) the establishment of joint production, marketing, purchasing, and storage activities; (2) methods to implement shifts in production among firms, including agreements to specialize in certain products or to merge management and production in whole or part; (3) investment in energy conservation or fuel conversion and in increased production efficiency and product quality; and (4) the development of new products or technologies. To facilitate these expanded goals, the new law provides a broad range of new tax incentives to complement the loan guarantees already available.

MITI's scope of activity under the 1983 revisions is broad indeed, but the law can hardly be considered a carte blanche for aggressive MITI intervention. The SDIL follows the pattern of the Petroleum Industry Law: MITI's powers are not necessarily so large as its expansive responsibilities would imply. While MITI may now take the initiative in fostering mergers and other types of interfirm behavior, the lack of an antitrust exemption means that the Fair Trade Commission retains a veto power over all such activity. Although the Commission had had initial approval power over capacity elimination cartels under the DIL (and continues to have such a power under the SDIL), its role was minimal thereafter because, once approved, cartels were legally immune from Antimonopoly Law attack. The SDIL merger provisions establish a framework within which the FTC can play an ongoing role. MITI may consult the FTC whenever it feels a proposal would affect competition policy; the Commission is required in turn to give its opinion of the proposal. Thereafter, should the Commission conclude that an approved cartel or merger is violating the Antimonopoly Law, it may so inform MITI and recommend changes. Given its continuing statutory power to institute criminal and civil actions directly against the firms involved, the FTC has become MITI's partner, at least in a negative sense, in the area of structurally depressed industry policy.

The restructuring of the Japanese petrochemical industry can give an idea of how the SDIL works in practice.[33] Although it had weathered the first oil shock relatively well, the petrochemical industry was among those hardest hit by the second. Its share of the Southeast Asian market declined dramatically, and imports began to take a significant share of Japan's domestic market for the first time. The cause was an increase in the cost of naphtha, the Japanese petrochemical industry's basic feedstock, from less than ¥6,500 per kiloliter in the early 1970s to over ¥55,000 by 1980. Because the domestic price of natural gas, the American industry's major feedstock, was controlled through this period, American producers were able to undersell Japanese producers by up to 30 percent by the early 1980s.

Contributing to the problem was MITI's policy of artificially increasing domestic naphtha prices to subsidize the Japanese petroleum industry. Under Article 12 of the PIL, to import naphtha one must register with the Agency of Natural Resources and Energy (ANRE), a MITI-affiliated and staffed agency. Although legally anyone can register, ANRE administrative guidance has limited the right largely to domestic petroleum companies. By giving petroleum refiners control over imports, ANRE was able to protect them when the price of imported naphtha dropped below that of domestic naphtha. That characteristic preference of stability in supply and demand over excessive competition was thought to be particularly necessary in the oil market because stable and economically healthy domestic oil companies were thought necessary to ensure secure and stable sources of petroleum in times of crisis. The result was an inefficient domestic oil industry with a MITI-approved lock on naphtha prices.

As long as the petrochemical companies were able to offset any gaps between foreign and domestic naphtha prices with efficient production processes, they were willing to live with this system because MITI's policies in other areas had been highly favorable to them. Just like steel before it, the petrochemical industry was chosen as a growth industry by MITI in the 1960s. As a result the industry boomed in that decade, and many MITI officials retired to high positions in the industry. By the 1980s, however, what had looked like a healthy boom began to be considered disastrous overexpansion, and the industry was willing to destroy its relationship with MITI by threatening to register to import naphtha itself. Supporting it was the Basic Industries Bureau (BIB) of MITI, with the result that the "naphtha war," as it was called, was not only between the oil and petrochemical industries but also between two competing factions within the Ministry of International Trade and Industry itself.

For discussion and suggested solutions of this problem, MITI relied on the *shingikai* process of industry–government consultation and cooperation. In April 1981 it referred the situation to the Chemical Industry Committee of the Industrial Structure Council, one of MITI's most important *shingikai*, which in turn created the Petrochemical Subcommittee in June 1981. The Subcommittee had seventeen members: five representatives of the petrochemical industry, four from user industries such as synthetic fibers, two from the petroleum industry, and six neutral mediators, who were expected to represent a broader perspective and to facilitate a compromise between the petrochemical and petroleum industries. This group included bankers, trading company officials, and an academic economist. One of the subcommittee members was both a member of the synthetic fiber industry trade association and a member of the federation of labor unions in the chemical industry. The members were generally managing directors of their firms or the equivalent.

MITI wanted discussion of the desirability and feasibility of two measures: reducing naphtha prices and restructuring the petrochemical industry. On December 8, 1981, after four meetings of the Chemical Industry Committee and six of its subcommittee, the Committee issued an interim report recommending that (1) the petrochemical industry should have access to low-cost feedstock and (2) petrochemical producers should be merged. The interim report stated that both steps were necessary for the industry to regain international competitiveness, but it gave no specifics on how either was to be achieved. The ambiguity involving the feedstock question was a victory for the Agency of Natural Resources and Energy and the petroleum industry. Opinions representing the petrochemical industry were excluded from the main body of the report and relegated to an appendix as "supplementary opinions." One of the most influential of the petrochemical industry representatives, the president of Shōwa Denkō, publicly expressed his dissatisfaction with the report. This discrepancy of views is unusual for a *shingikai* because such bodies are established for the purpose of submerging and disguising conflict, not airing or clarifying it. The seriousness of the conflict was further demonstrated in January 1982 when the petrochemical companies announced their intention to register to import naphtha directly if ANRE continued to ignore their demands.

Unlike Hyūga's threat to sue MITI during the Sumitomo Metals incident, the petrochemical companies' threat was not made out of desperation. The petrochemical industry had strong support from the Basic Industries Bureau within MITI and from the private sector, where there was a growing perception that ANRE's policy of protecting domestic oil companies had become an unnecessary drag on the economy. If anything, it was ANRE and the petroleum companies that were isolated, and ANRE's Director General had to face the possibility that his agency was about to lose its control over naphtha imports. In February, therefore, the Director General and the petroleum industry agreed to a compromise that gave petrochemical companies free access to imported naphtha through arrangements with the petroleum companies, which remained the direct importers. ANRE retained the power to determine domestic naphtha prices but agreed to hold them to import prices. The substance of the agreement was what the petrochemical industry had wanted, but the form left ANRE in control.

With the naphtha war successfully behind it, MITI was able to concentrate on the second item on the Industrial Structure Council's agenda, the restructuring of the petrochemical industry. The new naphtha policy had eliminated the price differential between imported and domestic feedstock and provided some help to the industry, but more important in MITI's view was the elimination of much of the industry's productive capacity and the merger of more than a dozen firms into three to five groups. With their role in the naphtha settlement fresh in the companies' minds, MITI bureaucrats felt that it was an excellent opportunity to persuade the industry to face up to the difficult choices ahead.

The final report of the Chemical Industry Committee, submitted to MITI on June 9, 1982, reflected this shift in concerns and focused on the elimination of excessive competition within the industry by scrapping productive capacity and by promoting joint efforts in the areas of capital investment, purchasing, marketing, and research and development. The report also recommended new legislation to replace and expand the DIL, due to expire one year later, so that the industry would be able to implement these measures under the supervision of MITI without fear of Antimonopoly Law attack. This recommended legislation, after many twists and turns and public debate, eventually became the Structurally Depressed Industries Law.

The final committee report was superficially what MITI had wanted, but it represented no more than a vague agreement by the dozen or so major petrochemical firms that structural reform was needed. As a means of reaching an intra-industry, product-by-product agreement on the tough questions of who would eliminate how much capacity, by what date, and under what terms, a new subcommittee, the Petrochemical Industry System Subcommittee (PISC), was established in July 1982; it consisted of the presidents of the leading petrochemical firms and neutral facilitators, including Chairman Arisawa Hiromi. The appointment of Arisawa, who is Professor Emeritus of Economics at the University of Tokyo, chair of both the general assembly of the Industrial Structure Council and the Chemical Industry Committee, and Japan's preeminent postwar industrial economist, demonstrated the importance of the issue and the difficulty anticipated in reaching agreement.

MITI wanted the new subcommittee process to consolidate the industry into three or four groups that would concentrate production in the most efficient facilities and coordinate purchasing and marketing. Suspicion within the industry was the main obstacle to consolidation, since long-time competitors were afraid that they would reduce their capacity only to find their rivals reneging on the agreement and profiting from the improved market conditions. The establishment of working product groups within the subcommittee had no immediate effect on this mutual distrust, and by the late summer of 1982, the economic situation had worsened further.

To break this impasse, MITI tried a different approach: in early October it sent the subcommittee members to Europe. The stated purpose was the study of structural reform in the European petrochemical industry, but the real purpose was to create personal relationships among the company presidents conducive to the reorganization of the industry. This approach seems to have worked. Participants claimed that the experience of traveling together built mutual trust, and the end of October marked a new flurry of activity. On October 18 Idemitsu Petrochemical announced that it was postponing completion of a planned ultramodern ethylene plant, and Shōwa Denkō announced three days later its plans to close a major plant. These initial steps were followed in late November by the PISC's publication of a "revitalization plan" including specific amounts of capacity to be eliminated by certain dates, a proposal to form groups to plan and execute the capacity elimination, and a call for antitrust immunity to facilitate the realization of these goals. The process of intra-industry consensus formation was complete and awaited only the bureaucratic imprimatur under the Structurally Depressed Industries Law.[34]

Given the economic and legal changes of the 1970s, perhaps the most striking aspect of the restructuring of the petrochemical industry under the SDIL was its similarity to the industrial policy process during the Sumitomo Metals incident. Then the Iron and Steel Federation was given a free hand to develop cartel policy within MITI guidelines. Seventeen years later, the Tokyo High Court's opinions in the Oil Cartel cases meant that trade association involvement had to be cloaked in the official guise of the Petrochemical Industry System Subcommittee, but the company presidents remained the central actors and the process remained intimate and informal. The major difference was the inclusion of the Fair Trade Commission as a major participant. The Commission retains its Antimonopoly Law power and, depending on the degree to which it wants to use it, can veto MITI's and industry's plans. When, for example, MITI and the petrochemical producers decided in early 1983 to concentrate all sales of certain products in three joint sale companies, the number had to be increased to four because of FTC fears about excessive market share. The Commission's power, however, is largely negative because its lack of personal and historical connections with industry means that it has little positive role in policymaking. The genius of the SDIL compromise is that it has incorporated the FTC into the previous structure and minimized the legal threat of the Antimonopoly Law without sacrificing the informal and consensual nature of the process.

Nor has the SDIL weakened MITI's power to determine to what extent and by whom outside interests will be represented in the industrial policy process. Such representation usually takes the form of membership on the various *shingikai*, but most of the work of *shingikai* is done by ad hoc subcommittees of various duration and status. As we saw in the case of the Industrial Structure Council, the Chemical Industry Committee, the Petrochemicals Subcommittee, and the Petrochemical Industry System Committee, the representation of outsiders on each advisory group tends to decline in proportion to the actual importance of the deliberations. And at the lowest level, the give-and-take necessary to devise the details of particular policies frequently occurs outside of the formal meetings and is coordinated by MITI bureaucrats who staff the committee or subcommittee.

The second major avenue of interest articulation in industrial policy is through the various subdivisions of MITI itself. Here again, the structure of the SDIL is consistent with prior practice. One way of interpreting the FTC's role under the SDIL is to think of the FTC as another bureau or section of MITI, whose special role is to evaluate and articulate the competitive effect of the policies of other MITI bureaus. Just as the pollution crisis led to the creation within MITI of an office specifically charged with reviewing the environmental aspect of MITI policy, the Oil Cartel cases strengthened the role of competition policy in the MITI process, albeit in the form of statutory consultation rather than bureaucratic institutionalization.

The overriding characteristic of industrial policy legislation such as the Structurally Depressed Industries Law is the attempt to limit the potential for open conflict, particularly conflict that might lead to the intervention of a neutral or independent third party such as the Fair Trade Commission or the courts. Although this approach does not prevent change in the substance of industrial policy—the presence of the FTC within the process may mean some shift toward pro-market policies—it limits the changes in its form and, most important, in the control of the agenda and direction of policy. Substantial shifts in the calculus of power occurred in the seventeen years between the Sumitomo Metals incident and the SDIL. The rise of the FTC and the internationalization and maturation of many sectors of the Japanese economy have strengthened the private sector, with the result that MITI can no longer bully individual firms as it did in 1965 and must instead rely on a variety of economic incentives to gain compliance with unpopular policy. The important constant is the bipolar and informal nature of the process, whatever the varying strengths and weaknesses of the parties involved.

The Implications of Informality

Informality in Japanese administrative policymaking is not limited to MITI or industrial policy. In 1981 the Administrative Management Agency sponsored a study whereby each major central government agency and many local governments were requested to report on their use of informal administrative guidance.[35] These reports indicate that informality is preferred by every level of government and in all areas of government–citizen contact. Informal action by necessity constitutes the vast majority of all administrative actions in all governments, but its use by Japanese agencies goes well beyond the informal give-and-take that surrounds an agency's implementation of its statutory duties to include the creation and operation of wide-ranging administrative systems with little or no statutory basis.[36] Further distinguishing Japanese bureaucratic informality from that in other countries is the legal environment within which it occurs. Broad delegations of authority to administrative agencies, particularly in areas of economic regulation, are inevitable, but in many jurisdictions the availability of judicial review significantly limits agency discretion by discovering implicit statutory standards or requiring the agency to create and abide by its own standards, by requiring certain procedures or written findings, or at the minimum by providing a public forum in which the agency must justify its action.[37] Though present in certain areas in some circumstances,[38] this judicial role is almost nonexistent in Japanese industrial policy because of the doctrines governing standing, justiciability, and scope of discretion. The result is a judicially unaccountable bureaucracy that operates without clear statutory limits even in relatively narrowly focused statutes like the SDIL.

Nor is there the kind of procedural formality that would restrain agency discretion even in the absence of substantive standards and effective judicial review.[39] The *shingikai* system is intended to bring into the policymaking process information and expertise from various different sources and to provide an open forum for the discussion of differences so that a consensus can emerge and a generally acceptable recommendation made to the appropriate ministry. To a certain extent and in some policy areas, the *shingikai* system does operate in this manner; the discord and debate on the various advisory bodies considering equal employment legislation and on the subcommittees of the Industrial Structure Council wrestling with the naphtha price dispute between the petroleum and petrochemical industries may indicate a growing substantive role for *shingikai*. But the usual pattern has historically been for the *shingikai* to cloak what is essentially a bipolar MITI–industry decision-making process. Given that MITI appoints the participants, provides their staff, and oversees the frequent informal consultation that separates the infrequent formal meetings, it is not surprising that the *shingikai* rarely play the central role in making policy. Their true function has been to legitimate policy made elsewhere. In many instances, as in the MITI–industry decision to restructure the petrochemical industry, that means ratifying past decisions. At other times, as when the Industrial Structural Council issues a document envisioning the economy of the future, it means preparing the ground for future decisions. Whatever the precise nature of the *shingikai* action, it remains beyond legal challenge since no *shingikai* report, no matter how final and no matter what its role in industrial policy, constitutes an administrative disposition. Nor do MITI's actions in appointing *shingikai* members, establishing their agenda, or ghost-writing their reports reach the level of legal formality necessary for judicial review.

It is important to stress that lack of legal accountability does not mean that industrial policy is insulated from outside pressure or that it serves only the interests of the businessmen and bureaucrats involved. As demonstrated by the role played by financial circles and economic federations in the Sumitomo Metals incident, the clash between the petrochemical and petroleum industries and their MITI protectors over naphtha imports, and the role of the FTC and academic economists in the drafting of the SDIL, industrial policy must answer to divergent and at times inconsistent demands. As those demands shift with changes in Japan's economic structure, the substance of industrial policy evolves. Shifts will often mean switching emphasis and protection from one industry to another, as in the naphtha war, or addressing entirely new problems, as in structurally depressed industries policy. It can mean introducing new considerations and interests into the decision-making calculus, as occurred to some degree in environmental policy in the early seventies and with competition policy in the eighties. But what does not change despite legal shocks like the Oil Cartel cases is the informal nature of the process, and although legal informality may not point one way or the other in terms of the substance of industrial policy, it has profound implications for the political and social context within which policy is made.

One such implication is informality's impact on interest group formation and articulation in Japan. Interest groups abound and are enormously successful in Japan in general and in industrial policy in particular. The informality of the process would be impossible without the existence of trade associations and economic federations like the Keidanren. But even though MITI would be hard-pressed to operate its industrial policy as it does without interest groups, the legal nature of the process itself is a strong obstacle to the formation of new interest groups, particularly voluntary associations representing wider, less intensely held interests such as environmental or consumer concerns. To understand why the legal context of industrial policy has this effect, one must be able to imagine a totally different legal context, one that would emphasize formality, accountability, and bureaucratic neutrality. Fortunately American administrative law doctrines provide precisely this contrast, and a brief overview of their effect on interest group formation in the United States can broaden our understanding of the effect of the very different Japanese doctrines.

In sharp contrast to Japan, the threshold doctrines that determine respectively who can challenge a particular act and what degree of finality and formality is necessary for the act to be judicially cognizable have been dramatically relaxed in recent decades in the United States. Although the reasoning of Japanese courts in standing and justiciability cases finds its echoes in American cases of the 1940s or

1950s, American courts have since relaxed these doctrines so that even undifferentiated members of the public who can show some particular actual injury will have standing, and even press conferences and opinion letters may be ripe for judicial review.[40]

Reinforcing the liberality of the threshold doctrines is the approach of American courts to the exercise of bureaucratic discretion.[41] Though they are as reluctant as Japanese courts to impose their judgment directly on the substance of an agency decision, they have forced agencies to justify the rationality of their decisions by requiring detailed findings and exhaustive and inclusive hearings and by generally emphasizing openness and neutrality throughout the decision-making process. One of the fundamental premises of judicial intervention in America has been a profound distrust of the informal, *ex parte* contacts that animate Japanese administrative life, resulting in substantial restrictions on their presence in American policymaking.[42] In doing so, the courts have been able to rely on the provisions of statutes like the Administrative Procedure Act and the Freedom of Information Act that specifically empower individuals and groups to use the legal system to keep the bureaucracy accountable, but much of the impetus has been in statutory interpretation as the federal courts and Congress have both worked to eliminate precisely the close, informal, collaborative relationship between the bureaucracy and business that is the lifeblood of Japanese industrial policy.

The centrality of these doctrines in American policymaking has led to a multipolar administrative process, and the almost total absence of parallel doctrinal developments in Japanese administrative law deserves some credit for maintaining the essentially bipolar nature of the industrial policy process in Japan.[43] In fact, this may be one instance where legal rules make an enormous difference in the way societies articulate grievances and how political support coalesces around those grievances to form interest groups. The wearing down of the Japanese environmental movement is one example, and the Japanese bureaucracy's aversion to any legally enforceable environmental impact assessment requirement similar to that contained in the American National Environmental Policy Act shows that the Ministries of International Trade and Industry, Transportation, and Construction are quite aware of the danger of giving outside groups a legal peg on which to hang their collective hat. The *Federation of Housewives* case, where consumers were denied standing to challenge FTC rules on fruit juice labeling, and the ultimate futility of Sumitomo President Hyūga's threat of legal action against MITI are further examples of how doc-trine prevents effective recourse to Japanese courts, which in turn eliminates an excellent forum for publicity and focus for organization as well as practically eliminating legal control of the bureaucracy.

A second implication of informality in industrial policy is its effect on the government–business relationship and on the tendency of pri-vate companies to comply voluntarily with MITI's informal guidance. MITI and business have worked to create a relationship of mutual trust and interdependence by institutionalizing the constant contact be-tween industry representatives and MITI officials at all levels, as was apparent in the three industrial policy case studies. History, personal contacts, common backgrounds, and intertwined futures all contribute to this relationship, but it is maintainable only because of the closed, informal nature of the industrial policy process whereby interim deci-sions are rarely challenged publicly and are frequently unknown outside the industrial policy community until they have become a virtual *fait accompli*. Another factor reinforcing this community of inter-ests is the sense of common destiny shared strongly by all Japanese. This phenomenon is often exaggerated, and there is nothing mystical about it, but to ignore its role would be an error. It is easier in Japan, therefore, to induce behavior by appeals to national interest than in the United States. Related factors are the professionalism and nonpolitical ethos of the bureaucracy, which lend credence to its evocations of the national interest. The effect of all this is to reinforce the consensual aspects of the decision-making process in those sectors of the econ-omy, such as steel, oil, and petrochemicals, in which history and eco-nomic conditions converge to make the MITI–industry relationship particularly interdependent.[44] Basic policy decisions in these sectors are rarely made without thorough consultation with the business and political elites. The result is that the goals of the public and the private sectors are frequently congruent, at least in the long term.

It would be a mistake, however, to dismiss compliance with MITI's informal policies as a by-product of "Japan, Inc.," obeyed simply because the interests of corporate and public officials are identical. The internal dynamics of the Japanese government are too complex for such simplified identity of interests to represent reality. But even if there were total harmony at the top, the question of compliance would remain since administrative guidance often favors some firms in an industry over others. There is a tendency for MITI to ask for equal sacrifices by all firms, but equality of sacrifice is hardly self-defining.

The emergence of perceived winners and losers is inevitable, and yet compliance, however reluctant, has been the rule.[45]

One reason is fear of economic disadvantage. Because of the nature of administrative guidance, sanctions are either legally informal or based on statutory provisions not involved in the administrative guidance. The Sumitomo Metals case is the best example of the latter, but others would include withholding permits for expansion or construction of facilities, zealous enforcement of environmental controls, and the like. In recent years as MITI's legal power has eroded, punitive sanctions have frequently been replaced by the withholding of subsidies as in SDIL cartels, but the underlying mechanism has remained unchanged. Economic pressure in either form can be brought against both the firm itself and members of its *keiretsu* or corporate group. Such pressure may come directly from MITI, or it may be applied by one of MITI's satellite agencies such as the Japan Development Bank in the form of delays in processing loan requests, or it may come from a wholly distinct branch of the government in the form of reduced procurement contracts.

This type of pressure, even when in the form of punitive retaliation, would be extremely hard to combat in the United States, but three factors make it even more so in Japan. First, the existence of corporate groups ironically makes their members more, rather than less, vulnerable to indirect sanction in some circumstances. Second, the difficulties of judicial review mean that judicial control of such bureaucratic arm-twisting is extremely unlikely. As we saw in the Sumitomo Metals case, even the most blatant retaliation may be beyond judicial control under Japanese administrative law doctrine. Third, and perhaps more important, the consultative policy process means that the reluctant firm will be facing not only MITI but an otherwise united industry as well. We saw this clearly in the way Sumitomo Metals' rivals rallied support for the MITI/Iron and Steel Federation position in 1965, and we saw in the "naphtha war" how dissent within an industry or competition between related industries can make MITI's task extremely difficult. Therefore, MITI's time-consuming and cumbersome process of building a public/private consensus in industrial policy, though in some ways a necessary product of its relative lack of specific formal powers, can become an important source of strength when enforcement against renegade firms is necessary.

These three strands of administrative process—the exclusion of independent outsiders, its consultative consensual character, and the virtual impossibility of attacking it legally from within or without—complement one another and create an environment in which good relations are the key to success in dealing with the government. Since universal rules cannot be applied to the process and outsiders are largely excluded, it remains extremely particularistic. Each problem is handled with attention to the public interest and to the general principles of fairness and equality, but without being constrained by any legally enforceable procedure for defining or achieving these goals. Short-term sacrifices are required, but MITI's long institutional memory benefits its friends as well as punishes its enemies. The process also works to blur the lines of responsibility, with the result that a dissatisfied firm cannot blame only MITI since the decision was made as much by the industry as by MITI. The end result is a relationship of diffuse and undefined mutual obligations where the balance of power between industry and government may vary but where the latter retains formal control. As in ANRE's reaction to the petrochemical industry's threat to register to import naphtha directly, MITI will often prefer to compromise on the substance of a dispute if it can thereby retain legal control of the process of decision.

This account does not attempt to present or evaluate Japanese industrial policy as economic policy. Nor are the incidents and industries discussed necessarily typical of the MITI–business relationship: steel, petroleum, and the declining industries of the eighties are all closely involved with and dependent on government in a way in which many other Japanese industries are not. In prosperous and independent industries like consumer electronics and automobiles, or in any situation where MITI has to act without wide industry support, the emphasis on consultation and consensus, an approach made necessary as well as desirable by MITI's lack of compulsory powers, works considerably less well than it does when trouble hits and firms and industries begin looking for government help.[46] It is, however, precisely these latter instances, where potential economic conflict is greatest and the government role most intrusive, that provide the best vehicle for this inquiry into the legal context of social conflict and change in Japan.

SIX

Toward a New Perspective on Japanese Law

THE PREVIOUS four chapters have demonstrated that Japanese law can play the same instrumental role in the pursuit of private interests and social goals that it plays in other industrial democracies, but the social implications of law extend beyond its instrumental importance. Law is more than a collection of ingenious devices to avoid or resolve disputes, advance particular interests, or legitimate a specific regime. As Clifford Geertz has argued, law does not just regulate behavior; it interprets behavior and, in doing so, gives it significance and meaning. To understand the significance of Japanese law, therefore, it is not enough to understand its role in social and political struggles; we must also understand the stories it tells, the symbols it deploys, the visions it projects, and how the Japanese use all of these to give meaning to their social life.[1]

The Ideology of Law in Japanese Society

In his article "The Ethics of Harmony and the Logic of the Antimonopoly Law"[2] published at the height of the MITI–FTC debate over the Structurally Depressed Industries Law, political commentator and retired MITI official Amaya Naohiro argued for the extension and strengthening of the SDIL and against the strict enforcement of the Antimonopoly Law. He based his argument on cultural imperatives and the American origin of the AML:

> Japan's history is much different from that of the United States. Japan did not establish the atomistic individual as the basic unit of society and rarely had individuals who "spun off" from society and lived by themselves. Today, as in the old days, the basic unit of Japanese society is not

"atomistic" individuals, but "molecule-like" groups. These groups consist of "villages" and "families." One may consider "families" as monomers and "villages" as polymers. Individuals live as an organic element of their groups within this group structure.

The fundamental ethic which supports a group has been "harmony." Such American values as individual freedom, equality, equal opportunity, and an open-door policy can be considered "foreign proteins" introduced into the traditional body of Japanese society.[3]

That American society also consists of interdependent groups, that Japanese "harmony" frequently masks the suppression of dissident or powerless groups, or that the stability of Japanese "monomers" and "polymers" is dependent ultimately on the satisfaction of their members' individual self-interests might not be denied by Amaya. Even the demonstration that the concepts embodied by the Antimonopoly Law have deep roots in Japanese history, a fact brought out by an FTC representative in a companion article in the same journal,[4] was essentially beside the point because Amaya had already successfully evoked the dominant ideology of Japanese law and society and linked it to the goals and methods of MITI's version of the SDIL.

Given the foreign origin of much of Japanese law, it is not surprising that many Japanese share Amaya's identification of law and litigation with Western individualism, a social characteristic that they contrast with a vision of Japanese society as consensual and harmonious.[5] Until recently, that contrast was usually seen as a shortcoming by scholars of law and development and interpreted either as a fundamental flaw in Japan's social and political development or as a lag in legal development that would disappear as Japanese legal institutions and attitudes caught up with economic and social conditions.[6] The assumed characteristics of Japanese law—the low number of lawyers, the weak role of litigation in dispute resolution, a politically irrelevant judiciary, the absence of detailed contracts and other forms of legal planning from commercial life, and the informal and particularistic relationship of government and business—were identified with premodern social values and legal backwardness.

As Amaya's article shows, however, two decades of increasing Japanese social and economic success vis-à-vis the West have led many observers to reverse the normative evaluation, so that sociolegal characteristics formerly seen as embarrassingly premodern are now celebrated as models for the overly individualistic and litigious West.[7] The "modern" legal system exemplified by the rule-centered model described in Chapter 1 has ceased to be the ideal and assumed destination of Japanese social and legal evolution. Instead, commentators envision a legal system that preserves the social interconnectiveness which they perceive as Japan's unique cultural foundation and which is immune to the corrupting influence of the same individualistic rights consciousness that previous observers had considered a prerequisite to a modern democracy.

For such commentators, the ideal legal system must fit their perception of Japanese society as based on consensus, the denial of individually defined self-interest, and the acceptance of a benevolent hierarchy. Such a legal system would not emphasize the legal function of individuals, since taking individuals as the elemental social unit denies that society is composed of groups each of which is greater than the sum of its members and which together constitute a society that is similarly greater than the sum of its constituent groups. Nor would legal rights and duties, even if wielded by groups rather than individuals, play a large role. Legally assertive interest groups pressing for the uniform application of universal norms to the concrete transactions of social life would destroy the particularistic web of relationships that animates Japanese society and prevent the circumstantial adjustment of group interests that constitutes the Japanese ideal of dispute resolution. This view of society and law is hostile to abstract rules serving as a guide to social action, but it is the abstract nature of the rules and the procedural formality and rationality of their application through litigation, more than the content of any given rule, that is anathema. Even when the rule embodies an appropriate norm, the process of its application denies the value of emotion and circumstance, both of which are essential to the survival of relationships among potentially antagonistic groups and to the normative dominance of consensus in the processes of social conflict and change.

The ideal characteristic of a legal system under this view of society is informality. Informality allows the control of social interaction, whether by private groups, the bureaucracy, or the judiciary, to be particularistic so that consensus can form the basis of dispute resolution. Consensus-based dispute resolution in turn eliminates the instrumental role of universal rules and minimizes the possibility of an individual or a single group using the legal system to challenge the dominant social consciousness while simultaneously enabling the legal system to satisfy the legitimate needs of particular individuals and groups.[8]

Informality also confirms the Japanese people's view of their society as harmonious and conflict-free. Necessary sanctions, including bureaucratic ones, can in most cases be private, indirect, and ambiguous, qualities that can often render them virtually invisible to society at large. Legal informality implies a lack of legally recognized sanctions and hence means legal voluntariness, which, combined with a disinclination to look beyond ideology to empirical reality, reinforces the perception of Japan as a conflict-free and harmonious society. When combined with a constant rhetoric of consensus and harmony, informality also masks the decision-making process and even the existence of decisions at all. Without a formal and open policymaking process, government policies can appear as the inevitable and natural results of custom and consensus rather than as the conscious political choices among mutually antagonistic interests that they actually are. Because they appear natural and inevitable, policy decisions are considered socially legitimate and are virtually immune to legal and political attack. If, by contrast, the same policies were based on clearly delineated statutory powers and decided by formal administrative processes, their political nature would be clear, and social and political debate about their widsom would be possible and appropriate.[9]

That most Japanese believe that their society and legal system largely conform to these ideals seems beyond contradiction if we take their rhetoric seriously. The response of commentators to the Equal Employment Opportunity Act is illustrative: criticism centered not so much on the concept of equality as on the use of law and legal sanctions to bring about social change. Law in this view should be limited to the affirmation of custom, and although it may function to recognize or declare social change, it should not lead, cause, or even contribute to such change. The concept of an instrumental law in Japanese society was literally inconceivable for most observers. Thus, virtually none of the many articles and editorials on either side of the EEOA debate even mentioned the *Sumitomo Cement* line of cases as contributing to the passage of the act, despite the provisions' meticulous paralleling of each of the *Sumitomo* line's doctrinal developments.[10] Instead of acknowledging that here was one instance of law leading social evolution, commentators preferred to characterize the act as solely the result of foreign pressure, as another of Amaya's "foreign proteins."

Similar sentiments abound in all four of the phenomena that we have examined: the Minister of Justice's rejection of antidiscrimination legislation on the ground that "discrimination is a matter of the heart, not the law"; the emphasis of Buraku Liberation League theorists on the spiritual and moral nature of denunciation and the importance of psychological intimacy between denouncer and denounced; the apocalyptic rhetoric of the fishermen and farmers who eventually sued industry in the Big Four pollution cases; the willingness of the presidents of large corporations to apologize personally and abjectly to their opponents and to society and their eventual agreement to pay additional compensation not required by judicial judgment; the assumption by the courts in the pollution cases that a moral, as opposed to legal, relationship existed between polluters and victims and their reliance on that relationship to impose legal obligations on industry and government; the readiness of observers to characterize parties attempting to vindicate legal rights—whether they be Sumitomo Metals or the villagers of Isotsu—as selfish and destructive of community and stability; and the tolerance of the courts and the legal system of forceful tactics such as direct negotiations and denunciation that clearly violate the fundamental norms of the legal system all speak to the dominance of nonlegal rhetoric and imagery in Japanese legal discourse. The same is true of the language of statutes themselves. Not only the Equal Employment Opportunity Act but also the Special Measures Law in the Buraku discrimination context, and the Structurally Depressed Industries and the Petroleum Industry Laws in the industrial policy context, attempt to induce particular social behavior not by granting government agencies formal legal power but by relying on moral exhortation urging citizens to "strive" to meet the goals of the statute.

The Operation of Law in Japanese Society

There are many ways of interpreting the insistence of the Japanese that their legal system functions on the basis of harmony, consensus, and compromise rather than legally binding rights and duties. One is to take each instance of rhetoric and analyze it in terms of the speaker's self-interest, what one might call the negation of Japanese legal imagery. Thus one would point out, *inter alia*, that as a retired MITI bureaucrat Amaya would naturally argue for weakening his former ministry's major rival in the setting of industrial policy; that, however high-minded were the stated goals of the Big Four plaintiffs, they did in fact ask for and receive large sums of money as a direct result of their supposedly selfless actions; and that the replacement of legal sanctions with moral suasion in statutes like the Special Measures Law for Assimilation Projects or the Equal Employment Opportunity Act precisely suits the interests of the Liberal Democratic Party and Japanese industry.

This mode of interpretation is not wrong—indeed, it is necessary to a complete understanding of the rhetoric and the law—but it can only partially capture their true meaning because it assumes that the images that the law evokes in statutes and court decisions and that citizens evoke in their discussion of law can be separated from the "real" motivations and consequences of social action. It denies the interdependence of legal consciousness and social action, a relationship that moved Clifford Geertz to describe law as society's way of "imagining the real."[11] To approach the full meaning of law in Japanese society, one must combine the instrumental analysis of power relationships and social results with an awareness that what people say and believe they are doing is part of social behavior. Thus a full analysis needs to recognize and examine the interdependence between the legal imagery of harmony, consensus, tradition, and litigation and its concrete influence on and role in the management of social conflict and change.

Cultural predispositions notwithstanding, it does not make sense to discuss these concepts, particularly the ideal of consensus, as if they somehow preexist law. In a liberal democracy like Japan, law determines what the power relationships within the group will be by defining who will be in the decision-making group and the kind and degree of sanctions available to them to achieve consensus. Since the decision rule is unanimity, the group must be carefully selected and managed: members must either share fundamentally complementary interests, or those with opposed interests must be excluded or suppressed. Given the preference for the appearance of harmony in Japan, exclusion is preferred to overt suppression, but quiet pressure on members' unrelated outside interests is entirely appropriate.[12]

A simplified review of the industrial policy process, perhaps the area where Japanese consensus and harmony are most frequently celebrated in the West, can illustrate how legal doctrine establishes concrete parameters for policymaking. As was true in the Sumitomo Metals incident of 1964–1965, the formation of the ill-fated oil cartels of 1973–1974, and the "naphtha war" of the 1980s, policy formation begins with informal discussions among MITI bureaucrats and representatives of the leading firms in the immediately concerned industry. When the problem cuts across many industries, this process may take place within a framework of subcommittees and study groups established by the appropriate *shingikai*. Once the basic problem is analyzed and a tentative solution identified, the group is broadened to include suppliers, customers, other affected industries, and related divisions of MITI and other ministries. Once an acceptable compromise is worked out at this level, the full *shingikai* is convened to ratify a formal proposal for MITI action, perhaps a draft statute or criteria for cartelization.

The time-consuming consultation in policy formation lays the groundwork for implementation because by the time a final detailed plan has been worked out, everyone with a recognized interest has had a chance to influence the result or at least to register his complaint. In those relatively rare occasions when circumstances change or one firm is recalcitrant, the group is not without means to compel compliance. In extreme instances like the Sumitomo Metals incident, publicly coordinated bullying by the trade association backed up by threats of indirect legal action by MITI may be necessary, but in the vast majority of cases pressure can be brought quietly on the dissident firm's *keiretsu* allies as well as on the firm itself.

As long as the pressure remains private, the power relationships within the process are disguised by the culturally laden rhetoric of consensus. Even when the use of power becomes overt, the underlying role of law in structuring the consensus and then protecting it from dissidents' attacks remains unspoken and unevaluated. But without statutes meticulously drafted to avoid both the creation of private causes of action and clear criteria for administrative discretion, the consensus makers could not maintain the virtual monopoly over the substance of policymaking and interpretation that they now enjoy; and without the careful nurturing of legal informality in administrative processes, partially through the threshold doctrines of standing and justiciability and partially through the avoidance of procedural formality in statutory drafting, the informality necessary to mask political and economic power would be impossible.

The result of opening up the process of industrial policy, it is imperative to note, would not necessarily be a change in its content. By and large, the substance of current policy enjoys broad support within Japanese society, especially by those most directly concerned, and there is no reason to think that exposing the political choices involved would lead to an immediate rejection of heretofore accepted policies. What would change, however, is the rhetoric of industrial policy: what had formerly appeared through the rose-tinted lens of consensus as the natural result of custom and culture would have to be discussed as the accommodation of conflicting interests. Reasoned accounts would have to be made for what would now emerge as conscious political decisions, and the application of indirect sanctions would have to be defended against charges of bureaucratic overreaching. In the long run the shift in formal legal power, whose initial effect would likely be limited to the power to question, would affect the way in which participants and observers thought about the industrial policy process and might eventually influence the substance of economic policy itself.

More important, however, such a shift would weaken the domination of legal discourse now exercised by the ideology of consensus. This ideology is at the heart of informality throughout the Japanese legal system. Industrial policy and MITI provide highly visible examples on a grand scale, but the same processes are at work in the mediation of environmental disputes and the compensation of pollution victims; the toleration of forceful tactics like denunciation and direct negotiations and the intensive bargaining that they foster in areas like affirmative action grants or superlegal tort compensation; and the attempt through the EEOA to remove employment discrimination from the public forum of the courts to the informality and unaccountability of Ministry of Labor mediation. In any of these or many other areas across Japan's legal landscape, recourse to formal processes, even if the substantive result remained constant, would mean that the management of social conflict would openly contradict the dominant Japanese vision of their society as harmonious and conflict-free. Any weakening of that vision or of the similar and interdependent vision of their legal system as informal and consensual would be much more destabilizing to Japanese society than any substantive changes in, for instance, the amount of tort compensation for pollution victims or the status of women in the workplace.

The essential paradox of consensus is that the better the process functions to control human behavior, the less important it becomes. Because unanimity is required, consensus works best when interests are complementary or when dissidents leave or are suppressed. When such actions are attempted on a social level in a democracy, there are severe limits to the effectiveness of exclusion and suppression. The more parties are excluded from the decision group, the smoother the process and the more complete the consensus, but the less likely it becomes that the result can be effectively extended to the rest of society. If those excluded are powerless or unaware of their exclusion, of course, it does not matter, but in Japan they frequently are neither, and both litigation and limited instrumental force are often available to refute the consensus, demand inclusion, or simply pursue one's own interests.

Whether one views the applicable consensus as the 1959 mediation agreement that reestablished "harmony" in Minamata or the postwar national consensus for economic growth, the Big Four cases demonstrate the potential of litigation in attacking consensus. They exposed the government's neglect of its most fundamental obligations and played a role reminiscent of the Tokugawa *ikki* and Ashio protest marches. The subsequent suits demanding legal accountability and procedural safeguards in environmental management, however, had no place in either the neo-Confucian ideology that animated Tokugawa Japan or the consensus model that had become its contemporary analogue. These suits were asking not for benevolent concern on the government's part, but for an enforceable right to participate in government policymaking and implementation according to a formal and legally defined procedure. These later plaintiffs were asking for legal checks on the process as well as the substance of government behavior rather than assurances of official concern. The government is willing to give sincere avowals of the latter; it abhors the former. The result was the series of legislative and administrative steps that at once reaffirmed government's concern, maintained procedural informality, and marginalized the environmental movement in Japan.

MITI's response to the Oil Cartel cases, as well as the process of economic policymaking in general, repeats the pattern of bureaucratic concern for the preservation of procedural informality in the face of judicial intrusions. The threat posed by the High Court opinions to the informal and vertical nature of industrial policy was effectively countered, at least for the immediate future, by the widening of the consensus group to include the Fair Trade Commission and its avoidance of direct legal coercion in the cartelization process. Although the FTC's inclusion and the generally increasing power of Japanese industry may mean some changes in substantive policies, this seems to have been of less concern to MITI than the maintenance of informal policymaking.

The Structurally Depressed Industries Law institutionalized and legitimated the continued use of *shingikai* and their myriad subcommittees and study groups, which give the impression of consideration of a wide variety of public concerns and interests while avoiding any loosening of control over the process of policymaking. As with the mediation and compensation systems in the pollution context, problems in industrial policy are heard and dealt with on an informal and bilateral basis. Interest groups play a major role in the form of the industry associations, economic federations, and so on, but the role is cooperative and informal rather than formal and adversarial. Equally important, the nature and number of participating groups are entirely within the bureaucracy's hands. As with the later environmental litigation, a major factor in MITI's ability to control both the participants and the process of participation is Japanese administrative law. Statutes like the SDIL combine with the doctrines of standing, justiciability, and so forth to enable the ministries to maintain control over the policymaking process and force participants, even industry representatives, into supplicatory roles. The process works smoothly because both the bureaucracy and business recognize their symbiotic identity of interest and because potentially disaffected parties are hindered in forming politically effective groups and denied any legal right to independent participation in the decision-making process.

When we compare the Burakumin and employment discrimination case studies with the pollution experience, the fit is somewhat more ambiguous. Both groups are pursuing norms which, if realized, could destabilize the corporate workplace, the perceived source of Japan's postwar social and economic success. In this sense they pose a greater potential threat than even the antipollution movement despite their current meager popular support; their goal of equal access and equal opportunity would mean a substantial restructuring of Japanese society. In spite of the clear constitutional norms supporting equality, contemporary social practice and government policy leave little room for equality for either women or minorities, not necessarily because of sincere beliefs that either group is unable to perform well but because the diversity and flexibility introduced into the workplace by women and minorities threaten to destroy the social and psychological basis of Japan's political stability and economic success. It is in this context that we should understand the tactics of denunciation and litigation and the government's response to them.

Although in both cases the process is incomplete and the outcome uncertain, the government response seems to be aimed at maintaining control over the process of social change rather than at preventing it. In this sense, tacit toleration of denunciation is understandable. In the middle and late 1960s two paths were open to the Buraku liberation movement: a path toward full integration with majority society through equal opportunity, or one toward the improvement of material conditions for Burakumin and a "separate but equal" type of material equality. The two paths are not mutually exclusive, but denunciation as a tactic is extremely limited in achieving integration, and the Buraku Liberation League has not even tried to use it in that direction in any consistent manner. The result has been continued insulation of the mainstream from the Buraku movement, which remains directed at local governments and incremental material advances within the current social and economic structure. To the extent that denunciation limits the BLL's ability to appeal effectively to the norm of equal opportunity, it is natural for the government to prefer it to litigation—it achieves incremental social progress without threatening the particularistic norms of justice that underlie the government's mode of social control. As long as the BLL is directing its energy and protest against the bureaucracy through denunciation rather than against basic public and private policies through the courts, the government can be sure of continued control over the pace and nature of the movement.

The Ministry of Labor's response to the women employees' litigation is consistent with this interpretation. Although adroit maneuvering by corporate personnel departments has managed to maintain discriminatory employment practices in the years since the *Sumitomo Cement* decision, most observers agree that bureaucratic measures against early retirement and similarly discredited practices are, though belated, effective and in good faith. This may not be true of the Ministry's response to demands for equal access to management track positions. Even here the official rhetoric is one of eventual equality, but the EEOA leaves the definition and enforcement of equality up to the Ministry. As with the Special Measures Law in the Buraku context, the EEOA may have been politically significant, but it leaves legal control squarely in government hands. Greater equality may result, but it will be on the bureaucracy's terms. This does not leave total discretion to the government; working women and their supporters will continue legal and political pressure and will influence the pace and nature of change through lobbying, participation on consulative bodies, and litigation, but the government will attempt mightily to keep the forum for the ultimate battles out of the courts and within the bureaucracy.

Maintaining control in this context, however, may not be so easy. The government may not be willing to meet the demands of the women's movement for completely equal opportunity to the extent that they have met those of pollution victims or Burakumin, and thus there will remain a larger number of dissatisfied potential plaintiffs to continue to push the legal norms in the direction of equality. Whether such plaintiffs will be successful is of course unclear at present, but if they are, we may see litigation continue to play the role that it has in the last fifteen years—that of reflecting and contributing to changing social norms and simultaneously forcing the pace of the government's response to such changes. Such continued success is uncertain, but even if it occurs, the limitations in popular support and judicial remedies, neither of which will have been strengthened by the passage of the EEOA, will mean that the ultimate forum for substantial change will likely remain bureaucratic, rather than legislative or judicial.

If we step back from these four phenomena and seek a more general perspective on the role of litigation in contemporary Japan, a number of observations can be made. First, litigation raising highly charged moral issues can serve the role historically played by peasant rebellions—that is, it can be a vehicle for popular protest against a neglectful regime. In circumstances where plaintiffs can demonstrate that they have been excluded not only from the political process but also from a fair share of social benefits, litigation can provide a forum for the dramatic presentation of their plight to the nation. Its formal processes and universalistic rhetoric help to identify political allies and rally popular support, win or lose, in a way that other political strategies such as protest marches or instrumental force along the lines of denunciation or direct negotiations cannot. In this type of litigation, the prime examples of which are the early pollution cases, process and form are all-important, and the role of the judge and substantive legal norms is secondary. In this sense protest litigation, at least at its initiation, is purely political and fits neither the judge-centered nor the rule-centered model of Chapter 1. If the cases become part of a successful political and social movement, however, the judges' role can acquire great social importance, and morally powerful opinions like those in the *Minamata* and *Kawamoto* cases can embody and declare the existence of a new social consensus that is politically binding on the society as a whole as well as the specific defendants.

It is much more difficult to evaluate the role of less morally charged litigation. The women's litigation presented here is susceptible to two mutually contradictory interpretations. The first would emphasize the continuing sex-based segregation in the workplace and the toothless quality of the EEOA and conclude that the formal doctrinal advances of the *Sumitomo Cement* line of cases have only hardened male attitudes and actually worsened the economic situation of female employees. This interpretation would be consistent with critiques of American social litigation that claim that even doctrinally successful litigation worsens the situation of the less powerful in society not only by diverting attention from more effective direct political action but also because their formal victories legitimate the continuation of substantive injustice.[13] The second possible interpretation would emphasize the effectiveness of the Ministry of Labor's belated enforcement of judicially developed doctrine and the egalitarian rhetoric of the EEOA. While acknowledging the small number of women directly benefited by successful litigation and the ultimate weaknesses of litigation as a lever for substantial political change, this view would argue that the judicial rhetoric of the *Sumitomo Cement* line of cases represented the "imagining" of a new order and thus that these cases are more politically powerful than their immediate material results would imply.[14] According to this interpretation, continued success in the courts would legally pressure the bureaucracy to interpret the EEOA to prohibit discrimination in areas heretofore untouched by judicial doctrine and simultaneously would contribute to a social consciousness that demanded such an interpretation.

It is much too early to tell whether women will be able to continue to litigate successfully in the face of the political force of the EEOA,[15] but no one would argue that litigation alone will be determinative in the future of female workers. Sex discrimination in employment will not escape the general rule that the Japanese government simply will not allow important social decisions to be made outside of bureaucratic influence. Whether in the morally charged Big Four cases or the incrementalist women's movement, it is the government that has been the major player. The defendants may be private companies and the doctrines private law, but the object of the struggle is official policy and attitudes. Even among activist lawyers with their strong antigovernment bias, there is the general expectation that the ultimate actor in any protest movement must be the government. Despite the experience of the Big Four and *Sumitomo Cement* line of cases, the concept of achieving even incremental social change directly through the legal system, that is, by setting legal precedents to be employed by subsequent plaintiffs independent of government participation, is largely absent today in Japan. So, too, is the broader concept of a private sector distinct from a public one where private actors determine their own destinies with little governmental involvement or interest. In this sense, the social conflict we have examined contains parallels to the industrial policy case study—the government is a central actor in the development of protest and response even in instances where the interaction is initially among private parties. The common denominator in conflict and consensus, in litigation and denunciation, is the primacy of politics over law. And it is a politics of consultation and identification with the bureaucrats; whether the vehicle is *shingikai*, denunciation, or litigation, effective avenues of social conflict, change, and control eventually lead to the government.

This centrality of the bureaucracy and denigration of independent legal action are often ascribed to the strength of Japanese traditional values, as are the other characteristics of the legal system emphasized here, particularism and informality. The Confucian world-order held no place for law distinct from politics, and no area of social life was immune from the reach of the political order. Similarly, the Tokugawa Period was marked by the same hierarchically organized, informal dispute resolution that permeates contemporary Japan. Then as now, the subjects' relationship with officialdom was one of dependence, with no third party like the judiciary applying universal rules to cover the encounter. Given these broad similarities, though, what are we to make of them? Are they related as cause and effect, or in some more ambiguous manner?

To address this issue, we must reverse the usual sequence of discussions of Japanese law and society and ask not what kind of society will produce a particularistic and informal legal system like that of Japan, but instead what social values would be encouraged by the type of legal system portrayed in these case studies. I adopt this view of the causal relationship not because I believe the legal system is immune to the influence of social values but in order to dramatize the incompleteness of the conventional view of law and society in non-Western cultures, which all too often assumes a unilateral influence of culture on law. The reversal of the usual sequence will also emphasize what has been a theme of this book: that many characteristics of Japanese law thought to be traditional are in fact the consequence of recent and conscious human choice and are best studied with the understanding that they are more than lingering remnants of a past society or the products of relatively immutable cultural values.

The issue of tradition is dramatically posed if one returns briefly to the fate of the Japanese government—business relationship if it were governed by the doctrines of American administrative law: the choice of *shingikai* members would be legally challenged as being nonrepresentative. The adoption by the *shingikai* of goals, plans, and methods for structural transformation of declining industries would be attacked by disgruntled outsiders as unfair to consumers or harmful to the environment or, as is occurring now in U.S.-Japanese relations, a violation of the principles of free trade. MITI initiatives to establish export or import cartels, as in the Sumitomo Metals case, would be immediately reviewable under the Administrative Procedure Act, and the criteria for firm production allocations would be scrutinized by a court using a much narrower scope of discretion. Perhaps even more disruptive would be the likelihood that dissatisfied competitors, customers, suppliers, and consumers would bring civil antitrust actions demanding treble damages against complying firms. Broadly drafted statutes like the SDIL would not eliminate the problem, since courts would require detailed administratively created criteria in the place of statutory criteria. These hypothetical situations are made more threatening by the likely effect of relaxed administrative law doctrines on the formation of outside interest groups. Many Japanese commentators on and participants in the current system would argue that it works so well and the participants are so disdainful of litigation that few would avail themselves of the possibility of litigation. Even if that appraisal, however implausible to many observers, is correct for those presently within the system, it certainly would not hold for those now excluded. It seems extremely unlikely that the availability of legal challenges would not be exploited by outside interest groups, which would in turn be strengthened organizationally by their new legal muscle, resulting in a self-strengthening sequence of litigation leading to stronger opposition groups and eventually more litigation.

Japanese bureaucrats are very aware of this possibility. Both the deliberate exclusion of private causes of action for discrimination in the Special Measures Law for Assimilation Projects and the Equal Employment Opportunity Law and the government's reactions to the possibility of increased litigation posed by proposals for a legally binding environmental impact assessment requirement clearly imply a hostility to independent legal action. Despite frequent comment about the role of cultural values in the government–business relationship, the bureaucrats' actions are eloquent testimony to their belief in the vital importance of legal doctrine in maintaining those values. There remains the question of causality—of whether legal doctrines and institutions reflect or create social consciousness—but this may, in fact, be the wrong question since it is clear that they are interdependent. The lack of legal options forces the businesses in the private sector into an informal, consultative relationship with the bureaucrats (and with one another), but the social consciousness that makes such a relationship appear natural and desirable is equally crucial to its continued vitality.

The interdependence of traditional values and contemporary legal doctrine is most apparent in the ongoing "harmony" of industrial policy. Informality and particularism are intended to avoid conflict by engendering interdependence and mutual trust, and the appearance of open conflict, as in the other three case studies, indicates a breakdown in the system and the appearance of "nontraditional" values and Western legalism. But even here the overt manipulation of the legal system to forestall the further spread of litigation and to reinvent the traditional consciousness demonstrates the importance of law. The pollution experience and the Buraku liberation movement also indicate the success of such manipulation. The women's movement and its use of litigation may present a potentially more serious threat, but it seems clear that the government intends to react to this challenge as it has in the past, that is, by asserting its primacy in the resolution of individual cases through administrative guidance and mediation and thereby maintaining control over the issue of the role of women in the workplace.

In this book I have attempted to question the easy assumption that the particularism and informality of Japanese law are the result of the continued strength of traditional values. I have argued that these values are maintained, if not created, by legal rules and institutions as well as by social inertia and that this legal structure is the result of conscious choice. Implicit in much of the discussion, however, is the related, perhaps more fundamental question of the origin of the traditional values themselves. If these values are consistently recreated and strengthened by conscious choice, one would be remiss to fail to inquire whether they in fact ever existed in past Japanese society at all. Might not what is "traditional" be not only maintained by present policy but also the total creation of such policy?

To an extent, of course, the answer must be yes. Whatever its origin, all ideology is constantly in need of servicing; it follows that ideology is constantly being modified, and it would be difficult to deny that it is in a sense new. But as with the causality question, this is the wrong inquiry. There is no question that the characteristics of hierarchy, harmony, and so on fostered by Japanese law were present in prewar or Tokugawa social consciousness, and to that extent they are a continuation of past values. But as recent scholarship on the peasant *ikki* demonstrates,[16] the totality of Tokugawa society cannot be captured by these characteristics any more than can that of contemporary society. Just as there are now, there were then contrary social currents in Japan that represented values quite antithetical to the conventional view of Japanese traditional values. What has happened is a conscious choice by those with the power to make and implement such choices about which traditions to maintain and which to discard and then how to maintain or foster those chosen. As we have seen, the manipulation of the legal system is one such method.

Eastern Technique, Western Virtue: American Images of Japanese Law

Sakuma Shōzan, a late Tokugawa reformer and advocate of learning from the West, created the phrase "Eastern morals, Western science,"[17] which became the catchword of Meiji modernization policy. Western learning was to be imported and adapted, but the Eastern spirit, most especially Japan's unique polity, was to be protected from Western corruption. Now, a little more than a hundred years after the opening of Japan, prominent American politicians, judges, and academics are calling for a reversal of the direction of cultural borrowing and the reform of the American legal system on the Japanese model. Whether this idea is phrased quaintly as "giving Confucius a chance" or in explicitly economic terms ("engineers make the pie grow larger; lawyers only decide how to divide it up"), the urge to learn from Japan is only one manifestation of a general dissatisfaction with the American legal system and the common perception that litigation in our country is inefficient, unfair, and rapidly increasing.[18]

Although varied and multifaceted, much of the dissatisfaction reflects a growing body of opinion that the American legal system is unnecessarily formal and complex. In this view, American society is overly dependent on legal solutions to social problems and yet so hamstrung by American lawyers' preoccupation with procedural justice that the legal system is required to deal with complicated social, economic, and political problems through an adversarial process that frequently loses sight of substantive justice in its obsession with procedural fairness. The result, one is told, is bewildering complexity in rules and procedures, great delays, enormous cost, and a system that may work superbly in the great cases—the brain surgery of litigation— where both sides have unlimited legal resources, but that denies access to either procedural or substantive justice to the great majority of Americans. According to this critique, the perverse response of the legal system to its acknowledged failings is invariably yet another layer of rules and formality, with the result that litigation has become a self-perpetuating, all-consuming machine producing legal justice totally out of touch with social reality.[19]

Some of the most thoughtful criticism has focused on government regulation and the doctrines of American administration law that allegedly make it more formal, costly, and time-consuming than necessary.[20] The combination of new forms of regulation and the emergence and participation of public interest groups in policy formation and enforcement has led to what many commentators believe is an explosion in judicial review of and intervention in bureaucratic proceedings.[21] The constant threat of litigation has arguably resulted in a policymaking process that is preoccupied with the formal vindication of procedural rights—what one commentator referred to as "central planning through litigation"[22]—and that is thereby too rigid to discern, much less implement, fair and efficient regulatory policy. Instead of being allowed to set wise public policy based on their professional competence, American bureaucrats are seen as being at the mercy of hordes of legal mercenaries engaged in a zero-sum struggle from which only the lawyers profit.

Whether the concern is an overly contentious society, unjust and expensive legal machinery, or a legally paralyzed bureaucracy, commentators uniformly propose increased legal informality as part of the solution.[23] These proposals vary from a romantic longing for a village elders' style of communal dispute resolution[24] to elaborate recommendations for specific reforms in the doctrines governing administrative procedure. The relevance of Japan's experience with legal informality to this very American controversy in unclear, but casual reference to Japan is frequent, and explicit proposals for adoption of one or more Japanese techniques or models are not uncommon. Unfortunately, such references to Japan are most often based on a unidimensional view of Japanese legal phenomena, because the American perspective on Japanese law has concentrated overwhelmingly on the informal settlement of individual disputes and virtually ignored the implications of informality for the legal system and for the course of social change as a whole. Of course the value of increased informality in American law cannot be determined from even the most thorough explication of the Japanese experience, but it may be useful to review some of the major themes of this book from the perspective of their implications for the United States.

Legal informality in America exists in a vastly different social context from that in Japan. The formality and preoccupation with process now so closely identified with the American legal system are not simply a product of lawyers' self-interest and professional training; they are also inextricably tied to the individualistic strain in our cultural tradition. From Alexis de Tocqueville to Amaya Naohiro, foreign observers have noted the strength of American individualism and its influence on Americans' concept of justice, and though Amaya's chemical metaphor is both simplistic and self-serving, modern observers of America have also noted an increasing dominance of radical—what Amaya called atomistic—individualism in American moral discourse.[25] One concomitant of this type of individualism is an overweening position given to the rhetoric of personal freedom and choice, which are often equated and reduced to the freedom to act autonomously in pursuit of one's own values and ideals. From this vision of self comes a vision of society as made up of individuals each free of others' demands and competing with one another in pursuit of unconnected and independent vision of the good.

The implications of such a social consciousness for the legal system and for conceptions of justice are profound. If society is built on individualism and competition and the only acknowledged common ground is enlightened self-interest, social life becomes a desperate contest and community nothing more than a temporary equilibrium among fundamentally unconnected and potentially antagonistic actors. Because mutual trust and personal relationships are contingent and make unreliable guides for resolving conflict, the rules of the contest and the mode of their application become all-important. And because the judge/referee, as another unconnected and self-interested individual, is not trustworthy in himself, the rules must be unambiguous and their application automatic and free of personal choice. In such a world where the paramount values are personal autonomy and choice, the rules are likely to be procedural rather than substantive and the mode of interpreting and applying these rules formal and logical rather than informal and consensual.

This vision of American society and justice, which corresponds closely to the rule-centered model of Chapter 1, is no more real than Amaya's vision of a 1980s village Japan. Nor does it account for the many other conflicting visions of law and society held by Americans. Just as Japan has traditions of dissension and conflict, America has traditions of community and substantive justice within which freedom and personal choice were merely means to greater and shared social ends.[26] But the perception of society as no more than the sum of its atomistic parts and of justice as the logical interplay of formal rules dominates contemporary America, not only in the rhetoric of national politics but also in the very way Americans define morality and justice.[27] That these visions of social life are contrary to the way Americans live, that they may in actuality not even be shared by a majority of Americans,[28] does not change the fact that legal informality in America is forced to exist in an intellectual and legal culture that is profoundly suspicious of the very practices that have made informality so apparently successful in the Japanese context.

Cultural attitudes are not the only obstacle to increasing legal informality in the United States, however. To return to the language of Clifford Geertz, Americans can learn to "imagine the real" in a way much more respectful of the web of relationships that unite them than that described by contemporary legal ideology. Neglected traditions of community and shared values could be revived, and the other voice of American moral discourse identified by Carol Gilligan—a voice that stresses relationships and connections rather than logic and rules— could by presented as the better part of all Americans rather than marginalized as feminine.[29] Culture alone could not prevent the informalization of American law—indeed, changes in the way the law portrays social reality will influence Americans' attitudes about society and justice just as surely as those attitudes have helped to shape the legal system. But advocates of the introduction of Japanese-style informality have not only to overcome cultural suspicion but also to devise ways to cope with institutional and structural aspects of both the formal legal system and society at large that are part of and have developed in response to the formalism that reformers want to decrease.

Perhaps the most important structural obstacles concern the legal role and nature of bureaucratic action. In each of the case studies of Japanese social conflict and change that we have examined, the government has played a leading role. Even in the pollution and employment discrimination areas where the government was initially largely inactive, once the level of conflict was perceived as serious, the bureaucracy intervened to regain control of the pace of social change, if not its direction. Invariably the mode of intervention has been legally informal: whether it was directive mediation in the Minamata incident and later throughout the environmental area, negotiations with the Buraku Liberation League and the establishment of a legally informal system of affirmative action in Osaka, Article 12 of the Equal Employment Opportunity Act giving the Ministry of Labor authority to "guide" future antidiscrimination efforts, or the consultative form of policymaking under the Structurally Depressed Industries Law, the result has always been broad discretionary power to manage conflict and allocate resources. The legal basis of the discretion has been legal informality, not only in terms of the doctrines of standing and justiciability that limit judicial review, but also in the absence of the formal procedures and open hearings that characterize American bureaucratic policymaking.

Similar problems in the United States also require governmental intervention, but a fundamental distrust of bureaucratic discretion has led to a legal and institutional environment hostile to legally informal bureaucratic action. In the first place, the encouragement of private enforcement by the creation of private causes of action and by awards of attorneys' fees and treble damages in fields such as the environment, discrimination, and antitrust has effectively delegated much of the policymaking function in these areas to private litigants and the courts rather than the bureaucracy. Since the courts have the last word on statutory interpretation, parallel judicial involvement not only dilutes enforcement authority, decreasing bureaucratic influence over potential plaintiffs and defendants; it also provides a continuing check on the agency's discretion in interpreting its statutory mandate. It is precisely this type of dilution of power and narrowing of discretion that the myriad institutional mediation schemes in Japanese law are intended to forestall. The clearest examples are perhaps the Equal Opportunity Mediation Commission created by the EEOA and the three-tier dispute resolution process established by the Law for the Resolution of Pollution Disputes, but the Structurally Declining Industries Law played the same role in relation to the Oil Cartel cases and the MITI–FTC relationship: it "informalized" a previously judicially interpreted relationship. Such bureaucratic schemes cover potential conflict in virtually all areas of society and constitute a dramatic statement of the importance accorded their policymaking monopoly by Japanese bureaucrats. At least for them, the maintenance of legal informality within bureaucratic institutions—the creation of mutual trust on which the compromise, consultation, and concessions of informal policymaking rely—would be severely compromised, if not rendered impossible, by simultaneous judicial activity in the same policy areas.

Even without private causes of action, however, informality in the Japanese sense would be difficult to maintain in the American bureaucratic setting. One of the keys to the many successes of Japanese bureaucrats—and, conversely, one of the causes of their occasional failures—has been their ability to limit the interests involved in informal policymaking so that the unanimity required by consensus could be attained. The doctrines governing judicial review of administrative action would make similar control exceedingly difficult in the United States. Standing, justiciability, and scope of discretion are all interpreted much more aggressively by American courts than by Japanese, and it is difficult to imagine their fundamental reformulation in the near future given continued distrust of unsupervised bureaucratic discretion in all sectors of American politics. Even if judicial review were limited, it is likely that the underlying rationale for, say, expanded standing would continue to be enforced at the level of intervention in administrative proceedings. Any attempts at consensual policymaking, therefore, would have to contend with interests that were potentially mutually antagonistic. Nor would it likely be possible for the sponsoring agency to choose only "reasonable" representatives of conflicting interests, as is largely the Japanese bureaucrats' prerogative in the *shingikai* process. On the contrary, lawyer representatives of each subgroup of each public interest or industry group would vie for a seat at the negotiation table and would use litigation or the threat thereof as leverage.

None of these factors or the many other aspects of the American legal environment at least ostensibly hostile to legal informality would necessarily prevent successfully increasing the use of Japanese-style policymaking. Informal bureaucratic activity has long coexisted with legal formality in the American government; informal dispute settlement is, or course, the norm rather than the exception in private disputes; and it should be possible to devise techniques to protect formal legal rights within informal settings.[30] Doing so, however, will have an impact beyond the immediate effect on the legal system. To the extent that greater informality means greater bureaucratic discretion, it will also mean greater power for a bureaucracy that cannot generally compare with the Japanese in terms of competence, training, prestige, support, or stability. Although elite bureaucracies exist in the United States and more could certainly be created, this is hardly the current political trend. More likely is the continued deterioration of bureaucratic expertise and resources, which would make the public role in informal policymaking much more episodic and haphazard in the United States than in Japan. The less effective the government role, the more danger there is that the result of informally negotiated policy will be either a return to the discredited era of brokered deals and captured agencies or an increased possibility of catastrophic errors, or both. Certainly firms like Sumitomo Metals would argue that brokered deals are not impossible in MITI's industrial policy, and no one would deny that Japanese pollution policy in the 1950s and 1960s was a profound physical, economic, and political disaster. Given the relative mediocrity of the American bureaucracy, the likelihood of such results becomes particularly high if, as seems necessary, closed meetings replace open hearings and the threat of both direct and collateral judicial scrutiny is reduced.

Finally, to return both to culture and the Japanese context, Americans should be aware, as were Meiji leaders like Sakuma Shōzan, that any fundamental reformation of their legal system will not simply increase efficiency or improve decision making; it will also change the way in which Americans imagine their society and conceptualize justice. There is without doubt an enormous amount we can and should learn from the Japanese visions of justice and society, especially at a time in American social history when the values of community and social responsibility seem particularly devalued. In learning, however, we must not lose sight of both the contexts and the implications of those visions. We must, for example, ask ourselves whether and to what extent we wish to move toward a legal culture where the Minister of Justice, when asked why he opposed legislation to make Buraku discrimination illegal, responded that "discrimination is a matter of the heart, not the law."

Notes

Except in citations to English-language sources, Japanese names are written in Japanese form, with surname followed by given name.

1. Models of Law and Social Change

1. In his influential article "The Myth of the Reluctant Litigant," *Journal of Japanese Studies*, 4 (1978), 359, John O. Haley notes that "the belief that the Japanese are an exceptionally nonlitigious people is remarkably pervasive" and, in note 1, cites more than ten works as a "sampling of sources." In characterizing this literature, Haley notes that Japanese and foreign commentators are "almost unanimous in attributing to the Japanese an unusual and deeply rooted cultural preference for informal, mediated settlement of private disputes and a corollary aversion to the formal mechanisms of judicial adjudication." Perhaps the most influential works Haley cites are those written by Kawashima Takeyoshi, including his classic *Nihonjin no hō ishiki* [The legal consciousness of the Japanese] (Tokyo: Iwanami Shoten, 1967) and his English article, "Dispute Resolution in Contemporary Japan," in *Law in Japan: The Legal Order in a Changing Society*, ed. Arthur T. von Mehren (Cambridge, Mass.: Harvard University Press, 1963), 41–72. Another influential English source for a cultural explanation of Japanese legal behavior is Yoshiyuki Noda, *Introduction to Japanese Law* (Tokyo: University of Tokyo Press, 1976), 159–183.

2. Chin Kim and Craig M. Lawson, "The Law of the Subtle Mind: The Traditional Japanese Conception of Law," *International and Comparative Law Quarterly*, 28 (1979), 491.

3. For a discussion of the number of legally trained personnel in Japan, see Isaac Shapiro, Michael Young, and Kōichirō Fujikura, *The Role of Law and Lawyers in Japan and the U.S.* (Washington, D.C.: Smithsonian Institute Roundtable Discussion, 1983). For a discussion of the Japanese litigation rate, see Haley, "Myth," 362–364; and Marc Galanter, "Reading the Landscape of Disputes: What We Know and Don't Know (and Think We Know) about Our Allegedly Contentious and Litigious Society," *UCLA Law Review*, 31 (1983), 4–72. For a discussion of institutional barriers, including those created by the courts themselves, see J. Mark

Ramseyer, "The Costs of the Consensual Myth: Antitrust Enforcement and Institutional Barriers to Litigation in Japan," *Yale Law Journal*, 94 (1985), 604–645; Masao Oki, "Japanese Rights' Consciousness: The Nature of Japan's Judicial System," *Look Japan*, 10 January 1984, 4; and John O. Haley, "Sheathing the Sword of Justice in Japan: An Essay on Law without Sanctions," *Journal of Japanese Studies*, 8 (1982), 265; see also Haley, "Myth."

In his "Myth" article, Haley traces officially established barriers to litigation from the "formidable system of procedural barriers" (p. 371) of the Tokugawa Period (1603–1868) that "coerced" litigants to conciliation and compromise rather than litigation; through the mandatory conciliation statutes of the prewar period which were implemented, according to Haley, not because of popular dissatisfaction with the courts but because of "concern on the part of the governing elite that litigation was destructive to a hierarchical social order based upon personal relationships" (p. 373); to the present government's clear policy of drastically limiting the number of lawyers and judges (p. 385). Although avoiding any direct characterization of governmental motives for the postwar policies, Haley argues that the combination of low numbers of licensed legal professionals and restrictive statutory and judicial doctrines has led, in his opinion, to a judiciary so institutionally weak that it has become, at least at times, "naked and powerless as a political organ" (p. 388).

4. For an insightful portrayal of the judiciary's role in brokering the interests involved in land use planning, see Michael Young, "Judicial Review of Administrative Guidance," *Columbia Law Review*, 84 (1984), 923. See also Margaret McKean, *Environmental Protest and Citizen Politics in Japan* (Berkeley: University of California Press, 1981); Lawrence Ward Beer, *Freedom of Expression in Japan* (Tokyo: Kodansha International, 1985); T. J. Pempel, *Policy and Politics in Japan: Creative Conservatism* (Philadelphia: Temple University Press, 1982); Naoki Kobayashi, "The Small and Medium-Sized Enterprises Organization Law," in *Japanese Politics: An Inside View*, ed. Hiroshi Itoh (Ithaca, N.Y.: Cornell University Press, 1973); and Tadashi Hanami, "Conflict and Its Resolution in Industrial Relations and Labor Law," in Ellis Krauss, Thomas P. Rohlen, and Patricia G. Steinhoff, *Conflict in Japan* (Honolulu: University of Hawaii Press, 1984). Note that the index in the last work contains not a single entry under "law," "litigation," or "lawyers." The reason, one might infer, is that although scholars are aware that law may play a significant role in specific contexts, they have not recognized it as a separate topic for general analysis.

5. I make no claim that law can achieve social change regardless of the political context. See, generally, Frances Fox Piven and Richard A. Cloward, *Poor People's Movements: Why They Succeed, How They Fail* (New York: Vintage Books, 1977).

6. The models assume the availability of and recourse to litigation and thus focus primarily on its function in social conflict. In that sense they represent a narrower perspective of law's role than do the case studies, which often include the absence of litigation. But the failure to litigate in the course of social conflict, whether because of doctrinal problems, judicial incapacity, or a subjective preference for informality, is itself necessarily and intimately connected to the role of litigation.

7. It will surprise no one to learn that the rule-centered model strongly resembles the American ideal of a "rule of law, not of men" or that, although widely acknowledged as unattainable, it retains a powerful influence on American attitudes toward law. See, for example, Jerome Frank, *Law and the Modern Mind* (Garden City: Anchor Books, 1963), where it is referred to as the "mechanistic" model; Owen M. Fiss, "Against Settlement," *Yale Law Journal*, 93 (1984), 1073, where it is referred to as the "dispute-resolution" model; and Abram Chayes, "The Role of the Judge in Public Law Litigation," *Harvard Law Review*, 89 (May 1976), 1281, where it is referred to as the "traditional" model.

8. The judge-centered model is loosely based on descriptions of recent developments in litigation in the United States. See Chayes, "Role of the Judge," and Fiss, "Against Settlement."

9. See Lon Fuller, "The Forms and Limits of Adjudication," *Harvard Law Review*, 92 (1978), 353. For an argument that, legitimate or not, the courts are unequipped to make public policy in the mode evoked by the model, see Donald L. Horowitz, *The Courts and Social Policy* (Washington, D.C.: Brookings Institute, 1977).

10. Although the distinctions among the declaration, formation, and enforcement of norms may be artificial, the rule-centered model of litigation assumes their validity. The judge-centered model not only denies their validity but also proclaims the legitimacy of an affirmative role for the courts in the process of social conflict and change.

11. There are enormous practical problems that would prevent the perfect penetration of official norms envisioned by the rule-centered model. Even without the practical objections, moreover, the ideal of the uniform application of universal legal norms is subject to the fundamental objection that it attributes to legal rules a single determinant meaning when applied over a host of particular settings. In fact most authoritative norms, whether propounded by legislatures or courts, are ambiguous and indeterminant. The judge-centered model of litigation, on the other hand, may describe with some accuracy what some American courts are doing in some cases, but at best it describes a role played by a few courts in one society at one stage in its political history. See Marc Galanter, "The Radiating Effects of Courts," in *Empirical Theories about Courts*, ed. K. Boyum and L. Mather (New York: Longman, 1983).

12. Judges do, of course, have a recognized policy role in Japan; see, for example, Tanase Takao, "Bengoshi no daitoshi shūchū to sono kinōteki igi—shokuiki kakudai to shakaiteki yakuwari no tenkan," *Hanrei Taimuzu* Bessatsu no. 3, *Gendai shakai to bengoshi* [Special Issue no. 3, Contemporary society and the lawyer] (1977), 45–85 (translated as "The Urbanization of Lawyers and Its Functional Significance: Expansion in the Range of Work Activities and Change in Social Role," *Law in Japan: An Annual*, 13 [1980], 20): "Saiban e no shinrai to saiban riyō kōdō" [Confidence in litigation and the utilization of litigation], *Minshō Hō Zasshi*, 80 (1979), 377; 80 (1978), 535; 81 (1979), 35; "Saiban no seisaku keisei kinō to funsō shori kinō" [The policymaking role of litigation and its dispute resolution role], *Minshō Hō Zasshi*, 75 (1976), 51; and Tanaka Shigeaki, "Saiban ni kitai sarete iru yakuwari" [The role expected of litigation], *Minshō Hō Zasshi*, 75 (1976), 31; "Shimin undō ni okeru kenri to saiban: sono hōteki senryaku no haikei to igi o

megutte" [Rights and litigation in citizens' movements: Focusing on their background and significance as a legal tactic], *Minshō Hō Zasshi*, 76 (1977), 633; 76 (1977), 779; 77 (1977), 161; and 77 (1977), 321. However, the more common appraisal is that the courts are relatively powerless; see, for example, John O. Haley's comment that the judiciary is so institutionally weak that it often appears "naked and powerless" when opposing government action ("Myth," p. 388).

13. One type of innovative Japanese statute now attracting attention in the West is that of establishing institutions for alternative dispute resolution in fields such as family and environmental disputes and the compensation of victims of industrial pollution. See Julian Gresser, Kōichirō Fujikura, and Akio Morishima, *Environmental Law in Japan* (Cambridge, Mass.: MIT Press, 1981), 285–349; and Taimie L. Bryant, "Mediation of Divorce Disputes in the Japanese Family Court System with Emphasis on the Tokyo Family Court," Ph.D. diss., University of California, Los Angeles, 1984.

14. See, for example, Aoki Michio et al., eds., *Ikki*, 6 vols. (Tokyo: Tokyo University Press, 1983), and Stephen Vlastos, "Tokugawa Peasant Movements in Fukushima: Conflict and Peasant Mobilization," Ph.D. diss., University of California, Berkeley, 1977, for evidence of conflict and rights consciousness in the Tokugawa Period.

15. Most observers would agree that this assumption is likely true. Certainly the Japanese think that it is true, as shown by the responses to a Kyoto University survey; see Kyoto University Law Faculty Dispute Resolution Seminar, "Hōishiki to funsō shori—hōishiki chōsa chūkan hōkoku" [Legal consciousness and the resolution of disputes: Survey of legal consciousness interim report] (1978). For empirical scholarship on the nature and extent of such informal mediation, see Rokumoto Kahei, *Minji funsō no hōteki kaiketsu* [The legal resolution of civil disputes] (Tokyo: Iwanami Shoten, 1971).

16. Civil Code sec. 770 provides for contested divorce when "there exists [a] grave reason for which it is difficult for [one of the spouses] to continue the marriage." For a thorough and insightful study of divorce mediation in the Japanese family courts, see Bryant, "Mediation of Divorce Disputes."

17. Sources for the general discussion of the role of the bureaucracy include Chalmers Johnson, "The Institutional Foundations of Japanese Industrial Policy," *California Management Review*, 27, no. 4 (1985), 59–69; Michio Muramatsu and Ellis S. Krauss, "Bureaucrats and Politicians in Policymaking: The Case of Japan," *The American Political Science Review*, 78 (1984), 126–146; Dan Fenno Henderson, *Foreign Enterprise in Japan* (Tokyo: Charles Tuttle, 1975), 195; and Chalmers Johnson, *MITI and the Japanese Miracle: The Growth of Industrial Policy, 1925–75* (Stanford: Stanford University Press, 1982), 38.

18. The term *triumvirate* comes from Henderson, *Foreign Enterprise*. It has also been described as a "triangular relationship" (Johnson, "Institutional Foundations," 60) and a "triad" (Muramatsu and Krauss, "Bureaucrats and Politicians," 128). This view of the bureaucracy's role has been challenged recently by, among others, Muramatsu and Krauss, who argue that it ignores a recent increase in the power of LDP politicians, overstates the degree of shared backgrounds between the politicians and bureaucrats (the latter come from considerably more elite backgrounds and have higher levels of education), and overlooks cleavages within

the generally homogeneous bureaucracy. Even they, however, agree that top bureaucrats and LDP politicians have remarkably similar views of the policymaking process and their respective roles therein and that the bureaucrats are at least the equal of the politicians in terms of influence over policymaking. Their major disagreement with the triumvirate interpretation is that, whatever the reality of business power, the perception of bureaucrats and politicians is that the influence of business on national policy is much weaker than that of either other group, particularly in areas other than economic policy. Chalmers Johnson, on the other hand, believes that the triangular description remains valid and that any recent increase in the power of the Diet politicians vis-à-vis the bureaucrats is cyclical and temporary. He continues to believe that "the bureaucracy makes policy and the Diet merely rubberstamps it," and that "big business maintains a skewed relationship with the other two power centers" ("Institutional Foundations," 60). Whatever the truth, it is clear that the bureaucracy remains extremely strong in Japan even when compared with Western European bureaucracies and particularly in comparison with that of the United States.

19. Muramatsu and Krauss, "Bureaucrats and Politicians," 128–129.

20. The tradition of judicial independence began in 1891 with the Otsu Affair. On May 11, 1891, a policeman in the city of Otsu made an attempt on the life of the Russian Crown Prince. Since the Penal Code did not have a special penalty for the attempted murder of foreign royalty, the maximum penalty was the same as it would have been if the attempt had been made upon the life of a normal Japanese citizen, namely, life imprisonment. The government, however, sought the death penalty by making the analogy between the attempt on foreign royalty and an attempt on Japanese royalty. In spite of strong pressure from the government, the judiciary did not accept the analogy and instead only sentenced the offender to life in prison; see Kenzō Takayanagi, "A Century of Innovation: The Development of Japanese Law, 1868–1961," in *Law in Japan*, ed. von Mehren, 9–10. This judicial independence continued through the Ashio copper mine incident discussed in Chapter 2 and is exemplified by contemporary cases such as *Japan v. Kawamoto*, 853 *Hanrei Jihō* 3, also discussed in Chapter 2, and the malapportionment cases of *Koshiyama v. Chairman, Tokyo Metropolitan Election Supervision Commission*, 18 *Minshū* 270, and *Kurokawa v. Chiba Election Commission*, 30 *Minshū* 225. In the malapportionment cases the courts held that the apportionment ratios between urban and rural electoral districts current during the subject elections were in violation of Article 14, paragraph 1 of the Constitution, which provides that elected representatives "shall be proportionate to the populaton." The Supreme Court stopped short of invalidating the elections, but the Diet has increased the number of seats for urban districts.

21. Part of the courts' reluctance to interfere with the administration except in the most extreme cases results from a European view of the separation of powers that strongly discourages judicial intervention. For a series of administrative review cases illustrating the courts' approach to bureaucratic discretion, see the excerpts and summaries of cases on pp. 170–181 (cases 76–81) in Ogawa Ichirō, ed., *Juristo: Gyōsei hanrei hyakusen*, I Bessatsu no. 61 (April 1979) [One hundred selected administrative cases, vol. 1] (Tokyo: Yūhikaku, 1979).

22. Henderson, *Foreign Enterprise*, 54.

23. See the works cited in note 3.

24. Japanese bureaucrats do, however, exhibit a fundamental ambivalence toward the political control of administrative action, at least when politics is defined as the clash of parochial interests. See generally Muramatsu and Krauss, "Bureaucrats and Politicians."

25. See Beer, *Freedom of Expression,* for an interdisciplinary study of one group of such cases.

26. On Tokugawa mediation, see Dan Fenno Henderson, *Conciliation and Japanese Law, Tokugawa and Modern,* vol. 1 (Seattle: University of Washington Press, 1965); on prewar mediation, see John O. Haley, "The Politics of Informal Justice: The Japanese Experience, 1922–1942," in *The Politics of Informal Justice,* ed. Richard Abel, vol. 2 (New York: Academic Press, 1982), 125–147; on divorce mediation, see Bryant, "Mediation of Divorce Disputes." See also Rokumoto, *Minji,* and the Kyoto University Survey cited in note 15.

27. The Special Measures Law for Assimilation Projects enacted to help eliminate Buraku discrimination is another example of a statute that purports to change social relations without changing mutual legal rights and obligations. One notable exception is the environmental field in general, where strict liability for certain kinds of environmental torts was statutorily established. See Gresser, Fujikura, and Morishima, *Environmental Law,* 22–24 and 288–289.

28. For examples of the role of courts in social conflict before World War II, see David A. Sneider, "Protest and Punishment in Prewar Japan: The Trials of the May 15th Incident of 1932" (unpublished paper, 1984, on file with the author), and F. G. Notehelfer, "Japan's First Pollution Incident," *Journal of Japanese Studies,* 1 (1975), 351–383.

2. Environmental Tragedy and Response

1. For background on the impact of pollution on LDP growth policies and the related political fallout, see Margaret McKean, *Environmental Protest and Citizen Politics in Japan* (Berkeley: University of California Press, 1981) and Norie Huddle and Michael Reich, *Island of Dreams: Environmental Crisis in Japan* (New York: Autumn Press, 1975). The four important pollution cases are the Judgment of June 30, 1971, Toyama District Court, 635 *Hanrei Jihō* 17, aff'd by Judgment of August 9, 1972, Nagoya High Court, 674 *Hanrei Jihō* 25 (Toyama Itai-itai disease case); Judgment of September 29, 1971 (Niigata Minamata disease case); Judgment of July 24, 1972, Tsu District Court (Yokkaichi Branch), 672 *Hanrei Jihō* 30 (Yokkaichi industrial asthma case); Judgment of March 20, 1973, Kumamoto District Court, 696 *Hanrei Jihō* 15 (Kumamoto Minamata disease case). They are translated on pages 57, 66, 86, and 106, respectively, in Julian Gresser, Kōichirō Fujikura, and Akio Morishima, *Environmental Law in Japan* (Cambridge, Mass.: MIT Press, 1981). For an account of the change in the development of governmental policies in the wake of these decisions, see ibid., 229–349; see also generally Environment Agency, *Quality of the Environment in Japan,* published annually by the Kōsei Kankyō Mondai Kenkyūkai, Tokyo. *Quality* is a condensed translation of the annual *Kankyō hakusho* [Environment white paper].

2. Huddle and Reich, *Island of Dreams,* 106–107. The Minamata pollution disaster and the devastating effects on the people who live there are discussed in

"Yokkaichi kōgai ni okeru jūmin katsudō" [Symposium: The residents' activities in the Yokkaichi pollution case], 514 *Juristo* 134 (1972) (hereafter cited as *Juristo* A), and in "Yokkaichi kōgai soshō ni okeru soshō katsudō" [Symposium: Litigation activities in the Yokkaichi pollution case], 514 *Juristo* 102 (1972) (hereafter cited as *Juristo* B). Other accounts of the incident are found in Ui Jun, "The Singularities of Japanese Pollution," *Japan Quarterly*, 19 (1972), 281; Ono Eiji, "Shimin undō to bengoshi" [Citizens' movements and lawyers], *Jiyu to Seigi*, 23 (1972), 7; Eugene Smith, "Minamata Japan: Life—Sacred and Profane," *Camera*, 18 (April 26, 1974), 35; and Tsuchimoto Noriaki, director, *Minamata: The Victims and Their World* (1972), movie script on file with the author. Perhaps the most detailed account of the events surrounding the Minamata incident can be found in the opinions of the Kumamoto District Court in the Kumamoto Minamata Disease case (see note 1) and in *Japan v. Kawamoto*, 853 *Hanrei Jihō* 3 (Judgment of the Tokyo High Court, June 14, 1977; hereafter cited as *Kawamoto*).

3. Reprinted in Huddle and Reich, *Island of Dreams*, 117.

4. The actual text of the notification read as follows: "From the result of the research so far, it is presumed that wastewater of the Chisso factory has contaminated the mud in the harbor, and shellfish have become poisonous due to chemicals in the waste, and that the disease is caused by eating a large amount of such fish and shellfish" (*Kawamoto*, p. 7).

5. Ibid.

6. Ibid. The manager of Chisso's Minamata plant and the president of Chisso Corporation were later tried and convicted of manslaughter.

7. For analysis and discussion of the legal doctrine in these cases, see generally Frank K. Upham, "After Minamata: Current Prospects and Problems in Japanese Environmental Litigation," *Ecology Law Quarterly*, 8 (1979), 213, and sources cited therein.

8. *Juristo* A, 132.

9. Ibid., 140.

10. Ibid., 129.

11. Ono, "Shimin," 13.

12. Ibid.

13. *Juristo* A, 133–134.

14. Tsuchimoto, "Minamata: Victims," 28.

15. Ibid., 72.

16. Ibid., 90.

17. *Juristo* B, 118.

18. For English-language legal analysis of, *inter alia*, the treatment of negligence and causation in the Big Four cases, see Bruce Aronson, "Compensation of Pollution-Related Health Damage in Japan," in *Social Science and Medicine*, ed. Michael Reich (forthcoming), and Tomohei Taniguchi, "A Commentary on the Legal Theory of the Four Major Pollution Cases," *Law in Japan: An Annual*, 9 (1976), 35.

19. Takanori Gotō, "What Is the Minamata Disease?" (unpublished paper, September 1975, on file with the author), 9–10. For similar statements and a fuller explanation of the role of direct negotiations, see Gotō Takanori, "Kyodai na shakai hanzai ni idomu: hō ni sogai sareta seikatsumin no 'jishu kōshōken' "

[Challenging an enormous crime against society: The "right of direct negotiations" of people deserted by the law], *Shimin*, 2 (1975), 142.

20. Gotō, "What Is the Minamata Disease?" 10.

21. *Kawamoto*, 4. The following chronology is drawn largely from the opinion of the Tokyo High Court in *Kawamoto*, note 2.

22. Huddle and Reich, *Island of Dreams*, 130.

23. For analysis and discussion of the legal doctrine in *Kawamoto*, see Frank K. Upham, "*Japan v. Kawamoto*: Judicial Limits on the State's Power to Indict," *Law in Japan: An Annual*, 13 (1980), 137, and sources cited therein.

24. *Kawamoto*, 11–12.

25. 984 *Hanrei Jihō* 37. The 15-person Supreme Court generally sits in three 5-person petty benches.

26. Ibid., 40.

27. For an analysis of citizens' movements in the environmental area and beyond, see McKean, *Environmental Protest*. See also Ellis S. Krauss and Bradford L. Simcock, "Citizens' Movements: The Growth and Impact of Environmental Protest in Japan"; Margaret A. McKean, "Political Socialization through Citizens' Movements"; and Jack G. Lewis, "Civic Protest in Mishima: Citizens' Movements and the Politics of the Environment in Contemporary Japan," in *Political Opposition and Local Politics in Japan*, ed. Kurt Steiner, Ellis Krauss, and Scott Flanagan (Princeton: Princeton University Press, 1980). Also instructive are Steve Reed, "Local Policy-Making in a Unitary State: The Case of Japanese Prefectures," Ph.D. diss., University of Michigan, 1979, and Tanaka Shigeaki, "Shimin undō ni okeru kenri to saiban: sono hōteki senryaku no haikei to igi o megutte" [Rights and litigation in citizens' movements: Focusing on their background and significance as a legal tactic], *Minshō Hō Zasshi*, 76 (1977), 633; 76 (1977), 779; 77 (1977), 161; and 77 (1977), 321.

28. Gresser, Fujikura, and Morishima, *Environmental Law*, 229–283.

29. *Kōgai funsō shori hō*, Law No. 108 of 1970, partially translated in Gresser, Fujikura, and Morishima, *Environmental Law*, 407–410. For discussion of the law see ibid., 325–349.

30. *Kōgai kenkō higai hoshō hō*, Law No. 111 of 1973. For discussion of the law see ibid., 285–323.

31. See Upham, "After Minamata," 219–224.

32. This description is based on documents received from an interview of MITI officials by the author in Tokyo, 1982.

33. For a discussion of the Osaka High Court opinion in the *Osaka Airport* case, see Upham, "After Minamata," 228–234 and 248–258.

34. For a discussion of the *Biwa* case, see ibid., 213–217 and 260–268.

35. These doctrines govern a plaintiff's standing to bring a lawsuit under the Administrative Case Litigation Law (ACLL) challenging "the exercise of public authority" (*kōkenryoku no kōshi*); the determination of justiciability or of what types of governmental action are appropriate for judicial review and at what stage in the bureaucratic process litigation can be brought; the degree of deference reviewing courts will show to bureaucratic discretion; and the possibility of enjoining ongoing official action under the ACLL. The nature and effect of these doctrines are

more fully discussed in the context of industrial policy in Chapter 5. For their effect in the environmental setting see Upham, "After Minamata," 225–248.

36. Judgment of the Supreme Court, Grand Bench, December 16, 1981, 1025 *Hanrei Jihō* 39. The Osaka High Court had allowed the plaintiffs to combine prospective injunctive relief against late-night flights with tort compensation for past injury. Both claims had been brought under the tort provisions of the Civil Code and the State Redress Law (*Kokka baishō hō*), which provides for tort suits against governmental entities, and had been governed by essentially the same private-law concepts that govern tort suits between private parties. Because they had based their injunctive claim on the essentially private law doctrines of the State Redress Law, the plaintiffs had avoided the much more stringent public law requirements for enjoining official bureaucratic action under the Administrative Case Litigation Law (ACLL). By characterizing the scheduling of flights at a publicly operated airport as "the exercise of public authority" (*kōkenryoku no kōshi*) and therefore enjoinable only under the ACLL, the Supreme Court reaffirmed the primacy of the ACLL and restrictive doctrines that govern it in any suit against the government that involves policymaking or implementation. For a discussion of the use of the State Redress Law up to the Osaka High Court decision, see Upham, "After Minamata," 225–234.

37. Robert N. Bellah, *Tokugawa Religion: The Values of Pre-Industrial Japan* (Boston: Beacon Press, 1970).

38. Irwin Scheiner, "Benevolent Lords and Honorable Peasants: Rebellion and Peasant Consciousness in Tokugawa Japan," in *Japanese Thought in the Tokugawa Period 1600–1868: Methods and Metaphors*, ed. Tetsuo Najita and Irwin Scheiner (Chicago: University of Chicago Press, 1978), 39–62.

39. This discussion of *ikki* is based on Namba Nobuo, "Hiyakushō ikki no hōishiki" [The legal consciousness of peasant rebellions], in *Ikki*, ed. Aoki Michio et al. vol. 4, *Seikatsu, bunka, shisō* [Life, culture, and thought] (Tokyo: Tokyo University Press, 1981) 43; Minagishi Kentarō, "Kinsei no hisabetsumin no tōsō" [The struggle of discriminated people in the Tokugawa Period], in *Ikki*, vol. 3, *Ikki no kōzō* [The structure of *ikki*], 52. See also Stephen Vlastos, "Tokugawa Peasant Movements in Fukushima: Conflict and Peasant Mobilization," Ph.D. diss., University of California, Berkeley, 1977. This discussion is also based on various published and unpublished materials concerning the 150-year-long struggle between majority and outcaste residents of Hozu Village, Kyoto Prefecture, regarding access to the village-owned commons, which were made available to me by Professor Igeta Ryōji of Doshisha University Law Faculty. See Igeta, "Meijikōki no kenritōsō no ichi jirei: mikaihō burakumin no byōdō iriai yōkyū" [One example of rights struggle in the latter half of Meiji: Demands by unliberated Burakumin for equal access to the commons], in *Nihon kindai kokka no hōkōzō* [The legal structure of the modern Japanese state], ed. Nihon Kindai Hōseishi Kenkyūkai (Tokyo: Bokutakusha, 1983), 481.

40. Scheiner, "Benevolent Lords," 55.

41. The account here is based largely on F. G. Notehelfer, "Japan's First Pollution Incident," *Journal of Japanese Studies* (1975), 351; Alan Stone, "The Japanese Muckrakers," *Journal of Japanese Studies* (1975), 385; and the record of the Ashio

trials in *Nihon seiji saiban shiroku (Meiji go)* [Historical records of Japanese political trials—Late Meiji], ed. Wagatsuma Sakae et al. (Tokyo: Daiichi Hōki, 1969).

42. For a description of the trials, see *Nihon seiji saiban*, 298–316.

3. Instrumental Violence and Buraku Liberation

1. See Michael Reich, "Toxic Politics: A Comparative Study of Public and Private Responses to Chemical Disasters in the United States, Italy, and Japan," Ph.D. diss., Yale University, 1981, for a detailed treatment of one such case, the Kanemi Oil poisoning incident. For a shorter treatment of the same incident, see Michael Reich, "Public and Private Responses to a Chemical Disaster in Japan: The Case of Kanemi Yushō," *Law in Japan: An Annual*, 16 (1983), 102. For a discussion of the motives behind such suits and the negotiations accompanying them, see Gotō Takanori, "Kyodai na shakai hanzai ni idomu: hō ni sogai sareta seikatsumin no 'jishu kōshōken' " [Challenging an enormous crime against society: The 'right of direct negotiations' of people deserted by the law], *Shimin*, 2 (1975), 142.

2. George De Vos and Hiroshi Wagatsuma, *Japan's Invisible Race: Caste in Culture and Personality* (Berkeley: University of California Press, 1966), is still invaluable for general background but is badly out of date on the political situation. For a description of recent political developments see I. Yoshino and S. Murakoshi, *The Invisible Visible Minority: Japan's Burakumin* (Osaka: Kaihō Shuppansha, 1977). See also Chong-Do Hah and Christopher C. Lapp, "Japanese Politics of Equality in Transition: The Case of the Burakumin," *Asian Survey*, 18 (1978), 487, and Martin Kaneko, "Buraku: Housing Conditions in a Discriminated Buraku Community in Japan," *Architectural Association Quarterly*, 10 (1978), 20.

3. For the pre-Meiji history of the Burakumin, see John Price, "A History of the Outcaste: Untouchability in Japan," in DeVos and Wagatsuma, *Japan's Invisible Race*, 6–60.

4. Whether their ancestors were farmers or were limited to outcaste occupations is a matter of great economic importance to rural Burakumin, because the income from commonly held village lands is distributed only to families whose ancestors were agriculturists and thus had the right to enter the commons (the *iriaiken*) to forage during the Tokugawa Period. The disagreement over whether or not outcastes held this right has been a constant source of conflict and litigation since the eighteenth century. For an account of the disputes arising from one village near Kyoto from 1802 through litigation in 1815, 1883, and 1908 up to its negotiated settlement in the 1960s, see Igeta Ryōji, "Meijikōki no kenritōsō no ichi jirei: mikaihō burakumin no byōdō iriai yōkyū" [One example of rights struggle in the latter half of Meiji: Demands by unliberated Burakumin for equal access to the commons], in *Nihon kindai kokka no hōkōzō* [The legal structure of the modern Japanese state], ed. Nihon Kindai Hōseishi Kenkyūkai (Tokyo: Bokutakusha, 1983), 481. See also *Yumita v. Muraishi*, Judgment of the Nagano District Court, March 13, 1973, in which the court ruled that the ancestors of the Burakumin plaintiffs had been agriculturists and that, therefore, the plaintiffs could share in the proceeds of the commons. The text of the opinion and relevant documents are reproduced in Aoki K., "Niboku iriaiken jiken to

hanketsu no igi" [The Niboku commons case and its significance], *Buraku Mondai Kenkyū*, 40 (1973), 34.

5. For an account of protests by the Tokugawa ancestors of the Burakumin, see Minagishi Kentarō, "Kinsei no hisabetsumin no tōsō" [The struggle of discriminated people in the Tokugawa Period], in *Ikki*, ed. Aoki Michio et al., vol. 3, *Ikki no kōzō* [The structure of *ikki*] (Tokyo: Tokyo University Press, 1981), 52.

6. *Eta kaihō rei*, Proclamation no. 61 of the Dajōkan.

7. The unlimited availability of the *koseki* for public inspection probably contributed more than any other single factor to the tenacity of Buraku discrimination. Until 1976, Article 10 of the *Koseki hō* (Family registry law) stated that the *koseki* was open to anyone who paid the fee. It was even possible to mail in the fee and receive a copy. It was easy, therefore, for employers, prospective in-laws, or the merely curious to determine who was of Buraku origin by merely seeing if they were registered in the 1873 census as "new commoners." Under pressure from the Suiheisha and their supporters in the 1920s, the Ministry of Justice repeatedly promised to limit access to the 1873 census and even to gather all such records in central locations to control their abuse more effectively. These promises and the various ministry directives meant to effectuate them were never fully implemented, although whether the ministry's failure was due to a lack of will or to local resistance is unclear. In any event, the result was continued access and discrimination into the 1970s, when the BLL convinced local governments to limit access on their own initiative. These efforts were met immediately by a series of lawsuits brought by private investigation firms, whose main business in Japan is conducting personal background checks (*mimoto chōsa*) for employers and prospective spouses. Although background checks are intended to discover such things as previous marriages, any family history of mental illness, or ancestors' criminal records or occupations, as well as outcaste origin, the closing of only the 1873 census records would affect significantly only those interested in Buraku status. The immediate and widespread reaction of the private detective agencies is, therefore, impressive anecdotal evidence of the strength of discrimination even in the 1970s.

The agencies' lawsuits, which demanded continued free access to the 1873 census based on Article 10 of the *Koseki hō*, were generally successful. See Nakagawa Jun, Miyai Tadao, Kokufu Takeshi, Satō Yoshihiko, and Tsuji Rō, "Koseki kōkai no gensoku to sono genkai" [The principle of an open family registry and its limitations], *Hanrei Taimuzu*, 349 (1977), 7, for a discussion of these cases and their aftermath. The eventual result was the amendment by the Diet of Article 10 of the law to limit severely access to an individual's *koseki* without the individual's permission (ibid., 33–36). For accounts of the use of the 1873 records in the 1960s and 1970s, and the attempts by the BLL and local governments to prevent it, I have relied on a newspaper file maintained by the Buraku Liberation Institute; I have copies of many of these articles on file.

8. For the history of Buraku liberation efforts and the governmental response in one city, see Osakashi dōwa mondai kenkyū shitsu [Osaka City *dōwa* Problem Research Office], *Osakashi dōwa jigyōshi* [The history of Osaka City *dōwa* projects] (1979).

9. Yagi Kōsuke, *Sabetsu kyūdan: sono shisō to rekishi* [Discrimination denunciation: Its thought and history] (Tokyo: Hihyōsha, 1976), 54–55.

10. For general descriptions of postwar activities up to 1960, see Osakashi, *Jigyōshi*, 113–123 and 162–198, and Hiroshi Wagatsuma, "Postwar Political Militance," in DeVos and Wagatsuma, *Japan's Invisible Race*, 68–87.

11. For an account of the formation of the Deliberative Council and the events leading up to its report, see Prime Minister's Office, *Dōwa taisaku no genkyō* [The present condition of *dōwa* policy], 5–19. The full text of the 1965 Report is appended on pp. 220–273.

12. *Dōwa taisaku jigyō tokubetsu sochi hō* (Law No. 60 of 1969). Originally set to expire after ten years, the law was extended by Law No. 102 of 1978. Translated in Buraku Liberation Research Institute, ed., *Long-Suffering Brothers and Sisters, Unite!* (Osaka: Kaihō Shuppansha, 1981), 259.

13. Judgment of June 3, 1975; 782 *Hanrei Jihō* 22. Reversed by the Osaka High Court, March 10, 1981, 996 *Hanrei Jihō* 34; appeal dismissed without discussion by Supreme Court, Decision of March 2, 1982.

14. The Kinoshita pamphlet read as follows: "Dear Member: (1) Are your working hours being respected? Can you leave school at 4:00 so that you have time to prepare at home? Aren't you taken away from your job and being forced to do work outside working hours? Do you just resign yourself to problems concerning assimilation [*dōwa*], grade promotion, etc., which cause you to be late no matter what you do? Also, do you have to give up work that you really want to do? (2) Aren't the rigid controls imposed in the name of normalization of education unwarranted? Cross district registration, special tutoring, assimilation [*dōwa*] matters, etc., are all extremely important, but under the pretexts of these programs, there arise the problems of transfers and overstaffing, of special home visits, of faculty seminars, and of restrictions on classes that are making work more and more difficult and distressing." 782 *Hanrei Jihō* 23, p. 29.

15. 782 *Hanrei Jihō* 23, pp. 24–25.

16. Ibid., p. 25.

17. Ibid., p. 26.

18. Ibid., p. 27.

19. Ibid.

20. Ibid.

21. See Hah and Lapp, "Japanese Politics," and Yoshino and Murakoshi, *The Invisible Visible Minority*, 89–95, for English treatments of the JCP–BLL rivalry. For a BLL-oriented account severely critical of the JCP, see Sawa Keitarō, *Sabetsu e no tenraku: nihon kyōsantō hihan* [Descent into discrimination: A critique of the Japanese Communist Party] (Tokyo: Asahi Shimbun Press, 1977). In general, the publications of the Buraku Mondai Kenkyūsho (Buraku Problems Research Institute) support the JCP view and those of the Buraku Kaihō Kenkyūsho (Buraku Liberation Research Institute) that of the BLL. The former publishes the monthly *Buraku* and the latter the monthly *Buraku Kaihō*.

22. For a valuable, albeit dated, English overview of the educational problems and policies concerning Burakumin, see Nobuo Shimahara, *Burakumin: A Japanese Minority and Education* (The Hague: Martinus Nijhoff, 1971). The Buraku Problems Research Institute publishes the quarterly *Dōwa Kyōiku Undō* [Assimilation education movement], which presents the JCP perspective. For the BLL perspective, see *Buraku Kaihō Kenkyū*, nos. 10 and 11 (1977), for a special series on the problems of Buraku education.

23. 782 *Hanrei Jihō* 23, p. 28.

24. The following account of the events following the April 9, 1969, denunciation is drawn primarily from the opinion in *Kinoshita v. Osaka City*, Judgment of the Osaka District Court, October 30, 1979, reported in 963 *Hanrei Jihō* 111. Other sources include a December 9, 1977, interview in Kyoto of Tsukada Toyuki, one of the plaintiffs in *Kinoshita*, and Plaintiffs' Brief submitted to Osaka District Court on June 20, 1977, in *Kinoshita*. The District Court opinion was affirmed by the Osaka High Court on December 16, 1980.

25. Tsukada interview, December 9, 1977.

26. 782 *Hanrei Jihō* 23, p. 31.

27. Ibid.

28. 996 *Hanrei Jihō* 34, p. 37.

29. 782 *Hanrei Jihō* 23, p. 31.

30. Ibid., pp. 31–32.

31. Ibid., p. 32.

32. 996 *Hanrei Jihō* 34, p. 35.

33. Ibid., p. 37.

34. Ibid.

35. Yamagami Ekirō, "Kaisetsu: hōteki chitsujo to iu 'gomu' teiki—Osaka kōsai hanketsu ni atatte" [Commentary: the rubberstamp of so-called legal order—The Osaka High Court judgment], *Kaihō Shimbun*, April 13, 1981, p. 2. See also "Yata kyōiku sabetsu saiban no imi" [The meaning of the Yata educational discrimination decision], *Shakai Shimpō*, April 10, 1981. *Shakai Shimpō* is the organ of the Japan Socialist Party.

36. Matsumoto Takeo, "Yata kyōiku sabetsu jiken—Osaka kōsai hanketsu no igi" [The Yata educational discrimination case—The significance of the Osaka High Court judgment], *Buraku Kaihō*, 166 (1981), 72.

37. Yoshioka Yoshiharu, "Futettei na 'kaidō' bōryoku e no danzai" [The inconsistent condemnation of BLL violence], *Akahata*, March 13, 1981.

38. Reproduced and translated in Buraku Institute, *Long-Suffering Brothers and Sisters*, Appendix E, 249.

39. The following description of explanations and theories of justification of denunciation draws largely on the following sources: Yagi Kōsuke, *Sabetsu kyūdan: sono shisō to rekishi* [Discrimination denunciation: Its thought and history] (Tokyo: Hihyōsha, 1976); Yagi Kōsuke, "Sabetsu kyūdan to ishiki kaizō" [Discrimination denunciation and the reconstruction of consciousness], in *Sabetsu no ishiki kōzō* [The structure of discriminatory consciousness] (Osaka: Kaihō Shuppansha, 1980); Murata Yasuo, *Sabetsu kyūdan to minshushugi* [Discrimination denunciation and democracy] (Tokyo: Meiji Tosho, 1977); and nos. 3, 4, 5, and 6 of a series of reports entitled *Kaihō riron no sōzō* [The making of liberation theory], available from the Buraku Liberation Research Institute, Osaka, Japan. See particularly Nishimura Ayumi, "Sabetsu kyūdan tōsō ni tsuite" [Regarding discrimination denunciation struggles] in no. 5, p. 184, and Uesugi Saichiro, "Sabetsu kyūdan tōsō ni tsuite" [Regarding discrimination denunciation struggles], in no. 4, p. 138. See also Oga Masayuki, "Sabetsu kyūdan to wa nanika?" [What is discrimination denunciation?] in no. 6, p. 216, and Taniguchi Shutarō, "Sabetsu kyūdan tōsō no shisō teki igi" [The intellectual significance of discrimination denunciation struggle], in no. 3, p. 620.

40. Buraku theorists dismiss the Civil Liberties Bureau of the Ministry of Justice as powerless to enforce their fundamental rights not only because it would mean depending on the government, but also because the Bureau has no formal legal power. See Yagi, *Shisō to rekishi*, 205–206.

41. Ibid., 211. For a mainstream view of Article 25 that agrees with the BLL's interpretation, see Osuga Akira, *Seizonkenron* [On the right to existence] (Tokyo: Nihon Hyōronsha, 1984).

42. Yagi, *Shisō to rekishi*, 233–234.

43. Ibid., 234–235.

44. Ibid., 232–233.

45. Oga, "Sabetsu kyūdan," 216–219.

46. Reprinted in Yagi, *Shisō to rekishi*, 241.

47. *Yumita v. Muraishi*. See note 4.

48. Nagano District Court (Ueda Branch), Judgment of March 20, 1965, reported in 410 *Hanrei Jihō* 13.

49. Judgment of Kōchi District Court, March 24, 1972, reported in 679 *Hanrei Jihō* 60.

50. Supreme Court, Second Petty Branch, Judgment of April 4, 1975.

51. For a fuller treatment, see Frank K. Upham, "Ten Years of Affirmative Action for Japanese Burakumin: A Preliminary Report on the Law on Special Measures for *Dōwa* Projects," *Law in Japan: An Annual*, 13 (1980), 39.

52. This practice was successfully attacked by a Communist-Party-affiliated Burakumin in the Naniwa One-Window Case, *Higashi v. Oshima* (Judgment of the Osaka High Court, July 30, 1979). See Upham, "Ten Years," 59–62. See also Kishiue Shigeo, "Kōsei na dōwa gyōsei e no ōkina tenkan e" [Toward a dramatic conversion to fair *dōwa* administration], *Buraku*, 33 (February 1981), 50.

53. The extreme sensitivity of the Japanese to the Buraku issue is illustrated by the fact that there was a journalistic taboo against any mention of the subject until the late 1960s. See Hah and Lapp, "Japanese Politics," 494. It is my unsupported impression that the *Asahi Shimbun*, which originally broke the taboo, is still the only major newspaper to give more than minimal attention to the issue.

54. An illustration of the desire by the Japanese to avoid any mention of the *dōwa* problem is the fact that the publishers of the Japanese translation of Edwin O. Reischauer's book *The Japanese* deleted all portions of the original that mentioned the Burakumin. The deletion was made without Professor Reischauer's prior permission, and he was notified of it only after it was too late for him to do anything about it. This incident was related in a letter from Professor Reischauer dated February 25, 1980, on file with the author.

55. See generally Upham, "Ten Years."

56. *Asahi Shimbun*, December 11, 1977. See also Tomonaga Kenzō, "Zenkoku jitai chōsa to tokubetsu sochi hō no kyōka enchō" [National survey data and the extension of the SML), *Buraku Kaihō*, 112 (1977), 36; Murakoshi Sueo, "Hisabetsu buraku no kihonteki jōkyō wa henka shita ka?" [Has the fundamental situation in discriminated Burakus changed?] *Buraku Kaihō*, 137 (1979), 45. See also the articles collected in "Tokushū: buraku no shigata wa dō kawatta ka?" [Special issue: How has employment in the Buraku changed?], *Buraku*, 30 (June 1978).

57. See the articles collected in "Tokushū: buraku no shigata."

58. *Asahi Shimbun,* December 10, 1976, p. 2.

59. One leading case is the Naniwa One-Window Case, *Higashi v. Oshima,* discussed in note 52. There are literally dozens of cases in several different district and high courts brought by JCP-associated plaintiffs against the BLL influence in *dōwa* administration. They take many forms, but two published cases similar to the Naniwa case are *Maeda v. Takase,* 887 *Hanrei Jihō* 66 (Judgment of the Kobe District Court, December 19, 1977) (concerning Nishiwaki City), and *Matsuoka v. Shindō,* 870 *Hanrei Jihō* 61 (Judgment of the Fukuoka High Court, September 13, 1977) (concerning Fukuoka City). See also generally the following materials collected by the JCP and on file with the author: *Osaka ni okeru 'dōwa mondai'* [The *'dōwa* problem'* in Osaka] (May 1975); *Fukuyamashi no dōwa gyōsei 'madoguchi ipponka' soshō shiryōshū* [Collection of materials on Fukuyama City's 'One-Window' *dōwa* litigation] (August 1977); *Fukuokashi ni okeru dōwa mondai saiban reishū* [Collected examples of Fukuoka City's *dōwa* problem litigation] (February 1978).

60. For one exception known as the "Yōka High School incident," see Susan J. Pharr, "In Search of Social Equality: A Case of Burakumin Protest," paper presented at the 30th Annual Meeting of the Midwest Conference on Asian Affairs, Columbia, Missouri, October 2, 1981.

61. Gotō, "Kyodai na shakai hanzai."

62. One example is William H. Simon, "The Ideology of Advocacy: Procedural Justice and Professional Ethics," *Wisconsin Law Review* (1978), 29.

4. Civil Rights Litigation and Equal Employment Opportunity

1. For other examples of the use of limited instrumental force, see Tadashi Hanami, *Labor Relations in Japan Today* (Tokyo: Kodansha International, 1979), 73–87, and cases cited therein; and 354 *Hanrei Taimuzu* (1978) and cases cited therein.

2. The full title of the legislation was *Koyō no bunya ni okeru danjo no kintō na kikai oyobi taigū no kakuho o sokushin suru tame no rōdōshō kankei hōritsu no seibi nado ni kansuru hōritsu* [An act for the adjustment of laws relating to the Ministry of Labor to promote the assurance of equality of opportunity and treatment for men and women in employment]. It substantially amended the Working Women's Welfare Law (*Kinrō fujin fukushi hō*), Law No. 113 of 1972, and renamed it the Act for the Assurance of Equality of Opportunity and Treatment for Men and Women in Employment and the Enhancement of the Welfare of Female Workers [*Koyō no bunya ni okeru danjo no kintō na kikai oyobi taigū no kakuho nado joshi rōdōsha no fukushi no zōshin ni kansuru hōritsu*]. It is this amended statute that contains the antidiscrimination provisions of the legislation and that is hereafter referred to as the Equal Employment Opportunity Act or EEOA. The legislation also amended the provisions of the Labor Standards Act (*Rōdō kijun hō*), Law No. 49 of 1947, that grant female workers special protection in working conditions. See note 13.

3. Unless otherwise noted, statistics in this chapter are from *Japanese Industrial Relations Series: Problems of Working Women,* published by the Japan Institute of Labor (an organ of the Ministry of Labor, hereafter cited as MOL) in 1981.

4. The 1982 figure is from MOL, *The Status of Women in Japan* (1983), 18. The female/male ratio peaked at 56.2 percent in 1978. See MOL, *Problems*, 12.

5. International Labor Organization announcement of March 22, 1984, as reported in *Yomiuri Shimbun*, March 23, 1984, p. 2.

6. The average work week for part-time female employees in 1980 was 31.6 hours. MOL, *Problems*, 12. The percentage of working women employed part time more than doubled from 8.9 percent in 1960 to 19.3 percent in 1980. Ibid., 11. For one instance of the use of women as "part-timers," see the description of the *Shinshirasuna* case in note 40.

For a discussion of the long-term threat that increasing rates of "part-time" and "temporary" employment pose to women and a pessimistic view of the chances of the EEOA creating real equality of opportunity, see Nakajima Michiko (with commentary by Teruoka Itsuko, Masuda Reiko, and Higuchi Keiko), "Josei no ima, soshite mirai wa? Josei to rōdō," *Sekai* (August 1985), 36 (translated and abridged as "Women Yesterday and Today—Women at Work," *Japan Echo*, 12, Summer 1985, 58). Nakajima fears that opening management track jobs to women without relieving any of the burden on women in the home will polarize working women into "those who work like men and those who work part time while doing the housework and bringing up the children." Nakajima and other women, including Teruoka, Masuda, and Higuchi, believe that the EEOA and other recent government action ostensibly aimed at improving working women's lot are actually intended to maintain and strengthen the sex-based division of labor within Japanese society by making it easier for housewives to move in and out of the labor market. The long-term result, according to this view, will be the creation of a two-tiered labor market with a largely female pool of low-paid "temporary" and "part-time" workers economically subsidizing a much smaller pool of largely male "permanent" employees. In addition to creating economic efficiency and personnel flexibility on the microeconomic level, this division of labor will solve a major impending social problem as well by encouraging working housewives to leave the labor market in their fifties to care for elderly in-laws. Given Japan's aging society and the government's determination that the elderly should be cared for privately within the "three-generation household," the availability of housewives to care for the elderly becomes an important social goal. It is the view of many women, therefore, that the current government efforts toward better working conditions for women and in particular for part-time and temporary workers are better interpreted as an attempt to strengthen the position of women as housewives rather than an attempt to increase the employment rights of all women. They phrase this distinction as "stress[ing] wives' prerogatives while ignor[ing] human rights." See Higuchi Keiko (with commentary by Teruoka Itsuko, Masuda Reiko, and Nakajima Michiko), "Josei no ima, soshite mirai wa? Josei to katei," *Sekai* (August 1985), 24 (translated and abridged as "Women Yesterday and Today—Women at Home," *Japan Echo*, 12, Summer 1985, 51). For a legal and economic analysis of the current status of part-time employees, see Hiroya Nakakubo, "Actual Conditions and Legal Problems Relating to Part-time Employment," *Japan Labor Bulletin*, 23 (January 1 and February 1, 1984), reprinted in Kazuo Sugeno, "Japanese Labor Law in Comparative Perspective" (unpublished teaching materials used at Harvard Law School, 1986).

7. For economists' views, see, for example, the comments by Ono Akira of Hitotsubashi University and Sano Yoko of Keio University quoted in "Japan's Secret Economic Weapon: Exploited Women," *Business Week*, March 4, 1985, p. 54, and the statements of Shibayama Emiko, women's labor specialist, translated in *Mainichi Daily News*, March 13, 1983. See also generally Nakajima, "Josei to rōdō," and Higuchi, "Josei to katei," discussed in note 6.

8. In 1982 the Prime Minister's Office reported that 22 percent of part-time employees work the same hours as regular employees, and 50 percent work more than 35 hours a week. *Mainichi Daily News*, March 13, 1983.

9. Ministry of Labor statistics, cited by *Asahi Shimbun*, September 29, 1981.

10. Yujiro Yamamoto, "Male Establishment Resists Female Workers," *The Asia Record* (May 1982), 84.

11. Ibid.

12. *Mainichi News*, March 13, 1983.

13. *Rōdō kijun hō*, Law No. 49 of 1947. Until this law's amendment in 1985 by the Equal Employment Opportunity Act, Articles 61 (working hours and rest days), 62 (night labor), 63 (dangerous or harmful work), and 64 (ban on underground work) limited the hours and types of work available to women. Article 65 (maternity leave), 66 (on-the-job nursing time), and 67 (menstruation leave) provided additional privileges to women workers. With certain exceptions, the EEOA relaxed but did not eliminate these provisions.

14. As with many other social phenomena of postwar Japan, such as permanent employment and low litigation rates, the clear distinction in familial sex roles relegating women to a purely domestic role is explained and justified as "traditional." The history of women's social status in Japan is beyond the scope of this book, but there is evidence that Japanese women, at least in rural Japan in the 1930s, have not always been as economically dependent on their husbands or played the role now frequently assumed to have always been theirs. See Robert J. Smith, "Japanese Village Women: Suye-Mura 1935–36," *The Journal of Japanese Studies*, 7 (1981), 259.

The debate over the passage of an equal employment opportunity law provided a series of examples of Japanese views toward woman's proper role in society, including Hasegawa Michiko, " 'Danjo koyō byōdō hō' wa bunka no seitaikei o hakai suru" [The "law for sexual equality in employment" will destroy our cultural ecosystem], *Chūō Kōron* (May 1984), 78; and "Equality of the Sexes Threatens Cultural Ecology," *Economic Eye* (June 1984), 23–26; Eiko Shinotsuka, "Women in the Labor Force," *Economic Eye* (September 1982), 22; Kimindo Kusaka, "Do Japanese Women Want Total Equality?" *Economic Eye* (June 1984), 19; Yayama Tarō, " 'Danjo koyō byōdō hō' wa nihon o tsubusu" [The "law for sexual equality in employment" will ruin Japan], *Shokun* (May 1984), 240; Ido Kazuo, Kōno Tadayoshi, and Sumiya Mikio, " 'Josei koyō' o ikanai teichaku saseruka?" [How should "women's employment" be made secure?], *Ekonomisuto* (April 17, 1984), 46; Hashimoto Hiroko, Kakuta Takuko, Sumiya Mikio, and Watanabe Michiko, "Hataraku josei ni totte, 'byōdō' to wa?" [What does "equality" mean to working women?], *Ekonomisuto* (October 2, 1984), 60; Ida Naotaka, Nakayama Tsuneo, Sumiya Mikio, and Watanabe Kazuro, "Kigyō no myōnichi o tou josei koyō" [The challenge to the future of the firm of female employment], *Ekonomisto* (July 3, 1984), 50.

15. For a general discussion of the dual structure of the Japanese economy, see Robert Cole, *Japanese Blue Collar: The Changing Tradition* (Berkeley: University of California Press, 1971).

16. For a doctrinal analysis in English of many of these cases, see Catherine Brown, "Japanese Approaches to Equal Rights for Women: The Legal Framework," *Law in Japan: An Annual*, 12 (1979), 29. In Japanese see Nakajima Michiko, "Danjo sabetsu saiban no gendankai" [The current stage of sex discrimination litigation], *Juristo*, 725 (1980), 39; Akamatsu Yoshiko, *Joshi rōdō hanrei (kaisetsu)* [Women's labor precedents (Commentary)] (Tokyo: Gakuyō Shobō, 1975).

17. Constitution of Japan, Article 14:   (1) All of the people are equal under the law and there shall be no discrimination in political, economic or social relations because of race, creed, sex, social status or family origin. (2) Peers and peerage shall not be recognized. (3) No privilege shall accompany any award of honor, decoration or distinction, nor shall any such award be valid beyond the lifetime of the individual who now holds or hereafter may receive it.

Article 24:   (1) Marriage shall be based only on the mutual consent of both sexes and it shall be maintained through mutual cooperation with the equal rights of husband and wife as a basis. (2) With regard to choice of spouse, property rights, inheritance, choice of domicile, divorce, and other matters pertaining to marriage and the family, laws shall be enacted from the standpoint of individual dignity and the essential equality of the sexes.

18. Labor Standards Act, Article 4:   The employer shall not discriminate women against men concerning wages by reason of the worker being a woman.

Article 3:   No employer shall discriminate against or for any worker by reason of nationality, creed or social status in wages, working hours, or other working conditions.

For the protective provisions of the Labor Standards Act, see note 13 above.

19. *Minpō*, Law No. 89 of 1896.

20. 17 *Rōshū* 1407.

21. Ibid., 1411.

22. Ibid., 1411–1412.

23. For an explanation of the Japanese wage structure and why it poses such a problem in these circumstances, see Cole, *Blue Collar*, 72–100.

24. 17 *Rōshū* 1407, p. 1419.

25. Ibid.

26. Ibid.

27. Ibid., p. 1421.

28. See, for example, Mitsui Shipbuilding case, 22 *Rōshū* 1163 (Judgment of the Osaka District Court, December 10, 1971). See Brown, "Japanese Approaches to Equal Rights," 34. See also Akamatsu, *Joshi*, 10.

29. See, for example, Judgment of the Tokyo District Court, July 1, 1969, reported in 20 *Rōshū* 715. See also Akamatsu, *Joshi*, 16, and Judgment of the Nagoya High Court, September 30, 1974 (The Nagoya Broadcasting case), 756 *Hanrei Jihō* 56. See Brown, "Japanese Approaches to Equal Rights," 36.

30. See, for example, Izu Cactus Park case, 882 *Rōdō Hōritsu Junpō* 89 (Judgment of the Tokyo High Court, February 26, 1975); aff'd, 896 *Rōdō Hōritsu Junpō* 136

(Judgment of the Supreme Court, August 29, 1975). See Brown, "Japanese Approaches to Equal Rights," 38; Akamatsu, *Joshi*, 28. *Izu Cactus Park* was followed in the Nissan Motors case, 998 *Hanrei Jihō* 3 (Judgment of the Supreme Court, Third Petty Bench, March 24, 1981). The only case known to me upholding different retirement ages, the Karatsu Red Cross Hospital case, 881 *Hanrei Jihō* 149, decided by the Saga District Court, November 8, 1977, was settled in the plaintiff's favor in 1983 while on appeal. For discussion of the District Court decision, see Brown, "Japanese Approaches to Equal Rights," 39.

31. See, for example, Toyokuni Industries case, 18 *Rōshū* 59 (Judgment of the Kobe District Court, September 26, 1967). See Brown, "Japanese Approaches to Equal Rights," 40. But see *Watanabe v. Furukawa Mining*, 21 *Rōshū* 1475 (Judgment of the Maebashi District Court, November 5, 1970); aff'd, Supreme Court, First Petty Bench, December 15, 1977.

32. Akamatsu, *Joshi*, excerpts thirty-five cases as of 1975 relating directly to women workers' litigation and lists 116 others in an appendix.

33. 21 *Rōshū* 1475 (Judgment of the Maebashi District Court, November 5, 1970); aff'd, Supreme Court, First Petty Bench, December 15, 1977. See Brown, "Japanese Approaches to Equal Rights," 40; Akamatsu, *Joshi*, 79.

34. 21 *Rōshū* 1475, p. 1495. Neither the District Court nor the Supreme Court considered the defendant's failure to fire the men in the five redundant staff positions to be a major weakness in the defendant's argument, possibly because the elimination of staff positions was beyond the personnel authority of the plant manager who had fired the plaintiff. See also *Watanabe v. Sandobikku Japan Co.*, 33 *Rōshū* 207 (Judgment of the Sapporo District Court, March 1, 1982). Japanese courts recognize an obligation to consider relative hardship in selecting persons for transfer or layoff. They are also traditionally more sympathetic to workers contesting individual layoffs than they are to those protesting their inclusion in collective dismissals.

The complexity of Japanese courts' treatment of the discharge of women during reductions in force is further illustrated by two subsequent cases, the Koparu case, 789 *Hanrei Jihō* 17 (Judgment of the Tokyo District Court, September 12, 1975), and the Nihon Kōkan (the steel company known as NKK in the West) case, 33 *Rōshū* 695 (Judgment of the Yokohama District Court, Kawasaki Branch, July 19, 1982). In *Koparu* the company and union agreed on criteria for the laying off of redundant employees during a recession. One criterion was that women with two or more children would be asked to resign, and two women fitting this criterion who did not resign were fired. They sued for reinstatement and were successful, the court finding no reasonable ground for singling out women on the basis of the number of their children. In *Nihon Kōkan* the company in conjunction with its union decided to reorganize completely and reduce from 14,000 to 6,000 the permanent labor force at its Keihin (Yokohama) plant as part of the construction of new facilities. One means chosen was to subcontract "peripheral work" (*shūhen gyōmu*) to wholly owned subsidiaries created specifically for this purpose. Except for those who could be transferred to other work in the plant, all employees engaged in peripheral work were to be discharged and rehired by the subsidiaries, presumably under less favorable conditions. Female employees, it was argued, were not transferable to ordinary work within the plant because the work either was hazardous, required shift work, or was otherwise inappropriate because of provisions in the Labor Standards Act restricting female employees' working conditions. One of the women discharged in accordance with this plan sued for reinstatement as a regular employee of the parent company, but unlike the court in *Koparu*, the *Nihon Kōkan* court accepted the defendant's argument that the protective provisions of the LSA made transfers of female employees difficult and that the defendant therefore had a valid business reason to discharge only women. For a discussion of these cases, including *Furukawa Mining*, and their role in labor law generally, see Sugeno Kazuo, *Rōdōhō* [Labor law] (Tokyo: Kōbundō, 1985), 113–128, and generally Hanami Tadashi, *Gendai no koyō byōdō* [Modern equality in employment] (Tokyo: Sanshōdō, 1986).

35. 321 *Hanrei Taimuzu* 162 (Judgment of the Akita District Court, April 10, 1975).

36. 17 *Rōshū* 1407, p. 1421.

37. Nakajima, "Danjo sabetsu saiban," 44. Perhaps the conclusive blow to discriminatory family allowances came with *Sugawara v. Iwate Bank*, 1215 *Rokeisokuho* 3 (Judgment of the Iwate District Court, March 28, 1985), excerpted and translated in Kazuo Sugeno, *Japanese Labor Law*. The wage regulations of the Iwate Bank provided for family allowances for all employees who were financially "responsible for their households" and defined "responsible" as "supporting his or her family with his or her salary, provided that if his or her spouse has an income which is beyond the upper limit for credit for a dependent spouse stipulated by the Income Tax Act, only [male employees] shall be regarded as being responsible for the household." In defense of its practices, the defendant referred to the Ministry of Welfare's (*Kōseishō*) interpretative rule for determining dependency for health insurance purposes, which regarded the husband as the primary breadwinner unless the wife's earnings surpassed the husband's by more than 30 percent. The court dismissed this and other arguments and found the practice in violation of Article 4 of the LSA. Shortly thereafter the Ministry of Welfare changed its method of determination of dependency for health insurance to comply with the court's opinion. Personal communication from Professor Sugeno Kazuo, June 1986.

38. Nakajima, "Danjo sabetsu saiban," 44. The legal impact of the *Sumitomo Cement* line of cases was only one factor in companies' increasing use of temporary and part-time employees. Others included their reluctance to increase the size of their permanent work force in the more volatile economic situation following the 1973 oil crisis and an increasing willingness of housewives to enter the labor force as part-time employees, caused partially by the failure of their husbands' salaries to keep up with inflation. Personal communication from Professor Sugeno Kazuo, June 1986.

39. See note 4 above.

40. The following discussion of *Iron and Steel Federation* is based on materials supplied by Nakajima Michiko, one of the plaintiffs' attorneys.

Another important pending action, which illustrates well the legal problems involved in the relegation of women to "part-time" positions, was filed in 1983 in the Nagoya District Court against the Shinshirasuna Electrical Machinery and Appliance Company by seven female "part-timers" with from nine to sixteen years of seniority. The plaintiffs are resisting the discriminatory discharge of "part-timers" at a time of economic pressure on the company and demanding compensation for past wage discrimination. According to the plaintiffs' complaint, the daily hours of regular employees in Shinshirasuna's plant were 8:30 A.M. to 5:20 P.M., while the hours of "part-timers" were 9:00 A.M. to 5:15 P.M. The wages of regular employees were determined by length of service, job classification, and performance. Wages of the female "part-time" employees, on the other hand, did not rise after the second year of service, despite their performing, at least in part, similar work. Of 83 total employees at the plant, only 22 were regular employees, the rest being either former regular employees rehired under another classification, employees under special contract, or "part-time" employees. Like *Iron and Steel Federation, Shinshirasuna* threatens the legal prerogatives of management in the classification of their employees and thereby the sexual division of labor within the firm in a much more fundamental way than the first generation of sex discrimination cases.

41. These doctrines are based on the guarantees of private property (Article 29) and autonomy (Article 22) of the Constitution of Japan. For a discussion of the doctrines in the context of a discriminatory discharge, in this case discrimination on grounds of political belief, see *Takano v. Mitsubishi Jushi K.K.*, 27 *Minshū* 1536, pp. 1541–46 (Judgment of the Supreme Court, December 12, 1973).

42. 961 *Hanrei Jihō* 41 (Judgment of the Tsu District Court, February 21, 1980).

43. 1076 *Hanrei Jihō* 40 (Judgment of the Nagoya High Court, April 28, 1983).

44. Ibid., 55.

45. Ibid., 55–56.

46. There are, however, significant characteristics of *Suzuka City* that distinguish it from other second-generation litigation and that illustrate potential limitations in its doctrinal approach. The most important is the public nature of the defendant. Unlike the *Sumitomo Cement* line of cases, which were based on Civil Code Articles 1–2 and 90, Yamamoto had to use Article 1 of the State Redress Law, which establishes tort liability for government entities in Japan. The law provides for compensation whenever a plaintiff can show that a "defect" (*kashi*) in government operations has harmed him. In *Suzuka City*, the "defect" is the violation of Article 14 of the Constitution and of Article 13 of the LPEL, which the *Suzuka* court characterized as embodying the ideals of the Constitution as well as providing an independent basis for equal treatment. The plaintiff in *Suzuka City*, therefore, theoretically had a substantial advantage over potential plaintiffs in the private sector, who must rely on Article 90's indirect application of constitutional values. It is important not to overstate the practical import of this distinction, however, since the Constitution and the specific statutes (the LSA, the LPEL, and so on) that directly prohibit certain forms of discrimination have been interpreted to prohibit only unreasonable discrimination. The test, therefore, is identical to the *Sumitomo Cement* reasonableness doctrine based on Article 90. Though certainly reason for caution, especially at this very early stage in the second-generation litigation, this distinction should not materially detract from the impact of this case.

A second limitation of the equal-pay approach of *Suzuka City* is the remedy. The plaintiff only requested back pay and damages. The defendant argued that the suit was in substance one for promotion since back pay was premised on promotion, and that the court had no power to intervene in discretionary personnel decisions.

It also denied that there was a legal right to promotion and asserted that a mere expectancy was not an adequate basis for a tort action. The court rejected these arguments with little discussion, noting only that the question of promotion was not directly addressed since the defendant had requested only damages for wage discrimination in promotion. This fine distinction was necessary in *Suzuka City* because asking for a judicial declaration that the plaintiff was entitled to promotion would have meant filing an administrative action under the Administrative Case Litigation Law (ACLL) instead of a tort suit under the State Redress Law. Just as many plaintiffs in second-generation pollution litigation—the *Osaka Airport* case is the prime example—sought civil tort remedies because of ACLL restrictions on injunctive relief, the plaintiff here wished to avoid the clear challenge to the city's power over personnel matters that an administrative suit would have created. In this sense the *Suzuka City* court's approach is open to the same result as the *Osaka Airport* case, where the Supreme Court eventually rules that private law tort actions via the State Redress Law could not be used to evade the ACLL's restrictions on injunctions. There the Supreme Court refused to accept the Osaka High Court's distinction between the airport's private and public law functions. Similarly the Supreme Court, either in ruling on the *Suzuka City* appeal or in a similar case, could reject this indirect, private law attack on governmental actions as well.

47. Personal communication to the author from an attorney related to the case.

48. See, for example, *Katei kiban jūjitsu kenkyū guruupu* [Family basis strengthening research group], *Katei kiban jūjitsu no tame no teigen* [A proposal for the strengthening of the family basis], Seisaku Kenkyūkai [Policy research group], May 29, 1980.

49. See, generally, Executive Committee of 1980 National Conference of Nongovernmental Organizations of Japan, *Japanese Women: Report of Mid-Decade April Meeting of 1980 National Conference of Nongovernmental Organizations of Japan* (1980; hereafter cited as Executive Committee). For discussion of the government's efforts to strengthen the position of housewives *qua* housewives, see Nakajima, "Josei to rōdō," Higuchi, "Josei to katei," and note 6 above.

50. According to a survey by Japan's Economic Planning Agency, a Japanese husband whose wife has a full-time job spends approximately 18 minutes per day on domestic chores; one whose wife has a part-time job, 36 minutes; and one whose wife is a full-time homemaker, 12 minutes. This was by far the least amount of time spent on housework by husbands in any of the eleven countries surveyed. See Sodei Takako, "Josei no shurō wa katei o hakai suru ka?" [Will women's working destroy the family?], *Ekonomisuto*, July 13, 1982, 28–33 (translated as "Family Stability in an Age of Working Women," *Japan Echo*, 9 (1980), 95–102).

51. Executive Committee, 27–28.

52. *Asahi Shimbun*, September 28, 1981, quoting survey by Seimei Hoken Bunka Sentaa [Life insurance culture center]. Public attitudes toward working women in Japan have followed the same pattern as those in the United States. See statistical analysis in Japan Economic Institute (JEI) Report no. 28A, July 29, 1983, p. 2.

53. Sodei, "Josei no shurō," 98.

54. JEI Report no. 28A, 2–5. For anecdotal accounts of successful female managers, see Susan Chira, "A Tough Ascent for Japanese Women," *New York Times*,

February 2, 1985; and Jane Condon, *A Half Step Behind: Japanese Women of the '80's* (New York: Dodd, Mead, 1985), 183–193.

55. *Asahi Shimbun*, July 16, 1982.

56. Tadashi Hanami, "Equality and Prohibition of Discrimination in Employment—Japan," in *Bulletin of the Institute for Labor Relations* (Bulletin 14, Equality and Prohibition of Discrimination in Employment), ed. R. Blanpain (Deventer, The Netherlands: Kluwer, 1985), 159–172.

57. Personal communication by Ministry of Labor officials.

58. Danjo byōdō mondai senmonka kaigi.

59. *Koyō ni okeru danjo byōdō no handan kijun no kangaekata ni tsuite*, presented to the Minister of Labor on May 8, 1982.

60. See Yayama, "Danjo koyō byōdō," 241, and an interview with Kitamura Hiroshi, director of the personnel management division of the Japan Federation of Employers' Associations (*Nikkeiren*), published as "Viewpoints: The Working Woman's Rights," *Asia Week*, March 2, 1984, p. 62.

61. For a sampling of such articles, see note 14.

62. Hasegawa, "Equality of the Sexes," 26.

63. Yayama, "Danjo koyō byōdō," 248.

64. In the many articles, editorials, and debates with which I am familiar (see those cited in note 14), the only mention of the *Sumitomo Cement* line of cases was by Moriyama Mayumi, a member of the House of Councilors in a debate with Professor Hasegawa Michiko in *Shokun* (May 1984), 268–277, 269.

65. *Asahi Shimbun*, March 27, 1984.

66. *New York Times*, April 14, 1984.

67. *Nihon Keizai Shimbun*, editorial, March 28, 1984.

68. *Japan Economic Institute Journal*, July 13, 1984, p. 2.

69. Because the defendant in *Suzuka City* was a public entity, the EEOA would not apply.

70. 42 USC §2000e et seq.

5. Legal Informality and Industrial Policy

1. This account does not attempt to present or evaluate Japanese industrial policy as economic policy. Nor are the incidents and industries discussed necessarily typical of the MITI–business relationship: steel, petroleum, and the declining industries of the 1980s are all closely involved with and dependent on government in a way in which most prosperous and established Japanese industries are not. It is, however, precisely these industries, where potential economic conflict is greatest and the government role most intrusive, that provide the best vehicle for this inquiry into the legal context of social conflict and change in Japan.

2. For general background on Japanese bureaucrats, see, for example, Michio Muramatsu and Ellis S. Krauss, "Bureaucrats and Politicians in Policymaking: The Case of Japan," *The American Political Science Review*, 78 (1984), 126. For the political and social history of MITI in particular, see Chalmers Johnson, *MITI and the Japanese Miracle* (Stanford: Stanford University Press, 1982).

3. Business–bureaucracy interdependence has strong roots in prewar Japanese economic and political history. See Johnson, *MITI*, 83–156.

4. See, for example, *Sangyō kōzō shingikai rei* [Order for the industrial structure council], Cabinet Order No. 79 of 1964 (revised Cabinet Order No. 208 of 1973).

5. *Tsūshō sangyō shō setchi hō* [MITI establishment law], Law No. 276 of 1952; *Gaikoku kawase oyobi gaikoku bōeki kanri hō* [Foreign exchange and foreign trade control law], Law No. 28 of 1949; *Sekiyugyō hō* [Petroleum industry law], Law No. 128 of 1962; *Tokutei fukyō sangyō antei rinji sochi hō* [Temporary measures law for the stabilization of depressed industries], Law No. 44 of 1978. The original Foreign Exchange and Foreign Trade Control Law, like many of Japan's basic postwar statutes, was drafted by Allied Occupation authorities. See John O. Haley, "Law, Culture and the Political Economy of Postwar Japan," paper delivered in Tokyo, January 6–11, 1986, at the Volume III Conference of the Japanese Political Economy Research Committee, p. 20.

6. Johnson, *MITI*, 194–195. The FECL has since been amended as part of the liberalization of Japanese trade laws. See Andrew B. Anderson, "The Law Partially Amending the FECL (Law No. 65, 1979)," *JASLS Reports*, 1 (May 1980).

7. Examples of standards such as the "public interest" or "convenience" are legion and include the statutes establishing most of the federal independent regulatory agencies. See, for example, Section 3(3) of The Transportation Act of 1920 amending the Interstate Commerce Act to require Interstate Commerce Commission approval of railroad consolidations upon a determination that they were in the "public interest." For a more recent example of how American courts deal with statutes with virtually no standards whatsoever, see Judge Leventhal's opinion in *Amalgamated Meat Cutters v. Connally*, 337 F. Supp. 737 (D.D.C. 1971), discussing the Economic Stabilization Act of 1970, Public Law No. 91–379, 84 Stat. 799 (1970).

8. Much is available in English on Japanese administrative law. See generally Kiminobu Hashimoto, "The Rule of Law: Some Aspects of Judicial Review of Administrative Actions," in *Law in Japan*, ed. Arthur T. von Mehren (Cambridge, Mass.: Harvard University Press, 1963), 239–273; Ichirō Ogawa, "Judicial Review of Administrative Actions in Japan," *Washington Law Review*, 43 (1968), 1075–1094; Nathaniel L. Nathanson and Yasuhiro Fujita, "The Right to Fair Hearing in Japanese Administrative Law," *Washington Law Review*, 45 (1970), 273–334; Ichirō Ogawa, "Several Problems Relating to Suits for the Affirmation of the Nullity of Administrative Acts," *Law in Japan: An Annual*, 6 (1973), 73–96; Kazuo Yamanouchi, "Administrative Guidance and the Rule of Law," *Law in Japan: An Annual*, 7 (1974), 22–33; Naohiko Harada, "Preventative Suits and Duty Imposing Suits in Administrative Litigation," *Law in Japan: An Annual*, 9 (1976), 63–82. See also volume 15 of *Law in Japan: An Annual* for a symposium on administrative guidance and the Oil Cartel cases.

General Japanese-language treatises used in this chapter include the following: Tanaka Jirō, *Shimpan gyōsei hō (jō)* [Administrative law, new edition I] (Tokyo: Kōbundō, 1976); Imamura Shigekazu, *Gyōseihō nyūmon (shimpan)* [Introduction to administrative law, new edition] (Tokyo: Yūhikaku, 1975); Yamamura Tsunetoshi, "Gyōsei soshō" [Administrative litigation], in *Kōgai gyōsei hō kōza* [Lectures on environmental administrative law], ed. Yamada Yukio and Narita Yoriaki (Tokyo: Gyōsei, 1976).

9. *Gyōsei jiken soshō hō*, Law No. 139 of 1963.

10. Judgment of the Supreme Court, February 24, 1955, discussed in Imamura, *Nyūmon*, 82–90. See also Tanaka, *Shimpan*, 326.

11. Judgment of the Supreme Court, January 19, 1962, 16 *Minshū* 57. Partially translated in Hideo Tanaka, *The Japanese Legal System* (Tokyo: University of Tokyo Press, 1976), 289. For discussion of this case and standing in general, see Harada Naohiko, *Uttae no rieki* [Interest to sue] (Tokyo: Kōbundō, 1973), particularly pp. 13–21.

12. *Shufu Rengōkai v. Kōsei Torihiki Iinkai* [Federation of Housewives v. Fair Trade Commission], Judgment of the Supreme Court, March 14, 1978, 882 *Hanrei Jihō* 3. For discussion of standing developments generally, see Frank Upham, "After Minamata: General Prospects and Problems in Japanese Environmental Litigation," *Ecology Law Quarterly*, 8 (1979), 239–244.

13. For an environmental case restricting administrative discretion, see, for example, Judgment of the Tokyo High Court, July 13, 1973, 710 *Hanrei Jihō* 23 (The Nikkō Tarō cedar case). For a discussion of how other courts in other contexts have broadened administrative discretion, see Michael Young, "Judicial Review of Administrative Guidance: Governmentally Encouraged Consensual Dispute Resolution in Japan," *Columbia Law Review*, 84 (1984), 923.

14. As the Japanese economy has matured and become more closely tied to the international economy, bureaucratic arm twisting has become more difficult. Most firms in most sectors are less dependent on government help and thus less susceptible to informal and indirect persuasion than are the firms and industries discussed in this chapter. Equally important, whenever the arm twisting can be interpreted as affecting access to Japanese markets, MITI actions face potentially intense scrutiny from Japan's trade partners. For a particularly well publicized recent incident, see the controversy surrounding the attempt by the Lions Oil Company, a small independent gasoline retailer, to import gasoline directly in defiance of MITI's "informal" administrative guidance restricting import of gasoline primarily to domestic Japanese refiners.

According to press reports, MITI was able to force Lions Oil to cease direct imports by convincing Lions' bankers to withdraw its credit. See the accounts in *Nihon Keizai Shimbun*, May 16, 1985, pp. 1–2; *The Japan Economic Journal*, May 21, 1985, p. 1; May 28, 1985, p. 9; and June 25, 1985, p. 9; *The Economist*, January 19, 1985, p. 66; *The Asian Wall Street Journal*, January 17, 1985, p. 13; and *The New York Times*, January 21, 1985, p. D10.

15. The discussion of land use planning cases in this section is drawn from Young, "Judicial Review." The use of informal "outlines," one form of administrative guidance, rather than duly enacted local ordinances is as ubiquitous on the local level as it is within central government ministries. See Gyōsei kanri kenkyū sentaa [Administrative Management Research Center], *Gyōseishidō ni kansuru chōsa kenkyū hōkokusho* [Report of survey research on administrative guidance], 1981, 150–164. For an analysis of local governments' use of administrative guidance in the particular area of affirmative action and welfare administration, see Frank Upham, "Ten Years of Affirmative Action for Japanese Burakumin: A Preliminary Report on the Law on Special Measures for Dōwa Projects," *Law in Japan: An Annual*, 13 (1980), 54–62.

16. The Sumitomo Metals incident is a *cause célèbre* among Japanese industrial policy aficionados. It is discussed, among other places, in Johnson, *MITI*, 268–271, and in Eugene Kaplan, *Japan: The Government–Business Relationship* (Washington,

D.C.: U.S. Dept. of Commerce, 1972), 146–148. The discussion in this section is based primarily on contemporary accounts in the *Nihon Keizai Shimbun [NKS]* from June 30, 1965, to August 29, 1966, and academic analyses including Kawasaki Hirotarō, "Gyōsei shidō no jittai—saikin no mittsu no keesu ni miru" [The real state of administrative guidance as seen in three recent incidents], *Juristo,* 342 (1966), 51, and Ogawa Ichirō et al., "Gyōsei shidō no kihon mondai" [Fundamental questions in administrative guidance], *Juristo,* 342 (1966), 38.

17. *NKS,* July 13, 1965, p. 1.

18. *Shiteki dokusen no kinshi oyobi kōsei torihiki no kakuho ni kansuru hōritsu* [Law concerning the prohibition of private monopolies and the maintenance of fair trade], Law No. 54 of 1947, trans. in H. Iyori and A. Uesugi, *The Antimonopoly Laws of Japan* (Tokyo: Kōsei Torihiki Kyōkai, 1983), 213–264.

19. *NKS,* November 20, 1965, p. 3.

20. *NKS,* December 3, 1965, p. 4.

21. The "fundamental reconsideration" promised by MITI Minister Miki took place during the first three months of 1966. First on December 28, 1965, MITI announced to the Market Policy Committee (MPC) of the Iron and Steel Federation the FY65 fourth-quarter quotas, which were identical to third-quarter quotas except for a decrease in that of Sumitomo to account for its overproduction in the third quarter. Thereafter the MPC and MITI created the Committee for the Adjustment of Fundamental Problems in the Steel Industry (*Tekkō kihon mondai chōsei iinkai*) to work out the details of the FY66 first-quarter quotas. The committee, which was chaired by a representative of Yawata Steel, reached final agreement in early March. The result was a wider choice of reference periods for the FY66 quota, including the use of January 1965–June 1965 as well as April 1964–March 1965 and July 1964–June 1965. The availability of the later period represents a minor concession to Sumitomo Metals' position, but it turned out to be of little significance economically because the informal cartel was discontinued in August 1966. *NKS,* December 28, 1965; January 11, 1966; March 8, 1966; March 30, 1966; July 1, 1966; and August 29, 1966. See also the account in the Sumitomo Metals official firm history made available to and on file with the author.

22. For a romanticized but not atypical explanation and justification of this attitude by a prominent retired MITI official, see Amaya Naohiro, "Wa no rinri to dokkinhō no ronri," *Bungei Shunjū,* 58, no. 12 (December 1980), 176–193. Translated as "Harmony and the Antimonopoly Law" in *Japan Echo,* 8, no. 1. (1981), 85–95. All translations of this article are my own and are not taken from *Japan Echo.*

23. In the opinion of one American observer of MITI and Japanese industrial policy, it is precisely the exclusion of outsiders that results in efficient policies: "[Effective industrial policy] requires that the bureaucracy directing economic development be protected from all but the most powerful interest groups so that it can set and achieve long-range industrial priorities. A system in which the full range of pressure and interest groups existing in a modern, open society has effective access to the government will surely not achieve economic development, at least under official auspices, whatever other values it may fulfill" (Johnson, *MITI,* 44).

24. *Kai v. Nippon Sekiyu, K.K.,* 1005 *Hanrei Jihō* 32 (Judgment of the Tokyo High Court, July 17, 1981; brought under Article 25 of the AML) and *Satō v. Sekiyu*

Renmei, 997 Hanrei Jihō (Judgment of the Yamagata District Court, March 31, 1981; brought under section 709–24 of the Civil Code). *Satō* has since been reversed by the Sendai High Court. For treatment of the civil cases, see J. Mark Ramseyer, "The Costs of the Consensual Myth: Antitrust Enforcement and Institutional Barriers to Litigation in Japan," *Yale Law Journal,* 94 (1985), 604. For discussion of the cases' implications for international business practices, see J. Mark Ramseyer, "Japanese Antitrust Enforcement after the Oil Embargo," *American Journal of Comparative Law,* 31 (1983), 395.

25. *Japan v. Idemitsu Kōsan et al.,* 985 *Hanrei Jihō* 3 (Judgment of the Tokyo High Court, September 26, 1980), trans. in J. Mark Ramseyer, "The Oil Cartel Criminal Cases: Translation and Postscript," *Law in Japan: An Annual,* 15 (1982), 57, affirmed in part and reversed in part, 1108 *Hanrei Jihō* 3 (Judgment of the Supreme Court, February 24, 1984); and *Japan v. Sekiyu Renmei,* 983 *Hanrei Jihō* 22 (Judgment of the Tokyo High Court, September 26, 1980), trans. in Ramseyer, "The Oil Cartel Criminal Cases," 57.

26. The draft bill was entitled the Special Measures Law for the Promotion of Designated Industries [*Tokutei sangyo shinkō rinji sochi hōan* or *Tokushinhō*], cabinet submission no. 151 of 1963. For Sahashi's attempt to get it enacted, see Johnson, *MITI,* 255–266. For an example of similar sentiments for a special law limited to the steel industry, see, for example, comment by Chairman Nagano of the Steel Subcommittee of the Industrial Structure Council in the aftermath of the Sumitomo Incident, *NKS,* March 30, 1966.

27. Thus, if the crude oil allocation in the Oil Cartel cases had been conducted under the instructions or authorization of MITI in order to enforce the supply plan system established by the PIL, and if that law had explicitly allowed the use of such allocations to carry out its provisions, then the allocations would have been legitimate activity. Even without such explicit statutory authority, in some circumstances the activities might still be legitimate and a finding of illegality precluded as long as the allocations were a necessary step in carrying out MITI's duties to regulate the supply and demand of petroleum and were conducted with the Ministry's approval or in pursuit of its guidance.

28. The DIL focused on the problem of excess capacity. MITI had estimated that from 20 to 40 percent of capacity of the four statutorily specified sectors was excessive, and the criteria for designating further industries limited designation to those suffering from permanent overcapacity such that the majority of their members were in substantial financial difficulty. Similarly, the Stabilization Plans drawn up jointly by MITI and the designated industry after consultation with the appropriate advisory commission (*shingikai*), industry representatives, and affected labor unions were limited to capacity elimination. The Stabilization Plan was to identify the types of facilities to be retired and to specify the manner and time period in which the process should take place.

29. Only one industry failed to dispose of 90 percent of its targeted capacity. It should be noted, however, that the attainment of particular targets in itself proves nothing about the causal effect of the DIL. The targets might have been met, or surpassed, without any governmental involvement whatsoever. Appraisals of the economic effect of the DIL, therefore, must await economic rather than legal analysis.

30. The Special Measures Law for the Promotion of Designated Industries (see note 26), as the draft law was called, arose out of a remarkably similar set of circumstances as that facing MITI and the declining industries in the late seventies. The immediate threat was trade liberalization, but liberalization was a threat only because MITI and industry believed that many sectors of Japan's economy were structurally unprepared for international competition. There were too many small-scale and undercapitalized companies engaged in what MITI calls "excessive" competition. Sahashi's draft was intended to give MITI the power to intervene in these sectors to achieve structural reforms remarkably similar to those envisioned by the SDIL: sales and production cartels and enforced mergers that would enable a more concentrated industry to compete successfully internationally. See Johnson, *MITI*, 255–266.

31. For a description of the powers and policies of MITI's prewar predecessors, see Johnson, *MITI*, chaps. 4 and 5 (pp. 116–197).

32. The FTC had one other powerful set of allies, the governments of Japan's trading partners. Although the effect is difficult to gauge, the eventual compromise reached by MITI and the FTC probably owes something to foreign, particularly American, pressure to limit the revisions as much as possible. For a summary of U.S. Trade Representative William Brock's fears regarding the SDIL, see William Chapman, "Another Battle in U.S.–Japan Trade War?" *Boston Globe*, February 27, 1983. See also John Pinder, Takashi Hosomi, and William Diebold, *Industrial Policy and the International Economy* (The Triangle Papers, no. 19, 1979); and *Opportunities in U.S.–Japan Relations: A Report Submitted to the President of the U.S. and the Prime Minister of Japan by the U.S.–Japan Advisory Commission* (September 1984).

33. This section is based largely on research done for me by Nakamura Reiko in 1983. For an interesting journalistic account by a participant in the process of the restructuring, see Tokunaga Yoshirō, *Nafusa sensō* [Naphtha war] (Tokyo: Nikkan Sekiyu Nyūsu, 1984).

34. As close attention to chronology will reveal, the SDIL was not in force during any of these events. The law authorizes and legitimates the industrial policy process but does not regulate or structure it. The process of restructuring the petrochemical industry with the contributions of the various *shingikai*, culminating in the PISC trip to Europe, was totally informal in the sense that it was not mandated or controlled by any statute. In the fall of 1982, when basic agreement among industry leaders was achieved, the SDIL had not even been drafted. By winter when the details on mergers and joint ventures were finalized, the structure of the SDIL was clear, but the statute was not enacted until the spring and did not become effective until June 1983. Thereafter, the necessary steps were taken to comply formally with the SDIL, but the substantive decisions had been made long before any legal guidelines governed the form, participants, or content of the procedure used. Though somewhat unusual in its relationship to the authorizing statute, the petrochemical reorganization is typical of the industrial policy process before and after the SDIL.

35. Gyōsei shidō kenkyūkai, *Gyōsei shidō ni kansuru chōsa hōkokusho* [Report of a study of administrative guidance] (1981).

36. Two familiar examples are the "outline guidance" schemes used to regulate urban land use in many Japanese municipalities, described and analyzed by

Michael Young in "Judicial Review," and the discussion of Osaka City affirmative action programs for Burakumin in Chapter 3. For fuller treatment of the latter, including analysis of how courts have dealt with outline guidance in the Buraku context, see Frank Upham, "Ten Years of Affirmative Action," 39.

37. See, *inter alia, Amalgamated Meat Cutters v. Connally*, 337 F. Supp. 737 (D.D.C. 1971); *Scenic Hudson Preservation Conf. v. Federal Power Commission*, 354 F.2d 608 (2d Cir. 1965) (*Scenic Hudson I*); *Scenic Hudson Preservation Conf. v. Federal Power Commission*, 453 F.2d 463 (2d Cir. 1971) (*Scenic Hudson II*); the contrasting concurring opinions of Judges Bazelon and Leventhal in *Ethyl Corp. v. Environmental Protection Agency*, 541 F.2d 1 (D.C. Cir. 1976, en banc), *cert. denied*, 426 U.S. 941 (1976); *Citizens to Preserve Overton Park, Inc. v. Volpe*, 401 U.S. 402 (1971) for examples of various American judicial techniques. But see *Vermont Yankee Nuclear Power Corp. v. Natural Resources Defense Council*, 435 U.S. 519 (1978) for emerging limits on some of these techniques.

38. For examples of similar techniques in Japanese administrative litigation, see Young, "Judicial Review," and Upham, "After Minamata."

39. To a certain extent this has been judicially required in the environmental area (see Upham, "After Minamata"), but it has not spread to other areas of bureaucratic decision making.

40. There are strong parallels between the evolution of American and Japanese standing doctrine. Both began with a requirement that the plaintiff show direct injury to a "legal right" narrowly defined to exclude, *inter alia*, economic injury. In *Alabama Power Co. v. Ickes*, 302 U.S. 464 (1964), for example, the Supreme Court dismissed an action by a private competitor of municipal power companies on the ground that "the mere fact that petitioner will sustain financial loss by reason of the unlawful competition" by allegedly illegally subsidized publicly owned utilities did not confer standing since the plaintiff had not suffered injury to a *legal* right. For discussion of a similar approach by Japanese courts, see Hideo Tanaka, *The Japanese Legal System* (Tokyo: Tokyo University Press, 1976), 689–692. This approach was abandoned in the United States by a series of cases culminating in the recognition of competitor standing in the *Association of Data Processing Service Organizations v. Camp*, 397 U.S. 150 (1970) and in Japan by the *Sakamoto* case (see note 11 above). The major difference between the two bodies of law—and it is a very important difference for our purposes—is that the American courts have gone well beyond *Data Processing* to adopt an "injury in fact" test that in its most extreme manifestations (see, for example, *United States v. SCRAP*, 412 U.S. 669 [1973]) allows almost anyone concerned to challenge governmental action. Although there have been several Japanese cases going beyond *Sakamoto*, primarily in the environmental area (see Tanaka, *Japanese Legal System*, 691–692, Harada, *Uttae no rieki*, 121–135, and Upham, "After Minamata," 241–244), after the *Federation of Housewives* case (see discussion in text at note 12) there is no reason to believe that the law of standing generally has moved far from the *Sakamoto* reasoning.

The contrast between American and Japanese doctrines governing the availability and timing of judicial review is even more stark, particularly when we focus on the review of informal administrative action. Cases like *National Automatic Laundry and Cleaning Council v. Schultz*, 443 F.2d 689 (D.C. Cir. 1971), where the court allowed judicial review of an advisory letter from the Administrator of the Fair

Wage and Hour Administration, stand in sharp contrast with the Japanese cases dealing with similar issues under the rubric of *shobunsei* (see discussion in text at notes 9 and 10). If the Japanese courts were to adopt the American approach to informal administrative action, many of the informal activities of, say, the Ministry of International Trade and Industry in industrial policy or the Ministry of Labor in equal employment policy would be subject to judicial scrutiny.

41. See generally the cases cited in note 40 above.

42. See, for example, *Home Box Office, Inc. v. Federal Communications Commission*, 567 F.2d 9 (D.C. Cir. 1977), *cert. denied*, 434 U.S. 829, *rehearing denied*, 434 U.S. 988 (1977). Under carefully controlled conditions, some *ex parte* contact is permissible; see, for example, *Action for Children's Television v. Federal Communications Commission*, 564 F.2d 458 (D.C. Cir. 1977).

43. See generally Richard Stewart, "The Reformation of American Administrative Law," *Harvard Law Review*, 88 (1975), 1669, for a description of the evolution of American administrative process.

44. In other sectors of the Japanese economy, particularly those such as automobile manufacturing that are highly successful, the relationship between MITI and the industry and MITI and individual firms is at best an arm's-length one and at times openly hostile. The number of firms that have defied MITI's suggestions are legion, and many have proved MITI completely wrong.

45. In addition to the example of Sumitomo Metals, another example of extreme (and public) reluctance is the confrontation between MITI and the Lions Oil Company described briefly in note 14.

46. That the informal and consensual nature of Japanese industrial policy which is a source of strength versus outsiders can become a source of weakness when consensus does not exist within an industry or in those rare instances when MITI is attempting to act on its own is well brought out by John O. Haley in his "Law, Culture and the Political Economy."

6. Toward a New Perspective on Japanese Law

1. See Clifford Geertz, *Local Knowledge* (New York: Basic Books, 1983), 175, and Mary Ann Glendon, "American Abortion Law in Comparative Perspective" (unpublished manuscript, 1985), 1.

2. Amaya Naohiro, "Wa no rinri to dokkinhō no ronri," *Bungei Shunjū*, 58 (December 1980), 176–193. Translated as "Harmony and the Antimonopoly Law" in *Japan Echo*, 8, no. 1 (1981), 85–95. All translations of this article are my own and are not taken from *Japan Echo*.

3. Ibid., 182.

4. Yasuda Osamu, "Shirarezu dokkinhō to kimyō na giron" [The unknown Antimonopoly Law and the strange argument], *Bungei Shunjū* 59 (January 1981), 420–426. Translated as "Strange Ideas on the Antimonopoly Law" in *Japan Echo*, 8, no. 1 (1981), 96–102.

5. Others include Noda Yoshiyuki, *Introduction to Japanese Law*, trans. Anthony H. Angelo (Tokyo: University of Tokyo Press, 1976), 159–183, and Isaiah Ben-Dasan, "The Japanese and the Jews," in Hideo Tanaka, *The Japanese Legal System* (Tokyo: University of Tokyo Press, 1976), 286–295.

6. Outstanding examples of this interpretation include Masao Maruyama, *Thought and Behaviour in Modern Japanese Politics* (London: Oxford University Press, 1963), 1–24, and Takeyoshi Kawashima, "Dispute Resolution in Contemporary Japan," in Arthur Taylor von Mehren, *Law in Japan: The Legal Order in a Changing Society* (Cambridge, Mass.: Harvard University Press, 1963), 41–72. Both have linked individualism with a modern legal system and a modern legal system with strong and stable democracy. In doing so, of course, they were well within the mainstream of postwar thought about the interrelationship of law, development, and individualism known as the law and development school. See Marc Galanter, "The Modernization of Law," in Lawrence M. Friedman and Stewart Macaulay, *Law and the Behavioral Sciences* (New York: Bobbs-Merrill, 1977), 1046–55. For the worldwide fate of this school, see David M. Trubek, "Scholars in Self-Estrangement: Some Reflections on the Crisis in Law and Development Studies in the United States," *Wisconsin Law Review* (1974), 1062.

7. Ezra Vogel, *Japan as Number One* (Cambridge, Mass.: Harvard University Press, 1979) and Thomas Rohlen, *For Harmony and Strength* (Berkeley: University of California Press, 1974) are examples of Western reappraisals. See particularly Rohlen's comments on p. 59 that the Confucian ideals underlying some Japanese corporations' spiritual training are better suited to contemporary organizational demands than Western individualism.

8. This idealized vision of the Japanese legal system corresponds closely to what Donald Black has termed a "conciliatory" legal system. See Donald Black, *The Behavior of Law* (New York: Academic Press, 1976), 4–5.

9. Maruyama Masao (see note 6 above) attributed Japan's descent into World War II to a failure to recognize decision-making responsibility among Japanese leaders in the 1930s. Presumably, if political decisions had been more clearly articulated and acknowledged, the increased debate would have forced political leaders to consider factors that remained hidden as long as policy was conceived as determined by inertia and thus not attributable to political choice. This interpretation may also help explain MITI's failure to gain additional formal legal power in the 1963 debate over the Special Measures Law for the Promotion of Designated Industries [*Tokushinhō*]; see the discussion in Chapter 5. Although what Sahashi was proposing meant in some ways little more than giving MITI formal power to do what it was already doing informally, the necessity of legislation and the ensuing public debate articulated the political choices and their implications for all to see. Sahashi's subsequent defeat may mean, therefore, that what is permissible under the guise of consensus becomes impermissible when closely and publicly examined. Although MITI denies that it ever wanted further compulsory powers, the intense public debate may also explain the failure to include additional exemptions from the Antimonopoly Law in the Structurally Depressed Industries Law.

The masking of responsibility for public decisions also allows government entities to extend their jurisdiction beyond statutory limits. Thus, local governments can use narrow statutory powers to enforce unrelated broad policy aims with no statutory foundation. See Michael Young, "Judicial Review of Administrative Guidance," *Columbia Law Review*, 84 (1984), 923.

10. See Chapter 4 for a sampling of the public debate over the EEOA. The only exception to the commentators' ignoring of the *Sumitomo Cement* line of cases

known to me is a single comment in the debate between Hasegawa Michiko and Moriyama Mayumi in *Shokun*, May 1984, p. 269.

11. Geertz, *Local Knowledge*, 173.

12. *Murahachibu* is the traditional method of exclusion in groups such as villages where actual physical exclusion is impossible. *Murahachibu* is still practiced in contemporary Japan and is at times brought before the Human Rights Conciliators. See Lawrence W. Beer and C. G. Weeramantry, "Human Rights in Japan: Some Protections and Problems," *Universal Human Rights*, 1 (1979), 13. In a sense, it was the threat of an analogous exclusion from the system of "industrial cooperation" symbolized by membership in organizations like the Keidanren that eventually forced Sumitomo Metals to agree to abide by MITI's cartel allocations.

13. William H. Simon, "The Ideology of Advocacy: Procedural Justice and Professional Ethics," *Wisconsin Law Review*, (1978), 29. See also Peter Gabel, "Reification in Legal Reasoning," in *Research in Law and Sociology*, vol. 3, ed. Steven Spitzer (Greenwich, Conn: JAI Press, 1981), 25.

14. In a slightly different context, this was the approach taken to American egalitarian judicial rhetoric in Duncan Kennedy, "Form and Substance in Private Law Adjudication," *Harvard Law Review*, 89 (1976), 1776–78. For fuller treatments of the ambiguous relationship between law and litigation and political and economic power, see, for example, E. P. Thompson, *Whigs and Hunters: The Origin of the Black Act* (New York: Pantheon Books, 1975), 245–269, and Isaac Balbus, "Commodity Form and Legal Form: An Essay on the 'Relative Autonomy' of the Law," *Law and Society Review*, 11 (1977), 571.

15. The EEOA contains no explicit or doctrinal obstacles to litigation if the prospective plaintiff can get past the new mediation machinery established within the Ministry of Labor, but it is very possible that courts will defer to the Ministry's interpretation of the statute and of terms like "equal opportunity."

16. See, for example, Namba Nobuo, "Hiyakushō ikki no hōishiki" [The legal consciousness of peasant rebellions], in *Ikki*, ed. Aoki Michio, vol. 4, *Seikatsu, Bunka, Shisō* [Life, culture, and thought] (Tokyo: Tokyo University Press, 1981), 43; and Stephen Vlastos, "Tokugawa Peasant Movements in Fukushima: Conflict and Peasant Mobilization," Ph.D. diss., University of California, Berkeley, 1977.

17. "Tōyō no dōtoku, seiyō no gakugei," translated as "Eastern Ethics and Western Science" in *Sources of Japanese Tradition*, ed. Wm. Theodore de Bary (compiled by Ryusaku Tsunoda, Wm. Theodore de Bary, and Donald Keene), vol. 2 (New York: Columbia University Press, 1958), 100.

18. Attorney General Joseph Lieberman of Connecticut, in a *New York Times* op. ed. article of July 9, 1984 ("Give Confucius a Chance"), and President Derek Bok of Harvard University, himself a former dean of Harvard Law School, in the *1981–82 Harvard University President's Report*, April 21, 1983, p. 6, are prominent examples of legal leaders advocating the consideration of Japanese values in American legal reforms. For an empirical analysis of this urge to learn from the East which, *inter alia*, questions whether litigation has actually increased or whether its nature has evolved so that it now threatens powerful and articulate groups, see Marc Galanter, "Reading the Landscape of Disputes: What We Know and Don't Know (and Think We Know) about Our Allegedly Contentious and Litigious Society," *UCLA Law Review*, 31 (1983), 37–62. For an explicit proposal for

American legislation along Japanese lines, see Stephen Soble, "A Proposal for the Administrative Compensation of Victims of Toxic Substance Pollution: A Model," *Harvard Journal of Legislation*, 14 (1977), 683.

Originally some of the impetus of this movement away from litigation and toward alternative forms of dispute resolution came from the left and from disillusionment about the amount of real social change possible through the courts. See, for example, Simon, "The Ideology of Advocacy"; Alan Freeman, "Legitimizing Racial Discrimination through Antidiscrimination Law: A Critical Review of Supreme Court Doctrine," *Minnesota Law Review*, 62 (1978), 1049; and Duncan Kennedy, "Form and Substance in the Private Law Adjudication," *Harvard Law Review*, 89 (1976), 1686. The movement for alternative modes of dispute resolution is now very much a mainstream phenomenon, with conservatives like Chief Justice Warren Burger among its proponents—so much so that early champions like Laura Nader have become vocal critics. For a perceptive and comprehensive critique of the current state of the movement, see Richard Abel, "The Contradictions of Informal Justice," in *The Politics of Informal Justice*, vol. 2, ed. Richard Abel (New York: Academic Press, 1982), 267.

19. See, for example, Bok, *1981–82 Report*, 6.

20. See Richard B. Stewart, "The Discontents of Legalism: Interest-Group Relations in Administrative Regulation," *Wisconsin Law Review* (1985), 655–686. I have profited greatly from an earlier draft of this article in writing this section. See also Richard B. Stewart, "Regulation, Innovation, and Administrative Law: A Conceptual Framework," *California Law Review*, 69 (1981), 1256; Lawrence Susskind and Alan Weinstein, "Towards a Theory of Environmental Dispute Resolution," *Boston College Environmental Affairs Law Review*, 9 (1980), 311; Philip J. Harter, "Negotiating Regulations: A Cure for Malaise," *Georgetown Law Journal*, 71 (1982), 1; and "Rethinking Regulation: Negotiation as an Alternative to Traditional Rulemaking," *Harvard Law Review*, 94 (1981), 1971.

21. Whether or not the number of administrative suits has actually increased is—as is the same question in regard to general litigation—unproved empirically. See Galanter, "Reading the Landscape of Disputes." Observers rely on anecdotal evidence such as the increase in the number of specialized Washington law firms and Bureau of National Affairs periodicals. See Stewart, "Discontents of Legalism."

22. Stewart, "Discontents of Legalism," 655.

23. Many commentators of the American scene ignore the already extensive use of informal techniques within the American legal system. See Harter, "Negotiating Regulations," 31–42 for a brief account of current informal activities in the administrative context.

24. See, for example, Chief Justice Warren E. Burger, "Our Vicious Legal Spiral," *Judges' Journal*, 16 (1977), 24 and 48.

25. Robert Bellah, Richard Madsen, William Sullivan, Ann Swidler, and Steven Tipton, *Habits of the Heart: Individualism and Commitment in American Life* (Berkeley: University of California Press, 1985).

26. Ibid., 28–31.

27. Carol Gilligan, *In a Different Voice: Psychological Theory and Women's Development* (Cambridge, Mass.: Harvard University Press, 1982).

28. Ibid. If the "different voice" that Gilligan describes is indeed a feminine one in the United States, then perhaps the majority voice is quite contrary to the dominant, male voice.

29. Ibid. As long as it is viewed as feminine, the voice of relationships will be stigmatized as being less valid or functional than the "masculine." One reaction by some American feminist lawyers has been to minimize its importance as merely the consciousness of female victims of male domination. See generally "Feminist Discourse, Moral Values, and the Law: A Conversation" (Isabel Marcus and Paul Spiegelman, moderators; Ellen C. DuBois, Mary C. Dunlap, Carol J. Gilligan, Catherine A. MacKinnon, and Carrie J. Menkel-Meadow, conversants), and particularly the comments of Catherine A. MacKinnon, *Buffalo Law Review*, 34 (1984), 18. The irony is that Gilligan's "masculine" voice is more likely merely American; it certainly does not describe the attitudes of male Japanese.

30. For one attempt, see Harter, "Negotiating Regulations."

Whether one should call it informality or not is unclear, but one proposed solution to formality, inefficiency, and delay in government regulation has been the shift from command and control regulation to reliance on market incentives. (Others are deregulation and the sale of governmental monopolies.) Though potentially very effective in enforcement and implementation, market mechanisms appear to have relatively little to offer in the area of initial policymaking, particularly in social regulation where the potential market forces are either inchoate or diffuse. In these areas—environmental protection and employment conditions are two well-known examples; competition policy may be a less well recognized one—the government will continue to be involved in the fundamental political choices, and increased informality will often mean increased discretion. See Stewart, "Discontents of Legalism."

Index

Administrative Case Litigation Law
(ACLL), 171
Administrative discretion. *See* Scope of
discretion
Administrative disposition, 170–171, 183
Administrative guidance: by Ministry of
Labor, 147–148, 155–156, 163; in land
use planning, 174–176; by MITI,
186–187; Administrative Management
Agency survey of, 198. *See also*
Administrative Law; Informality
Administrative law, 170–176; Japanese vs.
American, 200–202, 218–219, 221–227;
and policymaking, 211–214. *See also*
Judicial review; Justiciability; Scope of
discretion; Standing
Administrative Management Agency,
198
Administrative Procedure Act, 59–61
Agency of Natural Resources and Energy
(ANRE), 193, 194–195
Akita Bank case (1975), 137–138
Amakudari ("descending from heaven"),
167, 177, 181
Amaya, Naohiro, 205–206, 223
Antimonopoly Law (AML): in Sumitomo
Metals incident, 178, 181; in Oil Cartel
cases, 184–187; in petrochemical
industry restructuring, 190–192, 195,
197; American orgin of, 205–206
Arisawa, Hiromi, 195–196
Ashio mine, 69–72

Basic Industries Bureau (BIB), 193, 194
Basic Law for Environmental Pollution
Control (1967), 30, 58, 86
Bellah, Robert, 67

Big Four Pollution Suits, 18, 35; reasons
for filing, 37–42, 209; lawyers' role in,
42–44; and citizens' movements, 54; and
sex discrimination litigation, 156–160;
and consensus, 213. *See also* Pollution
problem
Buraku Liberation League (BLL), 78; and
informality, 26; origin, 84; struggle with
Japanese Communist Party, 91–96,
117–118; court ruling on denunciation
by, 96–103; denunciation ideology of,
105–111; and welfare benefits, 113; on
Buraku lists, 116; goals, 120–121
Buraku lists (*chimei sōkan*), 114–115,
116–117, 122–123
Burakumin: reasons for studying, 5; origin,
79; early discrimination against, 79–81;
development of liberation movement,
79–86; early use of denunciation by,
81–84; Deliberative Council report on,
84–86; Yata denunciation by, 87–96;
education of, 92–96; court ruling on
denunciation by, 96–103; theory and
political context of denunciation by,
103–123, 214–215; social programs for,
112–113; in media, 113–114;
employment discrimination against,
114–117, 122–123
Bureaucracy: political power of, 14–16;
management of social conflict by, 17,
21–27, 213–216, 224–225; leadership of,
21, 24–25; legal informality of, 21–27; in
pollution problem, 28; retirement from,
167, 177, 181. *See also* Government;
specific agencies
Business management: political power of,
14, 15; in pollution problem, 28;